The Documentary

The Documentary

Politics, Emotion, Culture

Belinda Smaill

palgrave
macmillan

First published 2010 by
PALGRAVE MACMILLAN

Palgrave Macmillan in the UK is an imprint of Macmillan Publishers Limited, registered in England, company number 785998, of Houndmills, Basingstoke, Hampshire RG21 6XS.

Palgrave Macmillan in the US is a division of St Martin's Press LLC, 175 Fifth Avenue, New York, NY 10010.

Palgrave Macmillan is the global academic imprint of the above companies and has companies and representatives throughout the world.

Palgrave® and Macmillan® are registered trademarks in the United States, the United Kingdom, Europe and other countries.

ISBN 978-0-230-23751-3   hardback

This book is printed on paper suitable for recycling and made from fully managed and sustained forest sources. Logging, pulping and manufacturing processes are expected to conform to the environmental regulations of the country of origin.

A catalogue record for this book is available from the British Library.

A catalog record for this book is available from the Library of Congress.

Printed and bound in Great Britain by
CPI Antony Rowe, Chippenham and Eastbourne

Contents

List of Illustrations

Acknowledgements

I am grateful to friends and colleagues in Film and Television Studies at Monash University in Melbourne who offered a supportive and enlivened intellectual environment during the completion of this book. In particular, I wish to thank those who read pieces and versions of chapters: Adrian Martin, Julia Vassilieva, Con Verevis, Deane Williams, and I would especially like to thank Therese Davis who offered particular support and intellectual engagement.

Earlier versions of chapters have appeared elsewhere and I thank the publishers for granting permission to reprint the following: 'The Documentaries of Kim Longinotto: Women, Change and Painful Modernity' in *Camera Obscura* 71 (2009) 43–74; 'Documentary Investigations and the Female Porn Star' in *Jump Cut: A Review of Contemporary Media* 51 (2009); 'Affective Authorship: Contemporary Asian Australian Documentary' in *Studies in Australasian Cinema* 2:2 (2008): 157–70; 'Injured Identities: Pain, Politics and Documentary' in *Studies in Documentary Film* 1:2 (2007) 151–63.

Part I Documentary and Pleasure

1
Introduction: Representation and Documentary Emotion

To speak about documentary is to immediately bring to mind the genre's associations with science, education and social responsibility, or what Bill Nichols has called the 'discourses of sobriety' (*Representing Reality* 3–4). In focusing on documentary and the emotions, this book is not proposing that these strong associations be bypassed, but rather that the emotionality inherent to sobriety should be more fully examined. This is an investigation into how individuals are positioned by documentary representation as subjects that are entrenched in the emotions, whether it is pleasure, hope, pain, empathy or disgust. The individuals I am referring to are, in some instances, film-makers, and in others, those who are featured in the documentary. By 'entrenched' I mean not simply that the poetics of the film, such as music, rhetoric or narrative,[1] frame individuals in ways that elicit emotional responses from viewers, but that emotion confers cultural meanings onto others. Emotions are not only private matters; they also circulate in the public sphere where they are fashioned across histories of signification, different media forms and other technologies of social life. Thus, two critical considerations guide my analysis in this book. The first examines how emotion is produced in particular documentaries and how the audience is addressed by this emotion. The second is concerned with the important cultural ramifications of this production and this address to the audience – I am interested in how emotionality marries with the social project of documentary in ways that make the non-fiction genre a compelling site for understanding how fantasies of self and other circulate through specific textual practices. This task requires a fresh approach, one that re-focuses debates around the study of documentary in order to account for the significance of the emotions in social life.

In the chapters that follow I explore how such an approach might take shape through a consideration of some contemporary trends in documentary and how these reference particular modes of selfhood. Each chapter presents a detailed investigation of the role of emotion in shaping perceptions of subjectivity in a defined social context. Collectively, these studies evaluate how different manifestations of the self are located by emotions in ways that effect their position within formations or technologies of power, such as the aesthetics of the text and the social conditions represented in the world of the documentary. Over the last decade a growing number of documentary films have gained theatrical release, signalling not only renewed commercial success, but also a new relevance for the genre in the eyes of film-makers and viewers. In looking more deeply at the way documentary circulates in the public sphere, this book goes some way towards understanding the basis of the popular appeal of documentary and documentary culture. By way of an introduction, I survey the different theoretical approaches to desire in documentary scholarship and establish how the expectations and assumptions that permeate the production, reception and critique of documentary are based in an emotional attachment to the form. I also outline the key propositions that underpin my approach, such as the role of object relations, the sociality of the emotions and the manner in which emotions can be perceived to work through documentary texts.

Focusing the emotions

To align documentaries with emotions such as pleasure, care, pain or disgust is to reference a number of epistemological questions that extend beyond the immediate concerns of film and media. There exists a long-standing opposition between feeling and thinking in Western thought and in the popular imagination. For some time, sectors of the humanities have been concerned with dismantling this perceived opposition.[2] In this spirit Isobel Armstrong writes, 'the power of affect needs to be included within a definition of thought and knowledge rather than theorised outside them, excluded from the rational' (87). Documentary's discourses of sobriety can be easily regarded as promoting the educative and the rational, and downplaying the experiential and the subjective. This characterisation presents a hierarchy that privileges knowledge while disavowing the importance of the emotions. The discourses of sobriety, as Nichols identifies them, include 'science, economics, politics, foreign policy, education, religion, welfare' (*Representing* 3) and other such institutions that represent instrumental power. It is significant that these discourses are closely aligned with another rationalist product of modernity: the public sphere.

The bourgeois public sphere, as theorised by Jurgen Habermas, was a zone of coordinated action where agreement was the outcome of deliberation. Consensus, in turn, frequently led to the establishment of assigned norms and values. Yet the process Habermas describes inevitably creates tensions between self and other, and between governance and social rights, that cannot be separated from emotional investments in the status of the individual and the well-being of the collective.[3] As scholars such as Lauren Berlant have persuasively argued, public spheres are worlds of affect at least as much as they are the outcome of rationality and rationalisation.[4] For Jim McGuigan, popular culture, including television and cinema, offers a mass-mediated aesthetic and emotional form of communication that is integral to perceptions of collective life. This kind of approach is prefigured in Miriam Hansen's important work on early cinema, in which she theorises Hollywood's role in facilitating a 'new sensorium' or 'vernacular modernism' in ways that impacted on the experiential horizon of audiences and eased the turbulence of accelerating modernisation. This work indicates that emotion can be thought of not only as a psychical response to particular stimulus, but also as integral to the way subjects experience public spheres at particular historical moments. Emotions shape worlds of experience and are vital to the way subjectivities are subordinated in and make sense of social formations. The emotions are tightly bound to the shifting terrain of technology, media, capitalism, globalisation and governmental politics, because all these apparatuses cater to and regulate the self.

In many ways, the non-fiction genre is closely aligned with the workings of the public sphere, most obviously because, as Jane Gaines theorises, documentaries engage the audience to produce 'a concrete continuity between ourselves and the world on the screen, a continuity that is felt as seen, and is seen as it is felt' (*The Production* 44).

Documentaries have the capacity to harness and focus emotions in ways that have a unique bearing on the social world and individuals they represent. Yet it is not enough to simply state that emotions influence our perceptions of public life and public figures. To understand how documentary texts tap into emotions, it is necessary to examine how emotions circulate socially. Emotions, such as anger, outrage, hope, apathy or pleasure, may be experienced simultaneously and collectively, but it does not follow that they are universal or culturally static. Emotions themselves are made meaningful by way of attitudes or social standards, and these standards are variable over time.⁵

Emotions frequently defy stasis and, as Sara Ahmed argues, they can move around through 'the movement or circulation of objects' (11). Moreover, she writes that while shared feelings are always present, 'emotions in their very intensity involve miscommunication, such that even when we have the same feeling, we don't necessarily have the same relationship to that feeling. Given that shared feelings are not about feeling the same feeling, or feeling-in-common, I suggest that it is the objects of emotion that circulate, rather than emotions as such' (10–11). I take up Ahmed's approach as a way to account for the capacity of emotions to confer value. Emotions can coalesce around an object and deem it boring, disgusting and/or, conversely, loved or invested with hope. In either case, value is distributed in ways that are tied to how the emotions move to give definition to an object in a particular instance. As emotions are not static, there is a constant shifting of the terms upon which objects are valued or de-valued. Given this, rather than simply being experienced and acted on by individuals as affect, emotions work in ways that are more mobile and malleable than this would imply.

To be more specific, in relation to filmic texts emotions exist relationally between subjects in ways that bind them to one another, including film-makers, critics, viewers and social actors in the texts. Emotions move along with histories of signification and, through this, become associated with and shape relationships with objects such as images and genres, a text and/or the institutions surrounding the text, in systematic ways. They also delineate and give meaning to objects, including bodies, communities, social practices and political regimes, through discursive processes. In this manner they also infuse perceptions of documentary subjects.

I have favoured the term 'emotion' largely over and above that of 'affect'. Both terms have become integral to a rich field of theory and critique that extends across a number of disciplines. Different disciplines take up the terms for different reasons and bestow on them different conceptual importance and even meaning. For this reason I do not wish to offer a definition in the first instance. More crucial is the way in which emotion can be understood to *operate* in relation to the contexts and textual practices under discussion. I will note, however, that in emphasising 'emotion' I am intending the term to include 'affect' – a term that is usually aligned with emotional responses, feelings and the domain of psychoanalysis, psychology and what is actually *felt*. Emotion, in this study, also encompasses a discourse of feeling, the signifiers of affect that are read without actually being experienced, and the way meaning can move in conjunction with or be assimilated to feeling.

In this respect, I am not signalling an attempt to bring a psycho-analytic approach to documentary studies. Yet such an approach is not inimical to my study of documentary and the emotions. Rather, the gratifications and disavowals facilitated by the genre extend across psychical and social realms. In this regard, there is an important distinction to be made between the approach taken in this book and discussions of cognitive affect in the cinema. Work in this area has examined how film genres and characters can engender emotional responses in the viewer.[6] Limited to fictional genres, notions of cognitive affect have usefully recognised the mutuality of emotions and reason, the importance of genre expectations in the audience and the role played by the imagination in the viewer's engagement with the film text. The emphasis here is on the film's form and narration and how these function to stimulate and direct the cognitive processes of the viewer. This work finds its precedence not in psychoanalysis, but in the work of Hugo Munsterberg. In his 1916 book, *The Film: A Psychological Study*, Munsterberg attends to a number of prescient issues, arguing that the expressions of actors and the formal qualities of early silent film are part of the imaginative and emotional experience of the cinema. While this work engages with the psychological effects of film, it differs greatly from the Lacanian film theory that emerged later in the century.

My aim is to focus only in part on documentary aesthetics and on how the sensibilities of the viewer might correspond to these.

More is to be gained from such an analysis if it is bracketed with, in the spirit of Hansen's work, the complex historical location of the texts, viewers, film-makers and genre. In contrast to cognitive approaches, which, for the most part, do not differentiate between broader social contexts of representation and reception, my acknowledgement of the sociality of the emotions recognises a need to grasp the particularity of historical contextualisation and its impact on textual production and circulation. This specificity is significant because emotion, themes and representations that pertain to particular public spheres do not always work with uniform effect. By this I mean that aversive emotions, such as loss or pain, can be transformative and can offer new avenues of possibility for marginalised subjects, and yet they can also facilitate stasis and maintain the conditions and discourses of the status quo. Similarly, emotions such as pleasure, desire, hope and optimism can work to cover *or* to further emancipatory forms of representation. Different moments and contexts produce different forms of prejudice and solidarity. In the next section I begin to look at how documentary, more specifically, might harness emotion. I survey some of the different theoretical approaches to desire in documentary scholarship in order to explore attitudes to and investments in the non-fiction genre itself.

Desire and documentary

If classical narrative cinema constructs a subject of desire through mechanisms akin to the psychoanalytic processes of identification and refusal in its spectator, the historical documentary – the documentary that seeks to intervene in history – mobilizes a subject of agency. This subject clearly desires too, but the desire is directed towards the social and political arenas of everyday experience as well as world-historical events shaping those lives and away from the purely psychosexual manifestations of lack and plenitude, differentiation and identification, which characterise the fetishistic forms of narrative desire. Of course there is no clear-cut distinction between inner and outer forms of desire; I want to suggest however that each has acquired different traits – narrative and documentary – to represent the Real.

Paula Rabinowitz, *They Must Be Represented* (23–4)

The conceptual approach to documentary that is fleshed out in the chapters of this book is indebted to the scholarship that has already emphasised the role of the emotions in documentary's social project. In a way that echoes the theorisation of fiction genres, much of this work has attended to questions of desire and pleasure. However, as Paula Rabinowitz's quote demonstrates, the study of documentary clearly demands different conceptual tools than those developed for the analysis of fiction. For Rabinowitz, documentary directs the spectator towards the social world rather than to the psychosexual identifications described through psychoanalytic film theory. Yet as Rabinowitz also observes, desire is not clear-cut. Whether it is fiction or non-fiction, the self as the viewer-subject is engaged by the fantasy on-screen through both social and intra-psychic registers. It is the nature of the fantasy that differs across genres.

In his essay 'The Imaginary Signifier', Christian Metz famously writes that 'the social regulation of the spectator's metapsychology [...] has as its function to set up good object relations with films [...]. The cinema is attended out of desire, a desire that it will please, not that it will displease [...] the institution as a whole has filmic pleasure alone as its aim' (18–19). The fact that this reference is made implicitly with regard to fiction film does not mean that it does not carry weight with documentary cinema. Like fiction film, documentary is attended in cinemas or viewed on television screens because it satisfies spectatorial desires. The psychoanalytical approaches that long dominated the theorisation of narrative filmic pleasure largely viewed this pleasure as a problem. This is perhaps the reason why so many words were devoted to its interrogation.[7]

The theorisation of documentary has seen desire as less of a problem but, equally, an exhaustive critique of desire and/or pleasure is often sidestepped on the path towards more pressing considerations or synthesised with other theoretical questions. The lack of coordinated theoretical attention to documentary pleasure is perhaps due to the preoccupation with the social concerns of the Griersonian project and direct or observational cinema. Hence, understandings of desire have appropriately become tied to the discourses of knowledge and their impact on documentary poetics and social subjectivity. In one such approach, Nichols poses the notion of 'epistephilia' – a desire for and pleasure in knowledge. This is a distinctive form of social engagement that is engendered by documentary, as its style and conventions activate the 'physical texture and social complexity of the historical world itself' (*Representing* 176).

In a way that parallels Rabinowitz's discussion, Nichols downplays the import of psychoanalytic mechanisms of desire in documentary spectatorship. The 'heightened attention to subjectivity [which] brings ego-centred and libidinous relations to the fore' (*Representing* 176) is the domain of the fiction film. While he does not dispute that documentary engages the psychic registers, Nichols' theory is much more focused on the social world and affective relations rather than on the psychosexual realm of fantasy. Hence, documentary engenders a mode of social subjectivity through the encounter with the text:

> The affective engagement of the viewer with social tensions and pleasures, conflicts and values – move the viewer away from the status of observer to that of participant. Something is at stake. Namely, our very subjectivity within the social arena. The move beyond observation to experience (coupled with understanding and interpretation, discovery and insight) opens a space for contestation.
>
> (194)

This passage testifies to Nichols' privileging of a trajectory towards social action; from experience, the encounter with the text, or observation, can lead to some kind of change not only in the perception of the viewer, but in the historical world itself. Drawing on Brecht and Lukacs, he argues that 'ideological struggle and political change follow from changes of habit that art, and the art of documentary, can provoke' (194).

Elizabeth Cowie offers a historical mapping of this relationship between desire and the non-fiction form. As she explains, the 'desire for reality as knowledge and as spectacle' (19) emerged in the earliest days of the cinema with new technologies of vision.[8] Thus she historically locates the form in discourses of desire. The 'pleasure of the visual and the desire for the "real"' (24) were, for Cowie, directly brought to bear on the scientific impulse to interrogate the visible. Importantly, this history binds the reception and production of non-fiction film to expectations of and desire for the visual and poetic presentation of reality. But as Cowie identifies, there is an anxiety that accompanies the desire for actuality. Because the image is variously both truthful and untruthful,

> the photographic image is the locus of ambivalent desire – for the true image and for the image that truly shows us things as we wish them to be. It is as well, of course, the locus of anxiety and thus of a repeated returning. Documentary films as recorded actuality therefore figure in both the discourse of science, as a means of obtaining the knowable in the world, and in the discourse of desire – that is, the wish to know the truth of the world, represented by the question invariably posed to actuality film, Is it really so, is it true?
>
> (25)

For his part, Michael Renov wishes to extend documentary desire further into the realm of the psyche. Indeed, Renov seeks to wrest non-fiction back from singularly conscious and rationalist understandings of the social realm in order to draw attention to the role of the unconscious in documentary spectatorial desire. For Renov, behind the production and interpretation of knowledge is the place in which fears, desires and impulses are in contestation. He argues that 'the documentary image functions in relation to both knowledge and desire, evidence and lure, with neither term exerting exclusive control' (*The Subject* 101). Further, Renov takes issue with the role of documentary desire in instigating social action – he views approaches such as those articulated by Nichols as a desire on the part of the *critic* to perceive the non-fiction discourses of sobriety to operate in tandem with social goals. Yet, significantly, he objects to Nichols' emphasis on documentary's connection to social praxis not necessarily because it is unfounded, but because it ignores the possibility for documentary to be aligned with a discourse of the delirious and the 'play of instincts' (*The Subject* 99).

The work of scholars such as Cowie, Renov and Nichols circles around different approaches to viewer desire, but they all corroborate the notion that the non-fiction form 'will please, rather than displease'. This is the case whether it is Nichols' social subject affectively engaged by the documentary text in the pleasures and vicissitudes of the historical world, Renov's understanding of documentary poetics as a base for knowledge, desire and ecstasy or Cowie's visual pleasure in the spectacle of actuality. Moreover, when Renov identifies the critic's own attachment to documentary, he echoes Metz's description of the cinema industry. For Metz, success with audiences and, thus, industry success, hinges on desire. The perpetuation of the cinema institution is based in desirous relationships which include the 'cinematic writer' as he is 'struck by the extreme concern he often reveals – a concern which gives him an odd resemblance to producer and consumer – to maintain good object relations with as many films as possible, and at any rate with the cinema as such' (20).

This characterisation of cinema is one that privileges emotional attachments, those of the spectator, the producer and, not least, the critic or cinema writer. There is a broader narrative in play here that indicates how the institution of documentary operates as an 'object', attracting a range of different critical, political and spectatorial investments. Further, all attachments entail the designation of good and bad objects. For example, if Cowie gestures towards the ambivalent anxiety around documentary, this should also be understood as a reference to a single object and its shifting status – it oscillates between good and bad. If documentary entails the desire for truthfulness, this also contains the possibility of the untruthful. The pleasure gleaned by the viewer is in the constant restoration of documentary as a source of knowledge. Confidence, and thus good (object) relations, is maintained because, in most cases, the expectation that documentary will convey knowledge about the historical world, that it will present the viewer with previously unknown historical truth, persists.

Subjectivity, knowledge and the historical documentary

One important category, the pointedly political documentary, manifests some of the most intense expectations around the documentary object. Here I wish to suggest just some ways of characterising audience investments in this kind of documentary practice. The social advocacy documentary has a long history that extends across European, British and American (North and South) traditions of film-making. The different groupings of documentaries and film-makers that constitute this tradition are expansive. When socio-political themes are present in documentary, they are often aligned, historically, with John Grierson's influence on the genre. Yet while Grierson may have been concerned with civic responsibility and collectivist influence, his conception of documentary was not a radical one – at most his was a reformist position, not at odds with the dominant social order. In contrast, Thomas Waugh uses the term 'committed documentary' to describe 'a specifically ideological undertaking, a declaration of solidarity with the goal of radical socio-political transformation' (xiv). At the heart of this definition is an alignment between the processes of material social change, the filmic object and the subjectivities associated with it. The committed documentary frequently bears the weight of political expectation and hope, as it assumes the status of a valued cinematic form that is invested with the capacity to trigger transformation.

In drawing a distinction between a Griersonian realist tradition and committed radical documentary practice, particularly the radical films emerging out of the counter cultures of the 1960s, Brian Winston couches his assessment in affective terms:

> The perennial unattractiveness of many documentaries, certainly many unvoyeuristic ones, to audiences must be acknowledged. This means, in effect, acknowledging the connotations of 'public education'. Audiences know full well that Grierson's public education purpose, however much glossed and disguised, is a virtual guarantee of boredom. For sixty years documentaries have gained nothing from being a 'discourse of sobriety' except marginalisation. It is possible to gloss Metz's remark that 'One is almost never totally bored by a movie' by adding 'unless it be a Griersonian documentary!'
>
> (*Claiming the Real* 254–5)

This characterisation is quite different from narratives that invest the 'discourses of sobriety' with the potential for instrumental power.

For Winston, far from embracing the educational impetus that dominated earlier documentary cinema, many documentary film-makers of the late 1960s and 1970s worked to stake out a new claim on the post-Griersonian stage, perceiving realist documentary rhetoric as an incumbrance. These include the feminist documentaries of the 1970s and 1980s such as *Union Maids* (1976) and *With Babies and Banners* (1978) and the historical compilation film, such as *The Atomic Café* (1982), *Seeing Red* (1983), *The Good Fight* (1984). While these documentaries were at times negatively critiqued for their inadequate standards of 'seriousness' or clarity when measured against the Griersonian tradition, for Winston a post-Griersonian cinema should be open to a range of different non-fiction traditions and the pursuit of new representational possibilities. The shift described here attempts a re-valuing of documentary in the eyes of audiences in order to revive the genre as a tool for social transformation; integral to this is a movement away from the restrictions posed by the precepts of realist documentary. This example points to one way in which documentary can be valued, de-valued or re-valued in the dialogue between audiences, critics and film-makers. If social advocacy documentary's status has been bolstered, as Winston suggests, this has been done, over a period of time and in different instances, in order to address new audiences, to rethink and reformulate particular modes of documentary or emphasise the aspects that are most successful with audiences.

Nevertheless the polarities of the emotions of pleasure and aversion, or simple alignments with, on the one hand, viewing pleasure, or with boredom or ideological dissatisfaction on the other, are inadequate when measured against examples that are less clear-cut. Documentaries that present the traumatic events of the past or ongoing lack and loss in ways that are linked to different affective goals are one case in point. The Holocaust documentary is significant in this respect. As a set of documentaries, those that focus on the Holocaust are pleasing not because they are pleasurable, but because they order and/or contribute to the recording and archiving of events that require memorialisation. Joshua Hirsch explores the ways in which such documentary, after the initial registering of a catastrophic historical event, must work to constantly reiterate the shocking nature of the original atrocities: 'Documentary images must be submitted to a narrative discourse the purpose of which is, if not to literally traumatize the spectator, at least to provoke a posttraumatic historical consciousness – a kind of textual compromise between the senselessness of the initial traumatic encounter and the sense-making apparatus of a fully integrated historical narrative [...]' (11). One fundamental issue at stake here is the value of a documentary discourse on trauma; either it invokes some actual form of trauma, or in some other way represents an originary moment of trauma to the spectator. As Hirsch notes, there is not a clear consensus among scholars on the manner in which trauma should be represented, but its place in the cinematic imaginary is undisputed. While these are not 'pleasing' texts, their production is necessary and valuable.

The emotions frequently define our relationship to documentary, as they do for all films. However, as conventions and themes are repeated across groupings of documentaries, more precise relationships emerge that begin to permeate these filmic languages: the political documentary and the desire for social change, the realist documentary and the boredom of education, trauma and the Holocaust documentary. Yet these brief examples can only gesture towards some aspects of the role of emotion in the relationship between histories of signification and the audience. How can we account more fully for the relationship between signification, ideology and the work of affect in ways that remain open to different histories of documentary practice and reception, as well as to a range of social contexts?

In this respect, I acknowledge Richard Dyer's important work on musicals and utopia. Dyer, in his analysis of utopia and Hollywood musicals seeks to account for the text's capacity to present feelings, which are both aesthetically and narratively authenticated (which he terms 'intensity'). In wanting to argue that emotions are coded and we learn how to respond to particular signs, he seeks to emphasise 'not the connections between signs and historical events, personages, or forces, but rather the history of signs themselves as they are produced in culture and history' (22). In this way, for Dyer, the entertainment forms he discusses present utopia as a set of feelings and so work at the level of sensibility in which an affective code is married with a mode of cultural production, the musical. Within this, 'to be effective, the utopian sensibility has to take off from the real experiences of the audience. Yet to do this, to draw attention to the gap between what is and what could be, is, ideologically speaking playing with fire' (25–6). The risk Dyer is referring to here is founded in the need to manage the contradictions between the desire for a utopian solution, a desire that is perpetuated by the capitalist system, and the social tensions and disenfranchisements in the experiential world of the audience. These disenfranchisements are also the product of capital.[9]

Dyer restricts his theorisation of emotional coding to utopianism and its realisation in entertainment, and the musical especially – one of the most politically conservative of film genres. Documentary offers a very different set of possibilities. While not all aspects of documentary fit easily within a category of entertainment, much of it does. It would seem that many of the ways in which documentary seeks to please, intersect with the potential for it to entertain.[10] Documentary may respond, as all entertainment does, to 'needs created by society' (24), but this is seldom in ways that consistently effect an orientation towards a singular utopian solution. Among non-fiction film, the rich tradition of social advocacy film-making, or Holocaust documentary, as I have noted, complicates this. While the sensibilities of the documentary are specific to the form and to particular examples therein, Dyer alerts us to the role emotions play in the ordering of the topography of ideology in which filmic texts and the history of signs are entrenched. So far I have perceived documentary as a particular kind of object or set of objects. In the next section, I wish to expand on how emotions influence the connections between viewers and documentaries. This requires a fuller discussion of the relations between selves and the objects of their emotional attachments.

Object relations and subjective performance

Metz draws on the work of Melanie Klein at the outset of his analysis and this is instructive. Kleinian psychoanalysis is distinguished by its emphasis on object relations, a set of theoretical concerns that has not been sufficiently explored in film studies,[11] especially in respect to documentary. Objects are all entities with which one forms an emotional relationship. Phantasies revolve around the relation between the self and good and bad objects and, while these begin in infancy, Klein understands that 'all aspects of mental life are bound up with object relations' (52), and thus also with affective identifications. The good object primarily is the mother[12] (and previous to this, the mother's breast), which becomes internalised through a process of introjection, and works as a source of inner strength, peace, hope and comfort as an internal object throughout life. In this respect, unlike Freud, Klein offers a notion of the self that is reliant on human relations (in the first instance, the mother), placing an emphasis on intersubjectivity. For Klein, the 'real objects and imaginary figures, both external and internal, are bound up with each other' (141). Emotions and perceptions of real events and people in the world are directly influenced by phantasies. The turn to 'external good objects as a means to disprove all anxieties' (145) is also a way to avoid reactivating the depressive position of early childhood development, which indicates the importance of maintaining trust in external objects and values.

Object relations pertain to the internal, psychic world of the individual, but also to relations between individuals and the social-historical world. In this way, psychoanalysis can be taken beyond the limits of the cinematic apparatus and brought to bear on the social expectations, perceptions and discourses of cinema and documentary in particular. To understand documentary through pre-established 'good object relations' is to position the form within theoretical approaches to cinema, while also opening the way for more precise genre considerations. Documentary may function in the manner in which Metz describes the cinema institution broadly – its very existence, through a circuit of commercial return and audience attendance (or television ratings and DVD distribution which are more crucial in the case of the commerce of documentary) testifies to the form's fulfilment of good object requirements. Yet this still offers only broad conceptualisations of what is perhaps the most diverse of film genres.

Here I have described one dimension of the emotions that propels expectations among spectators and critics. Beyond an understanding of how good object relations might be maintained at the level of genre, there are more specific questions at stake below this broad level of categorisation. I am interested in how the figure of the cultural other – the individual who is defined by how far removed they are from the life world or subjectivity of the viewer – emerges as a particularly cogent object of desire in documentary. This may materialise in a range of different ways. The desire that is apparent as scopophilia is inevitably concerned with sexualised desire for the other. Alternatively, desire might take the form of an anticipation to possess or assimilate the other through gaining knowledge, or to observe/experience, as the narrative progresses, their triumph or failure. All these assume a type of feeling for the other. This is often present as empathy but not exclusively – it may also take the form of disgust, hope or fear. Spectatorial desire can also be directed as a hope for some kind of transformation in the world of the documentary, and thus in the world of the social actor represented.

Beyond this, as I have noted, is the desire for the documentary to trigger social change. In offering a sense of connection between the world of social events and the viewer, committed or political documentaries most obviously work to activate, or are activated by, this emotion.

In one respect, emotion can shape our relationship to the genre and the other who is represented on screen. But there is a second analytical possibility at stake here; emotion is key to the representation of filmic subjects and the construction of intersubjectivity in film. Because representations frame individuals as social agents, and as socially conditioned selves, they are presented as subjects in the text. Thus, they exhibit motives that are not limited to our understanding of them as objects. As I will discuss in later chapters, subjects in documentary may desire, for example, self-actualisation and success, social change, self-determination or sexual agency. Moreover, the creator – the film-maker or doco-auteur – can similarly be cast as subject or object depending on how their point of view or motivation is signified and posed as part of a documentary's address to the viewer. It could be argued that in their traditional position behind the camera, the documentary film-maker is always the subject of the documentary, as it is their perspective the viewer sees from. Cinema studies took up psychoanalysis principally to formulate a theory of the subject, a subject that has been explored, most thoroughly, in relation to the 'coherence of meaning and vision' (De Lauretis 138) that positions the spectator within an apparatus of looks. I resist a notion that exclusively defines diegetic subjectivity as one that relies on the look or perspective of the camera as a surrogate for point of view.

This aspect of apparatus theory has, for some time, not been sufficient as an analytical tool. Given this, how might the non-fiction genre contribute to a detailed rethinking of conceptualisations of the construction of intersubjectivity in film? It is seldom the case in documentary that the viewer is asked to look from the perspective of the individuals whose stories are being conveyed, as if from the eye of the camera or through identification with their gaze. Documentary audiences have become accustomed to the fantasy of perspective in documentary being composed through the terms of the intersubjective. In other words, perspectives of selfhood work relationally and as a dialogue between the viewer and the performance of the character on the screen. It is through *performance* that subjects become epistemologically intelligible to the viewer, through observation. It is also through performance that individuals are positioned as social actors and desiring agents in documentary. This intersubjectivity is highlighted by Lisa Cartwright, who notes: 'In an era dominated by the scholarly claim that the media shape opinion and ideology, we would do well to remember that what also moderates media reception is observation of other people, and immersion in the affective relationships that pass between bodies and among communities, on screen and off' (32). Following this, Cartwright's endeavour is to rethink psychoanalytic film theory through a consideration of object relations, but despite the emphasis on off-screen associations, her approach remains primarily concerned with the close reading of text/spectator relations. I contend that to fully grasp the way documentary circulates among constituencies of viewers, the socio-historical worlds in which documentaries are embedded (that is say, the worlds they represent, the worlds viewers inhabit, and the correlation between these) must be accounted for. Within these public realms, the film-maker frequently exists not simply as the *subject* of representation, but also as the *object* of various emotions. If the documentary, attributed to the vision of the film-maker, makes an argument that, in turn, infers the presence of an author-subject, this author also attracts feelings of hope and trust as they objectify the desires of constituencies of viewers. But they should not be considered as ideal objects; as the figure of Michael Moore demonstrates, the doco-auteur can quickly become a bad object if they are associated with deception and a deficit of authenticity.

In this book I will sort through the various ways in which performances, and performativity, are relevant to documentary. In seeking to account for the expanding formal and aesthetic parameters of documentary, Bruzzi argues that all documentaries are 'performative acts' (1). Documentaries are increasingly employing dramatic effects and image manipulation to argue their point and the further from the established conventions of observational and expository form documentaries move, the more performative the approach. As I discuss in my chapter on 'civic love' and the new style of reflexive film-making, this signals, specifically, the presence of a particular doco-auteur. Perhaps even more salient, however, is the more obvious performance of the social actor in the diegesis. This performance, as I have noted, frequently offers the most compelling point of engagement for the audience. It would be naïve to read these performances as unmediated presentations of a self that are not subordinated to the film-maker's vision. Yet to simply understand these representations of subjectivity as outcomes of the production process is to ignore how this process can function as a site of dialogue between film-maker and filmed. While the finished documentary is ultimately out of the control of those depicted, the performance indicates a negotiation between the capacity for the subject to speak and the context in which that speech is enabled.

This points to a more fundamental concern in discussions of subjectivity – the way human individuals are constituted with social capacities and capabilities and the extent to which, and how, such social subjects are determined by the norms and values to which they are subjected. These questions contribute to what Nikolas Rose refers to as 'the problem of the self' (xvi) in sociological thought. It is not my aim to confront this problem or to present a revised theory of the self. Rather, the chapters that follow seek to elucidate particular representational practices that offer articulations of selfhood in defined circumstances and texts. In each case the social technologies, norms and discourses (and the performances) are specific to the themes of the documentaries in question. Suffice to say that my approach is consistently underpinned by the notion that subjects are subordinated to power in ways that both subject the self to that power *and* produce social agents. Judith Butler captures this contradiction when she writes, 'subjection consists precisely in the fundamental dependency on a discourse we never chose but that, paradoxically, initiates and sustains our agency' (*The Psychic Life of Power* 2). Further to this, because the book is concerned with the representation of subjectivity, and minoritarian subjectivities in particular, a reoccurring concern in the case studies is the relation between self and other, whether it is between character and viewer or only between individuals in the text. As I will argue, this manifests in many of the documentaries as an issue of responsibility – the responsibility of responding to or acknowledging the plight of the other, or to conduct oneself in the most appropriate way as a member of the body politic.

Notes on organisation

In this introduction, I have explored various concepts within a film-studies frame that reference the long-standing relationship between the institution of cinema and documentary. While this disciplinary focus informs my approach, I acknowledge that documentary is an expansive category that encompasses not only cinema, but also a variety of mediums, from photography, literature and painting through to the range of popular factual programming and current affairs that can be found on television. This abundance indicates the richness of the area. Staking out a terrain within this profusion of forms, I am concerned primarily with audio-visual examples of documentary.

The ways in which the viewer-subject is addressed and interpellated by documentary alters according to the differing contexts of reception. The intersubjective relationship between viewer and viewed must also differ. The differences between television and cinema and how they construct the viewer or spectator have been most theorised by scholars. The differences hinge on the distinction between the darkened space of the cinema and the everyday environment of the domestic realm. One engages the psychical mechanisms of the unconscious and the other must accommodate the viewer distracted by the rhythms of the private sphere. Significantly both provide the conditions for intimate connections and viewing practices. While the distinction between these two is important, there is still more at stake.

The avenues for viewing documentary have become increasingly fractured; perhaps more so than any other genre of 'old' mass media. Hence, documentary defies any privileged association with a specific forum for reception. One-off independent documentaries comfortably transgress the boundaries between theatrical release and television. Yet in recent decades the small screen has become integral to documentary distribution. Significant influences on the mode of the televisual address might include the distinctions between the commercial and public broadcasting of documentary, the predominance of non-fiction programming on increasingly popular 'History' or 'Discovery' channels, underground or commercial DVD distribution and also Internet streaming. The proliferating avenues for documentary reception on the small screen has, undoubtedly, contributed to the revival of theatrically released documentary and the increasing openness of audiences to consuming non-fiction on the large screen. Even within the category of 'theatrical' screening important differences in reception exist between mainstream commercial cinema, art-house release, film festivals and, for social advocacy documentary, small-scale educational and activist-oriented screening contexts.

My analysis does not disregard the importance of reception, but it is more concerned with the social worlds in which documentaries circulate than the detail of sites of reception and the methods of research pertaining to these. The primary avenue for viewing these texts is via the small screen and many of the documentaries here are shot and distributed on digital formats rather than film. Although my approach draws significantly on the theoretical traditions of film studies, the notion that documentaries find a home across a variety of audio-visual media is acknowledged throughout the arguments in this book. As each grouping of documentary is considered in the following chapters, the prevalent forum for distribution underpins my assumptions about the effect and circulation of the texts.

The focus on the connections forged between emotions and politics has motivated the concerns of each chapter. Necessarily the documentaries explored here concentrate on the expression of minoritarian subjectivity, countercultural movements or the particulars of class, ethnicity, gender and age. While many of the film-makers and films discussed in this book have gained great notoriety, such as the award-winning *Born into Brothels* or the documentaries in the next chapter that examine the pornography industry, many, such as the Asian Australian authored documentaries, are less known. The chapters are organised around trends in documentary and the subjectivities that are most visibly aligned with these groupings of films or television series. Following this, the chapters explore how these subjects are shaped by their relationship to a narrow band of emotions, such as pleasure, disgust, pain, loss, care, hope and nostalgia. In each chapter, the work of these emotions is considered in respect to the specific aesthetic, social and historical features of the documentaries under discussion.

The second chapter in Part I continues the discussion of pleasure and desire through examining documentaries about the pornography industry. The focus of this chapter is the figure of the female porn star, a frequent object of fascination and scrutiny in these documentaries. This discussion explores the intersecting histories of documentary and moving image pornography and the way both contribute to the sexualisation of the female body. Yet in contemporary popular culture, narratives that frame female sexual agency, often identified as post-feminist narratives, complicate the construction of women as objects rather than as subjects of desire. Key here is not only the pleasure promised by the figure of the porn star, but also the abjection and disgust that often troubles representations of the body. In focusing on three documentaries – *Sex: The Annabel Chong Story* (1999), *Inside Deep Throat* (2005) and *The Girl Next Door* (2000) – this chapter locates these female subjects, and female desire, within historical and contemporary narratives of female sexuality. In exploring these documentaries, this chapter takes up the relationship between desire, pleasure and documentary initiated in this introduction and looks at it in detail and in relation to a defined set of texts and cultural assumptions.

Part II looks at the representation of pain, the subjectivity of the disempowered other and their claims for agency and recognition. Chapter 3 identifies the problem faced by documentaries that seek to give voice to groups of individuals marginalised within civil society. Here I take up Wendy Brown's theory of 'wounded attachments' as a point of departure, to explore how the articulation of pain in identity politics can leave these subjects in stasis, attached to their own social exclusion. Focusing on two documentaries in particular, *Fix: The Story of an Addicted City* (2002) and *Rize* (2005), I locate this rhetorical move, and the spectacle of anguish and suffering, in relation to the history of the victim documentary. This chapter evaluates the potential for these documentaries to represent pain and subjectivity in ways that imagine a social future that is transformed and without pain. Chapter 4 examines the work of British film-maker Kim Longinotto. This chapter discusses four of her most recent and most well-known documentaries: *Divorce Iranian Style* (1998), *Runaway* (2001), *The Day I will Never Forget* (2002) and *Sisters in Law* (2005). Extending the analysis of pain developed in the previous chapter, here I explore how the documentaries weave together the activity of expressing pain or witnessing the pain of others (both physical and psychical) and confronting disenfranchisement. Significantly, this is a specifically gendered pain as it is women who are cast as both the subaltern and the agents of social transformation. Rather than a self-subversion, pain is rendered as part of the process of translation that is central to Longinotto's practice.

Part III focuses on the confluence of different emotions that, in combination, work to signal the presence of the film-maker. Chapter 5 explores the production of Asian Australian subjects as documentary authors in four prominent Australian documentaries produced over the previous decade: *Chinese Takeaway* (Mitzi Goldman, 2002), *Sadness: A Monologue by William Yang* (Tony Ayres, 1999), *The Finished People* (Khoa Do, 2003) and *Letters to Ali* (Clara Law, 2004). Emotions of loss and care mark not only the diasporic subjects but also the relation between text and audience. My reading of these subjectivities moves beyond established theories of diasporic identity construction and politics to explore how these Asian Australian authors act as a locus for the circulation of particular emotions in the context of an Australian cultural imaginary. Included within this dynamic of loss are not only the bereavements of loved ones, but also the losses that are bound to the movements of modernity, such as the lost fullness which is the promise of diaspora, the failure or absence of universal citizenship and the lack of safety in life lived in advanced capitalism.

Chapter 6 looks further at the labour of care in the authorial performance. Here I focus on well-known international documentaries that critique corporate capitalism, in particular *The Corporation* (2003), *Enron: The Smartest Guys in the Room* (2005) and *Supersize Me* (2004). This is an examination of how 'civic love', as one particular manifestation of authorial care, coalesces around the documentary film-maker. Less to do with actual love, this is a form of civic devotion and loyalty to the social collective that references the style of critique and citizenship associated with the figure of Socrates. Yet this notion of care operates in tandem with the sensibilities of irony and subversion that characterise the aesthetics of contemporary activist movements.

Part IV is concerned with the questions of temporality and the emotions that pertain to the past and the future, such as hope and nostalgia. Chapter 7 is concerned with documentaries that offer children an avenue through which to perform the self. It tracks the interplay between the objectification of children and the rendering of child subjectivity in relation to a politics of hopefulness and futurity and the unique ways documentary expresses the transitional state of childhood. In particular, I assess the representation of childhood in *Born into Brothels*, a recent award-winning American documentary focused on impoverished children in Kolkata. In the final chapter I look at the important relationship between tele-vision and docu-mentary through the lens of reality television. As television's fore-most non-fiction form, reality programming has been understood by scholars to highlight the emotions in ways that set it apart from traditional documentary modes. This chapter seeks to revise this characterisation and explores how the example of *Australian Idol*, and the *Idol* franchise more broadly, offers conceptualisations of history and historical subjects that are akin to those of the civic ethos of much traditional documentary. Through an examination of multicultural pasts and the recycling of popular music, I explore how the series might offer a space for reading history at the level of lived affective experience.

2
Pleasure and Disgust: Desire and the Female Porn Star

Since the mid-nineties documentary film-makers have become increasingly interested in exploring the world of pornography. These productions have come to represent one of the most marketable trends in contemporary documentary, particularly in terms of DVD distribution. These documentaries frequently seek to investigate the culture and production of pornography and often take the form of a 'behind the scenes' exposé of the industry and the individuals who work in it. Perhaps more than any other media form, pornography is shaped by and attracts a great deal of strong feeling. The documentary about the pornography industry, or what I term the 'pornography documentary', similarly activates a range of emotions and a number of these emotions centre on the figure of the female porn star. In this chapter, I look in particular at three of these documentaries: *Sex: The Annabelle Chong Story* (2000), *The Girl Next Door* (2000) and *Inside Deep Throat* (2004).

In exploring desire, this chapter looks further at the notion that spectators engage with filmic texts out of pleasure. This expectation of pleasure is closely allied with the question of desire – the desire to see, to know and to experience. In this sense, desire is an agentic experience, linked to hoping and wishing, that anticipates other emotions. In film theory, desire has been posed primarily in the Freudian sense as sexual desire. The subjects and objects of desire I focus on here, the women in the documentaries, are located in a web of desire that is composed of not only sexual desire, but also of the forms of wishing that motivate the self-determining agent and the pleasurable scene of knowledge that documentary promises.

In Christian Hansen, Catherine Needham and Bill Nichols' discussion of pornography and ethnography, they argue that 'both pornography and ethnography promise something they cannot deliver: the ultimate pleasure of knowing the Other. On this promise of cultural or sexual knowledge they depend, but they are also condemned to do nothing more than make it available for representation' (225). In other words, as viewers we desire pleasure but will never be pleased entirely (in pornography we extract pleasure but this is never the pleasure that is represented), we desire to know but cannot fully appropriate the knowledge that is represented (knowledge of the cultural other in the case of ethnography). Hansen, Needham and Nichols' formulation is instructive for a number of reasons. The representation of women in the pornography documentary appeals to the viewer's desire for knowledge about the other. This desire is based in pre-existing expectations and what is already known about the aesthetic qualities of documentary and pornography. Yet the pornography documentary emerges at a historical moment when female subjectivity and desire occupy a site of particular fascination and struggle. If these documentaries are organised around the pleasure of knowing the other, and thus engage a narrative desire that works at the intersection of pornography and documentary, how is (heterosexual) female desire, or the female as desiring subject, positioned in the documentaries?

Claire Johnston writes that 'in order to counter objectification in the cinema, our collective fantasies must be released: women's cinema must embody the working through of desire: such an objective demands the use of the entertainment film' (31). The problem of desire and female subjectivity in film has occupied scholars for some time, yet the terms of this problem have shifted greatly from the 1970s when Johnston was writing. The quest to release collective female fantasies has become complicated by the proliferation of sexual discourses in the contemporary media sphere, many of which attempt to attend to female desire. The sphere of popular culture in which pornography documentaries circulate is one that has seen mainstream representations explore what 'female sexual agency' might mean, most notably in the much discussed examples of *Sex and the City* or *Bridget Jones's Diary*. This sphere has emphasised female desire and pleasure, yet not necessarily on the terms second wave feminism might intend.[1] I focus in on the figure of the female porn star and how she is produced at the intersection of popular feminism, and narratives of female agency, and the historical conventions of genre that seek to organise desire.[2]

Pornography and non-fiction histories

The thematic and technological concerns that influenced early cinema offer important insights into the convergence of the prehistory of documentary cinema and moving image pornography. At this juncture, specific reading formations pertaining to the female body were set in motion. Theorisations of early cinema and other even earlier forms of visual culture in the latter decades of the nineteenth century suggest that these prehistories are constituted through a single apparatus of vision that ordered the relationship between pleasure, the body and cinematic technology. Tom Gunning draws on the writings of Sergei Eisenstein to describe early cinema[3] as a 'cinema of attractions' or a mode of visuality that emphasised the fascination in display, rather than the storytelling function that was later to govern classical cinema. These actuality films included travel film and topicals (short films depicting current events), re-enactments and scenes of everyday life. They emphasised the pleasure of vision and presented an illusion of actuality on the screen in a way that prefigures the documentary proper. Yet in a manner that sits uncomfortably with Grierson's documentary project of social betterment, actuality films and a cinema of the attractions adhere to, for Gunning, a metapsychology emerging from a 'lust of the eye'. Gunning identifies an aesthetic of attractions that encompasses the pleasure in looking at novelty, aggressive sensations that infer the threat of injury (such as a speeding train) and a sexualised fascination with the body evident in films that present female nudity, revealing clothing and other moments of gendered bodily display ('Now You See It' 4).

Sensations, movement or the presentation of the body were thus central to the apparatus of early cinema and to the changing culture out of which it emerged. The 'lust of the eye' indicates a sensibility of the time concerned with the affective and the corporeal possibilities of thrilling and pleasurable experiences. Documentary's connection to science and the status of its 'truth telling' qualities is established not in the Griersonian era that documentary is most frequently associated with, but in a longer history of modern science and the development of photographic technology within that history. Ethnography, in the form of travel films which record indigenous peoples at home and abroad, perpetuate this discourse of science within a focus on the body of the other. Yet more importantly for a consideration of documentary and pornography, the pleasure in and desire for indexical evidence about the world and the body's place in it becomes sexualised and specifically focused on the female body as early as the 1880s. An important precursor to Gunning's gendered bodily display can be found in Eadweard Muybridge's photographic series' that were set to motion by way of the 'zoopraxiscope', a cinematic device that was a precursor to film.[4]

Muybridge's photographs, for Linda Williams, capture not only the visual spectacle and 'truth' of moving bodies through new forms of visual apparatus, but are also a social apparatus that positions women as the objects of vision rather than its subjects. In the photographs, women's bodies are reproduced by way of existing understandings of the gendered disciplining of the body. As Williams identifies, women are fetishised in the images through self-conscious gestures (such as a running woman grasping her breast or raising a hand to the mouth) and through the use of props (such as a newspaper, a smoking cigarette or a fully made up bed that the woman lies down on). These gestures differ greatly from the male models' engagement in sports and heightened physical movement (*Hard Core* 39–40). The point here is not so much the status of women's bodies as objects, but the way these images, produced putatively to satisfy questions of science and measurement, betray an aestheticisation and fantasy of the sexualised body. Woman is marked through her associations with erotic meaning and thus by her difference and her lack.

This is important in the development of cinema because, as Williams theorises, 'by denying the woman-in-movement any existence apart from these marks of difference, Muybridge himself could be said to have begun the cinematic tradition of fetishization that exerts mastery over difference' (*Hard Core* 42). Inevitably, these projections became as much an investigation of the nature of motion as a forum for the voyeuristic and pornographic reception of female sexuality for a largely male audience. Muybridge's work exists at the crossroads of two trajectories: (1) a lineage of modern science that assimilates the camera as an inscription device and thus a truth-telling instrument, and this is a perception that goes on to structure the later social importance of documentary and (2) the establishment of cinema's gendered looking relations that rely on the function of voyeurism and fetishisation that were articulated much later by Laura Mulvey. These looking relations are posed, in Muybridge's work, through the pleasure in the investigation of the naked female and male bodies and, as such, echo one of the preoccupations of moving-image pornography.

As Catherine Russell observes, the activities Muybridge's models perform are largely those that would have been associated with the working classes (72). Adding to this, the models, particularly the women, would have been working-class individuals of the time. This awareness then contributes another dimension to the dialectic between the upper class, educated audience for these projections and the emphasis on the physicality of the models which aligns them with the natural world rather than with 'culture'. The mastery over difference noted by Williams takes on added weight and complexity in the case of working-class women. As I will discuss, class becomes an important feature in understandings of contemporary pornography.

The confluence of technological, social and imaginative developments that mark the prehistory of moving image pornography and documentary cinema demonstrate how both were part of an apparatus of vision that was facilitated by the pleasure in knowledge underpinning science and its instrument, photography. This desire coalesced around the body whether it was the thrills, sensation and display of the cinema of attractions, the body of the other in ethnography or the body in motion of the zoopraxiscope. This historical signification of the body impacts on the discourses of non-fiction and pornography by establishing the female body as an object of desire in ways that are tied to the function of display and non-fiction spectacle. The effects that follow from the co-mingling of these two related systems of vision and desire find an important point of documentary articulation, later, in the figure of the female porn star. Representations in the pornography documentary offer the female porn star as an object of pleasure and as an object of knowledge. In the case of the latter, it is the question of female sexual agency that is scrutinised within the narrative.

Beyond *Not a Love Story*: Sex, documentary and the contemporary public sphere

A much-discussed early example of the documentary representation of the pornography industry offers an important point of reference for the popularisation of feminist-derived narratives of female sexual subjectivity. In *Not a Love Story: A Film about Pornography* (1981) by Canadian film-maker, Bonnie Klein, feminist commentators, writers and men and women who worked in the sex industry were interviewed regarding the malignant and misogynist nature of the pornography business. For decades, this film has been a source of critique for feminist scholars drawn to question the film's reductive anti-pornography stance.[5] It is not my aim here to retrace this work, but rather to point to the way the documentary exemplifies the emotionalism of the pornography debate more broadly and to highlight the problem of definitively organising the classification and reception of visual texts about pornography.

In the first instance, Susanna Paasonen describes *Not a Love Story*, based in the radical feminist principles of the 1970s, as 'saturated with expressions of feeling' (47). The documentary gives voice to a range of emotions, from the discomfort of a male actor in the face of having to perform scenes of physical domination, through to the anger and sorrow of feminist activists, or the boredom of those who discuss their work doing live sex shows. Paasonen theorises, more broadly, the Anglo-American anti-pornography movement and its consistent recourse to a rhetoric of hurt, anger and fear as 'a discourse of negative affect' (47). This indicates the significance of affect in the critical reception of pornography. It also presents, for Paasonen, an aspect of pornography that has not been sufficiently explored by scholars: 'While there has been a renewed interest in studies of pornography, the seemingly evident connections of affect and pornography have not been addressed in much detail' (47). Within this, she places an emphasis on the dearth of attention to desire or fascination and their importance to the critical and popular circulation of pornography. As I explore, desire works in complex and paradoxical ways in relation to the pornography documentary.

Paula Rabinowitz also highlights the documentary's appeal to the emotions when she writes that *Not A Love Story* is

one of the most popular and highest grossing documentaries ever produced by the Canadian Film Board; however, audiences in a nation with restrictions on the public display of pornography are not necessarily seeing a tale of mourning and outrage; many are watching for the crotch shots that are meant to horrify, not titillate.

(*They Must Be Represented* 2)

Rabinowitz is referring to the multiple affective registers in the documentary and its capacity to be simultaneously compelling and saddening or appalling. She echoes B. Ruby Rich's suggestion that the 'antiporn film is an acceptable replacement for porn itself [...], the question is whether this outcry becomes itself a handmaiden to titillation, whether this alleged look of horror is not perhaps a most sophisticated form of voyeurism' (*Anti-porn* 58). A single viewer may produce these differing, or ambivalent, readings or they may be the divergent readings of different collectives of viewers. Such a variation in potential readings presents a very specific issue for the pornography documentary's aesthetic organisation. The recent proliferation of documentaries about pornography has, to varying degrees, assimilated the fascination, or titillation, Rabinowtiz and Rich refer to overtly into the text and into marketing and distribution material. They address a viewer who desires knowledge about pornography (documentary) as well as pornographic representation (pornography).

This is an address that frequently seeks to inform and educate the viewer about the sensational or the problematic and exploitative nature of the industry, but also offers the pleasurable viewing experience in which the sexual spectacle is always immanent, but almost never fully realised. The ambivalence that arises here is largely due to pornography's status as a mode of non-fiction and the way that it purports to truthfully present sexual activity and sexualised bodies. However, these documentaries, in spite of the extra-textual address of their marketing, are narratively organised in ways that ultimately forgo sexual arousal for epistephilia, a desire for and pleasure in knowledge.

This strategic address is bound up with the modes of distribution the documentaries enjoy. Independently produced one-off documentaries may be featured on the film festival circuit, but are largely distributed commercially for individual sale and a number can be found in video stores in 'special interest' or documentary sections. These documentaries range from narratives about personalities in the industry: *The Secret Lives of Adult Stars* (2004), *Thinking XXX* (2004), *Hard Trip* (2003), *Porn Star: The Legend of Ron Jeremy* (2001), *Sex: The Annabel Chong Story*, *The Girl Next Door*; the documentation of film productions: *Debbie Does Dallas Uncovered* (2005), *Exposed: The Making of a Legend* (2004), *Inside*

Deep Throat; and documentaries examining the culture and/or industry in a broader fashion: *Rated X: A Journey Through Porn* (1999), *Pornography: The Secret History of Civilisation* (2000), *Skin for Sale* (*La Piel Vendida*) (2004). While almost all of these documentaries feature nudity, none could be categorised as X-rated hardcore pornography. Significantly, these documentaries offer epistephilic satisfaction while also presenting a discursive, narrative focus on sex and eroticised bodies within the legitimacy offered by the expectations of the documentary genre. This is also often the legitimacy of more mainstream avenues of reception such as art-house cinemas and television.

The relationship between these documentaries and television is important and deserves further discussion. If documentary has become cemented as a primarily televisual form (albeit one that has enjoyed heightened periods of cinematic exhibition), the pornography documentary has, within this, secured its own television niche. Over the last decade, broadcast and subscription television has found an audience for this programming in markets such as Australia, the US and the UK either in the form of one-off documentaries, short-run seasons or series' continuing across a number of seasons. For example, in the US, cable channel HBO has produced the *Real Sex* (2001–) series as a 'magazine'-style half-hour slot. Another example is the *Cathouse* (2005–2007) series, set in the *Moonlite BunnyRanch*, a legal brothel in Nevada. In Australia, the pornography documentary finds a free-to-air television release on SBS television[6] where, in recent years, the time slot after 10 p.m. on Friday nights has featured local and international documentaries concerned with sexual themes and explicit sexual content. As a mix of these two examples, the UK has featured documentary series and one-off programming on much free-to-air television, most notably Channel 4 and 5. A number of HBO series' have made their way into British television. This programming has been described as 'docuporn', with the programming, particularly in the late-night schedule, more focused on the potential for arousal than the epistephilic function of documentary.[7] Within this abundance of programming, there is a broad range of approaches to the industry and the representation of women.

The breadth of individual documentaries and television series is suggestive of the status of sexualised representations in the contemporary public sphere. Sensibilities in the current moment contrast greatly with those of the early 80s when *Not A Love Story* was released. This was a time coloured by the polemicised feminist debates around anti-pornography and anti-censorship that feature in the documentary. Also influential was the highly visible movement towards the mainstreaming of pornography with the moment of 'porno chic' and the theatrical release of narrative feature length film such as *Deep Throat* (1972) and *The Devil in Miss Jones* (1973). These films heightened public debate among activists and scholars. *Not A Love Story* emerged out of and contributed to an intensely affectively charged domain, and while the earlier documentary reflects this environment and emphasises an activist agenda, contemporary pornography documentaries largely seek to entertain.

This current trend in documentary successfully appeals to a constituency of viewers not because it presents an illicit margin to the mainstream, but because it furthers an already enlivened sexualisation of public life. Williams describes this movement in a comprehensive way, so I quote her at length:

> Discussions and representations of sex that were once deemed obscene, in the literal sense of being off (ob) the public scene, have today insistently appeared in the new public/private realms of internet and home video. The term that I have coined to describe this paradoxical state of affairs is on/scenity: the gesture by which a culture brings on to its public arena the very organs, acts, bodies, and pleasures that have heretofore been designated ob/scene and kept literally off-scene. [...] On/scene is a way of signalling not just that pornographies are proliferating but that once off (ob) scene sexual scenarios have been brought into the public sphere.
>
> (*Porn Studies* 3)

This on/scenity is fostered, for Williams, not only through changing media technologies such as home video and later the Internet, but also by way of the public staging of incidents such as the Clinton/ Lewinsky affair and the Starr report that followed. In a British context, Brian McNair has observed the sexualisation of the public sphere and the media. He argues that a democratisation and diversification of sexual discourse has occurred. As my discussion of the eroticisation of the female body in historical non-fiction representation suggests, the sexualisation of media forms is not a new phenomenon. Yet the contemporary climate, as McNair and Williams' accounts make clear, presents a shift in the ideologies that inform the representation of sexualised imagery. This is a shift that occurs through a number of different registers.

The most visible shift concerns a certain popularised figuration of female sexuality based on a narrative of freedom, self-maximisation, choice and individualism. This conception of subjectivity references not only neo-liberal values but also the gains of second wave feminism. I am referring to what many scholars identify as a post-feminist[8] dynamic that effectively references the gains of feminism but, in Angela McRobbie's words, also presents an 'active, sustained, and repetitive repudiation or repression of feminism' (257). This mode of femininity appropriates choice and self-empowerment in ways that would not be possible without histories of feminist politics and yet feminism is cast as outmoded and no longer necessary. This popular cultural movement into 'post-feminism' minimises the complexities of power relations and gender inequalities through focusing on individual aspirations and the appropriation of social capital through maximising sexual capital. This often occurs through a self-sexualisation and commodification of the female body, sometimes with an ironic and knowing tone. Social sensibilities, especially where young women are concerned, do not protest sexual objectification, but rather play with the gaze in ways that embrace or enact sexism as a form of sexual agency. For many scholars, it is on these terms that female pleasure and sexuality is now frequently 'on/scene' in popular cultural forms such as narrative fiction film, print media, advertising and television.

Prominent examples of this can be found in the romantic comedy genre with films such as *Bridget Jones's Diary*. As McRobbie notes, this film presents a contradiction (on terms set down by second wave feminism) – Jones is an independent single career woman in her thirties who aspires to attain the fantasy of a traditional wedding and marriage. Also in a British context, 'girl power' films, such as *Bend it Like Beckham* (2002), as Justine Ashby observes, 'somehow managed to link being sexy with being ballsy, to celebrate female camaraderie while privileging individualism. In short, the very logic of "girl power" confounded any real attempt to politicize it' (129).

There are still more televisual examples that foreground modes of sexual agency while retreating from feminist precepts. These include examples in the realm of reality programming such as *Pussycat Dolls Present: The Search for the Next Doll* and the *Next Top Model* format. Seeking to utilise their appearance as markers of status and currency within the sexual economy as a way to fulfil their desires, these women derail the terms of feminism's collective empowerment.

If, as Feona Attwood writes, this sexualisation of culture has also inaugurated a fragmentation of moral consensus around sex and the proliferating discourses of permissiveness (80), this uncertainty has been assuaged by a new morality of individualism and an ideal of self-maximisation. This re-valuation supports pornography's shift into the mainstream imaginary as much of the popular critique, moral disdain and gendered scepticism surrounding the form is overshadowed (to some degree) by an unconditional validation of men and women as equally drawn desiring sexual subjects. Hence, the social world in which the new pornography documentaries circulate is one in which reading formations are now conditioned by this greater visibility of sexual discourses. Society also accepts a narrative of female subjectivity more widely rendered by way of the assertion of sexual desire and autonomy, albeit often without recourse to the recognition of gendered sexual hierarchies. I now turn to an exploration of how this narrative of female sexuality can be understood with regard to the pornography documentary, particularly considering the systems of vision and desire that inform these documentaries.

Documentary and the female subject

Gough Lewis's *Sex: The Annabelle Chong Story*, Christine Fugate's *The Girl Next Door* and Fenton Bailey and Randy Barbato's *Inside Deep Throat* attend to the experiences of women working in the pornography industry. Produced in a contemporary media sphere that has seen the popular refiguring of female desire, they present biographical documentary narratives of the female self and, at first glance, seem to pose this self as desiring subject. Each of these documentaries is in wide circulation on DVD release and each has also had significant exposure on the international film festival circuit. *Sex: The Annabel Chong Story* and *Inside Deep Throat* have enjoyed short-run theatrical release in an art-house cinema context, while *The Girl Next*

Figure 2.1 Annabel Chong in *Sex: The Annabel Chong Story* (Gough Lewis 1999). Courtesy of Omni Int/Greycat/The Kobal Collection/Jesse Fischer

Door was produced for, and first shown on, PBS in the US. Each of these examples takes as its narrative basis an exploration of an aspect of the industry and in so doing seeks to make visible knowledge and information that is not evident in pornographic films themselves. *Sex: The Annabel Chong Story* and *The Girl Next Door* investigate the perspectives and experiences of well-known women who act in moving-image pornography; Annabel Chong in the former and Stacy Valentine in the latter. *Inside Deep Throat* differs in that it examines the context out of which the 1972 film was made and the controversy surrounding it and its popular legacy. The star of the original film, Linda Lovelace (Linda Boreman), is one of a number of figures associated with the film who feature in this documentary account (Figure 2.2).

Made over the course of two years, *The Girl Next Door* follows Valentine at the height of her career. There are many interviews with Valentine and the observational camera also documents her appearances on set, her relationship with fellow actor, Julian, her family and friends and her excursions to the tanning salon, a plastic surgeon and

Figure 2.2   Linda Lovelace: Courtesy of The Kobal Collection.

a hypnotherapist. The opening credits appear over scenes of Valentine, other actors and crew preparing for a shoot. Following this and address-ing the camera Valentine states: 'I never really had anything that I was really good at. I'd envy those people that played basketball all through high school and all through college. They had something they were really good at and I just never had that. I'm really good at sex [...] I'm very confident in my sexual capabilities.' This begins Valentine's consistent self-narration which throughout the documentary focuses on her desire for fame, markers of success in the industry and personal success in relationships. In an early scene after reflecting on her expe-riences with an abusive husband in her hometown of Oklahoma, she states: 'I have the future to look forward to and its very bright.' She also observes that in the pornography 'business women are the money makers'. In contrast with Valentine's articulation of success as an outcome of labour, Annabel Chong references different discourses to support her formulation of herself as desiring subject.

Featuring interviews with Chong (Grace Quek), (Figure 2.1) friends, family and producers and actors in the industry, *Sex: The Annabel Chong Story* explores Chong's life as a student at the University of Southern California and her work in the pornography industry. In particular, the narrative revolves around the making of a film, *The World's Biggest Gang Bang* (1995), in which she has intercourse with 251 men in a single session, setting a world record. In a way that differs from Valentine's positioning, Chong is from what she defines as a 'middle class' Singaporean Chinese family, is an accomplished student and employs a language of feminist critique to narrate her own perspectives of her work. In an interview on a British television show, 'The Girlie Show', which is featured in the documentary, Chong states her motivation in participating in this event: 'I wanted to shake people up from their complacency and all the stereotypes with [sic] women being passive sexual objects [...]. On a personal level I just wanted to explore my own sexuality.' Both Chong and Valentine articulate themselves as desiring subjects and as motivated by the pleasure experienced in sex. Both voice a certain aspirational individualism, Valentine through discourses of labour and Chong through a language of gendered power relations, in which the self can be worked on and maximised through personal choice within a sexual economy.

In comparison with these two examples, Lovelace is not central to the narrative of *Inside Deep Throat*. As the star of the original film, her life is explored alongside that of co-star, Harry Reems and director, Gerard Damiano. Due to her death in 2002, Lovelace's story is represented through interviews with those who worked on the film and also through interviews with her sister, friend and daughter. Lovelace herself appears by way of archived interviews, appearances on talk shows, in photographs and through sequences of *Deep Throat* that are featured in the documentary. This portrayal, which spans the life of the star from her involvement in the film to her death, is one that oscillates between casting Lovelace as a freely choosing, desiring agent and one at the mercy of the sex industry. The archival sequences that feature Lovelace speaking to camera seem to render her as self-propelling and yet others commenting on her life and actions describe her as less than fully aware of the consequences of her actions and, as Damiano states, needing 'someone to tell her what to do'.

One aspect emphasised in the narrative is Lovelace's well-known transition from porn star to anti-pornography activist. Among the footage featuring Lovelace is a sequence of her testimony to the Meese Commission in the 1980s, in which she supported the investigation's agenda to document the harmful effects of pornography.

In her testimony, Lovelace described her participation in *Deep Throat* as resulting from coercion by her husband of the time, Chuck Traynor. Significantly, after Lovelace left the industry, Traynor went on to marry and manage her main competitor, Marilyn Chambers. In a sequence late in *Inside Deep Throat*, Lovelace is shown speaking about her decision to return to the industry and do a photographic spread for *Playboy* magazine at the age of 51, at a time when she is struggling to make a living. *Inside Deep Throat* signifies the indeterminacy of Lovelace as a freely choosing, desiring subject across the course of her life and the documentary.

Each of the three documentaries has sequences in which women express their subjective desire to maximise their social aspirations through utilising sexual capital. The pleasure in and desire for sex is also expressed. In this regard, the representation of the self draws on the conditions of possibility afforded by popular post-feminist narratives. Yet in another respect, the ambivalence that is so evident in the representation of Lovelace also plagues the other two examples as the documentary performances enacted by the women cannot provide a clear placement of female pleasure. These performances in front of the camera effect unstable positions within the textual economy of desire.

As Nichols notes, the documentary form engenders a wish for the depiction of social actors who are adept at 'virtual performance'. This is a performance that 'presents the logic of actual performance without signs of conscious awareness that this presentation is an act' (*Representing* 122). This performance relies upon a system of meanings surrounding vocal tone, gesture and posture that signify authenticity. In *Sex: The Annabelle Chong Story*, Chong demonstrates compelling expressive qualities that construct her as a forceful centre for the narrative. Contributing to this is her mannered performance in interviews and in her direct address to the camera. This presentation of the self is rendered in ways that throw its authenticity into question; hers frequently appears as an actual performance. When she professes her enjoyment of her work in front of the camera, the uneasiness of her embodied presentation works to signify it as a performance. Moreover, in the scenes featured from *The World's Biggest Gang Bang*, Chong's performance during the event, particularly as it is signified in her facial expressions, is ambivalent and could easily be understood as pain rather than ecstasy. Further to this, a reading of Chong's performance must, in ways that differ from Valentine and Lovelace, consider the intensely racialised framing of women of colour who work in the pornography industry.

In the case of Asian women, this is a designation that often locates them as either overtly sexualised or submissive. This coding then marks the possibility for Chong to be cast not only as a sexual object, but also as a trope of racialised Asian femininity. Yet in some respects, the awkwardness and instability of Chong's performance minimises the full impact of this stereotyping. There are a number of dimensions to Chong's character and these often become evident at different moments in the documentary. In some instances, Chong is rendered as a victim exploited by the sex industry and as the survivor of a gang rape, an event that is recounted as she revisits the scene of the attack on a visit to London. She is also shown as the dutiful daughter of conservative parents who only in the course of production become aware of her sex work. Racialised stereotyping is unsettled as the performance confuses any straightforward imposition of classificatory terms. Moreover, the self-narration that is sustained throughout much of the documentary presents Chong as a subject of feminist critique and *also* as hyper-sexual. In this respect, Celine Parrenas Shimizu goes further to describe Chong as a new subject of feminism – an Asian female sexual pervert. For Parrenas Shimizu, in *The World's Biggest Gang Bang* Chong appropriates 'technologies of the camera and the contest for perversity in porn in order to diagnose conventional understanding of female sexuality as bound and limited' (178–9).

Valentine also offers a very compelling character portrait, but one that exists as a more unselfconscious presentation of the self, seemingly a reproduction of the everyday. This performance offers an image of Valentine as financially successful and accomplished as an award-winning actor. However, her personal relationships and her compulsion for different technologies of body management, such as dieting and plastic surgery, cast her in a constant state of anxiety around her ability to maximise the self. In the case of Lovelace, she offers different statements at different times in the course of her life that also function more persuasively as virtual performance, yet collectively, as noted above, they refuse any clear account of her subjective status. Instead they offer a representation of the subject in process, oscillating dramatically between conceptions of her identity through sexual freedom and through describing her sex work as coerced and the result of abuse.

However, while the question of asserting female desire may be a central consideration for the women themselves, the documentary text is oriented towards engaging the viewer's desire for knowledge about the truth of the porn star's participation in the meta-structure of consent. This then becomes a focus on the authenticity of the performance and their value as objects of knowledge, rather than as subjects in the narrative. The performance is a point of pleasurable scrutiny for viewers as it is the locus of the defining question asked of the women, 'is their professed pleasure an authentic pleasure'? Bruzzi observes the importance of performance in documentary reception when she notes 'performance – the enactment of the documentary specifically for the cameras – will always be at the heart of the non-fiction film' (155). The documentary value of these women, as it is presented in the texts, lies in their position as objects of scrutiny; the realisation of their subjective aspiration and pleasure are second-ary. While all documentary performances are inherently unstable as forms of expression, there is an ambivalence to these ones that present them as a particular site of anxious pleasure for the viewer.

The address to the camera about the intimate details of their sexual experience combines with the ambivalences I have described to encourage a seeking out of the most 'truthful' aspects of these performances. This becomes a truth that can never be determined and the testimonies offered by the women can only be read as an indication of the viewer's incomplete knowledge and the undecid-ability of the 'realness' of this intimacy. Significantly, any potential that exists in these performances to emphasise female pleasure is deferred, as the ambivalence of their performances is privileged thus heightening their value as objects of investigation in the docu-mentaries. This eclipsing of subjectivity is further inscribed in the relationship between spectator and text through the framing of the body in pornography documentary.

Subjectivity and the body: Disgust, agency and abjection

Representations of the female porn star cannot escape the signifi-cance of the body as a powerful site of meaning. As I have noted, non-fiction film's promise of a pleasurable experience of actuality has, since early cinema, consistently centred on the spectacle of the female body. This expectation has persisted in the pornography documentary as it continues to organise a relationship between viewer and text in which there is an anticipation that the body will function as an object of pleasure. However, these documentaries frame the body in ways that are less straightforward than the simple display of clothed or naked bodies in silent cinema. It is the endeavour to render subjectivity in the documentary narrative that is constantly troubled by the body's status as sexual and cinematic object. The body always plays a crucial role in the constitution of subjectivity and, in turn, the meaning and valuation of the body is itself produced through the terms of the social. In this respect, the body profoundly influences the location of Chong, Valentine and Lovelace within an economy of desire. As I have argued, the expectation that the body will function as the primary object of pleasure is thwarted as desire is redirected onto the subjective performance as a locus of investigation. Moreover, it is also thwarted by the attempt to represent female subjectivity *and* the body of pornography, creating boundary confusion associated with disgust responses and further complicating the work of the emotions in these documentaries.

One of the compelling aspects of the intimate enunciation of the self in the works is the wilful transgression of bodily boundaries. In *Sex: The Annabel Chong Story* and *The Girl Next Door*, Chong and Valentine make statements in interviews about the different sexual acts they perform and their proficiency in this regard. Owing to censorship classifications, while scenes of intercourse are shown, actual penetration is never included in the frame. In the case of Chong, scenes from *The World's Biggest Gang Bang* are shown progressively throughout the documentary. Excerpts from a number of her other films are also shown. Fewer explicit sex scenes are shown in *The Girl Next Door*, but Valentine is also shown on-set with a camera crew filming her in the course of production. In contrast, *Inside Deep Throat* does feature scenes of sexual penetration. Sequences from *Deep Throat* are, sporadically, cut into the documentary narrative. Two of the scenes featured show Lovelace engaging in fellatio, the practice that is associated with her stardom and around which the fictional premise of *Deep Throat* is based. These excerpts function inter-textually as the pornographic and visual centre of the documentary, much in the way that they do in the narrative of *Deep Throat*.

The question of how documentary evidence of penetration is offered to the viewer is significant because disgust responses are primarily a function for protecting and maintaining the boundaries of the self. Disgust is an emotion, but it is one that bears a decisive relation to an object: 'Disgust is a feeling about something and in response to something, not just raw unattached feeling' (W. I. Miller, 8). This echoes Freud's description of disgust as a response formation that revolves around the body. The orifices that mark the boundary between outside and inside are saturated with potential to elicit disgust. For Julia Kristeva, the ambiguous status of the boundary threshold of the body has the potential, as it is recognised as abject, to obliterate subjectivity as one recognises oneself also as a corporeal object (5). Such a threshold includes bodily fluids and excretions. These, for Miller, also entail 'the danger of defilement' (8). This is a culturally, psychically and historically embedded understanding of the body that accounts as much for our impulses towards our own bodies as those of others.

While objects are not inherently disgusting, meaning can be organised in particular ways to produce disgust. Highly contaminating, an association alone is enough to render a previously pristine object disgusting. Thus, the threat of defilement through association or contact can evoke a disgust response. The bodily thresholds that demonstrate this capacity in the documentaries are the mouth, the vagina and also the anus. Both Chong and Valentine make reference to the activity and their experience of double penetration. While this is never offered visual representation, in *Sex: The Annabel Chong Story* as Chong discusses her first experience of anal sex in voiceover a less explicit sequence from one of her films is shown, suggesting that this is a feature of her moving-image sex work. For Miller, while all orifices are vulnerable areas for emissions and contaminations, the anus is the essence of lowness and untouchability. Of course, the vagina, as a site of fear, hatred and disgust, has a well-documented history. It is also often framed through a discourse of untouchability, but in a way that is highly gendered and corresponds with entrenched misogynist narratives.

In another important acknowledgement of the malleability of bodily boundaries, *The Girl Next Door* features an explicit presentation of Valentine undergoing a liposuction procedure as part of her cosmetic surgery programme. This scene, in which Valentine is unconscious and on the operating table, shows the incision in her stomach and the suction instrument as it probes inside her torso. In a later sequence, collagen is injected into Valentine's lips. The camera also presents images of Valentine in the surgeon's office as he draws on her body to record the regions that will be effected by implants and removals. In this example, because the border, the skin, is transformed into an object it becomes abject. Moreover, in each of the three documentaries the camera consistently centres the *mise en scène* on the naked, or semi-naked female body. This effectively functions not as a sexualising representation, but as a reminder of the vulnerability of the border or the contact zone that is open to aversive or unclean associations.

My aim is not to propose that sex is inherently disgusting, or that sexualised female subjectivity is disgusting, rather that the conjoint non-fiction figuring of the body *and* subjectivity produces an emphasis on the permeability of boundaries that brings about a recognition of the body's abjection. In the documentary about pornography the reactions of disgust that comprise abjection are featured in a way that is not always the case in pornographic representation. The pornography documentary works in a way that pornography seldom does because pornography is less concerned with the articulation of subjectivity. The pleasure of knowing the other, even by way of unverifiable performance, as a coherent subject is central to the narrative desire engendered in this mode of documentary. Yet this subjectivity, once posed, is overtaken by references to the boundary sites that once polluted or transgressed, threaten the very basis of subjectivity. Thus, there is a movement from subjectivity to the threatening recognition of corporeal object. For Kristeva, abjection confounds desire: 'It beseeches, worries, and fascinates desire, which nevertheless, does not let itself be seduced. Apprehensive, desire turns aside; sickened, it rejects' (1). If abjection moves to the forefront of the viewer's relationship with the object of narrative desire, the female porn star, this can be aligned with what Nichols describes as the 'magnitude' of the text (*Representing*). Magnitude describes an effect of the text that is less aligned with the discourses of sobriety and the historical world than a subjective intensity that privileges how the text is *experienced*. In this way, the logic or formal structure that might shape the biographical narratives and articulations of the self in the pornography documentary are minimised in the face of the weight of meaning carried by the body.

Laura U. Marks's notion of the documentary fetish provides a way to think through the affective dimensions of this experience more fully. Wresting the term back from its monopolisation in psychoanalysis, she notes that the fetish is anything defined by its relation to a powerful object: 'All fetishes are translations into a material object of some sort of affect; the fetish described by psychoanalysis is only one of these' (225). Documentary film, as a material object or set of objects, has a fetishlike quality manifest through its relation to the real. The materiality of the documentary is the fetish that transfers the intensity of the object of representation. It transfers the impression 'of the fleetingness of the senses to a recording medium, both its intensity and its evanescence, requires that the fetishlike quality of the audiovisual image be acknowledged' (Marks 231). There is then a tactile, inferred relation between the text and what it represents. This accounts for the historical layers of meaning that leave a trace on the object represented, such as the gendered body, and may be activated by the viewer. In this sense, that which is not explicitly stated, or represented in the filmic language of audio-visual signification, bears weight through the manner in which it is transferred.

The pornography documentary offers a unique example of this function of materiality. The logic of form and narrative, and even indexicality, is surpassed by the experience of the female body and its potential for abjection. Although many scenes of bodily penetration, orifices and fluids are invisible in the documentaries in that they are not featured in the frame, they have great magnitude that is transferred to the experience of the text. The scenes that present Chong's ten-hour sex event are highly affecting because they act as a conduit for what the viewer knows and senses but only partially sees. The experience enabled by the documentary text again impacts upon the placement of female desire. It is not only that the tactility of the body eclipses the self-narrativisation of the female subjects, but also if the body is deemed abject, what is considered disgusting must be expelled or disavowed in order for a stable speaking position to be established. As Elizabeth Grosz observes, for Kristeva, '"proper" sociality and subjectivity are based on the expulsion or exclusion of the improper, the unclean, and the disorderly elements of its corporeal existence that must be separated from its "clean and proper" self' ('The Body' 86). In these documentaries, the constant statements and visual suggestion of the transgression of bodily boundaries and the dwelling in the contact zone of the ambiguous and 'unclean' serve to destabilise women as speaking and desiring subjects within the economy of desire in which these examples are entrenched. Subjectivity's anchoring in the body translates into a troubling encounter with the documentary form and with the disgust reactions to corporeality, rather than articulating a fully realised notion of female sexual pleasure.

The problem of sexual capital

This recognition of bad feeling about the body impacts on the female porn star's place in popular cultural narratives of sexual capital (post-feminist narratives) that helped give rise to the popularity of the pornography documentary. This is because the revised permissive, active sexuality that offers a new post-feminist image for women is also one that comes hand in hand with struggles over exclusive taste formations. There is, as Attwood points out, an important confluence of gender, class, race and sexuality in the contemporary sexualisation of culture. For Attwood, examples such as *Sex and the City* rely upon a form of femininity that casts sex as 'fun' in a way that can only be figured within a bourgeois culture of taste and discerning consumption. The discourse is one in which promiscuous sexuality is 'classy'.

At stake is the mode of sexuality rather than economic capital. 'Available constructions of a female sexuality in which activity and power are expressed in terms of "low" characteristics – for example, in pornography and other forms of obscene or bawdy culture – are firmly eschewed here' (Attwood 85). Moreover, bourgeois sexuality is defined against that which is associated with the low. Although the classy pursuit of sex for pleasure may offer a new figuration of womanhood, this construction of the bourgeois body has a longer historical lineage. As Mikhail Bakhtin has theorised, the rejection of that which is low and the suppression of the corporeal or the grotesque body were integral in the formulation of the 'classical body' of the emerging bourgeoisie of the sixteenth century. The body, since this time, has borne the social coding of class as the gross materiality of the lower aspects of the body are transposed onto the lower social classes. This is a political distancing as those 'civilised' qualities which are difficult to attain, such as refinement, taste, etiquette and the regulation of bodily instincts and behaviour, become the standards of the bourgeois subject.

Laura Kipnis poses this historical opposition as important for an understanding of some modes of pornography, such as that seen on the pages of *Hustler*. She writes that 'the transcoding between the body and the social sets up the mechanisms through which the body is a privileged political trope of lower social classes, and through which bodily grossness operates as a critique of dominant ideology. The power of grossness is predicated on its opposition *from and to* high discourses' (emphasis in original 376). Subjecthood in high culture is therefore constituted through the exclusion and disavowal of the vulgar material body. On these terms, the female porn actor cannot properly recuperate sexual capital because she is over-identified with the lower stratum of the social and the corporeal. This occurs regardless of the actual class background of the women.

The women in *Sex: The Annabel Chong Story*, *Inside Deep Throat* and *The Girl Next Door* present differing manifestations of the experience of being a porn star but all speak to female (hetero)sexual pleasure in ways that cannot find a central place in the documentaries structuring fantasies. The women are caught in the non-fiction ordering of desire and value by the very terms on which subjectivity seeks to enter representation, the ambivalence of the documentary performance on the one hand and the body on the other. Adding to this is the women's failure to acquire cultural capital in ways that would locate them alongside the ascending and enterprising new woman. Yet in another respect, the documentaries, through failing in the stakes of this ideological impetus, reveal the way post-feminism can only offer exclusive, uncomplicated resolutions to the problem of female desire. The documentaries indicate something more profound in the displaced femininity that falls outside the borders of easily assimilable sexuality. Further, if abjection is caused by the disturbing of established systems and orders, they reference the *difficulty* of the body, its materiality and the textual complexity of representing and accessing the actuality of female desire within the scope of what remains a masculine erotic imaginary in popular culture.

Post-feminism's seemingly uncomplicated popular characterisation of femininity and sexuality covers over the ambivalences of subjectivity.

Offering an alternative to this is the example of porn star and performance artist, Annie Sprinkle. In addition to featuring in many porn films in the 1970s and early 1980s, Sprinkle has produced a number of one-woman performances and published a handful of books. Much of Sprinkle's contemporary work is strongly biographical and she has featured in a small number of documentaries. These include *Annie Sprinkle's Herstory of Porn* (1998), directed by Sprinkle, and *Sacred Sex* (Cynthia Connop 1992). These representations offer a significant contrast to the three documentaries discussed here.

While they similarly work to offer the female porn star as an object of pleasure and as an object of knowledge, Sprinkle's performances differ from those already discussed as they are more explicitly engaged in the activity of denaturalising femininity and the question of agency. If she seeks to maximise the self, this is often done through art practice rather than capitalising within a sexual economy. Belonging to a different epoch (that of second wave feminism), Sprinkle's rhetorical and physical gestures are able to achieve what Chong's can only hint at; she denaturalises gender and highlights the instability of speaking positions. In her documentary appearances, Sprinkle describes how she takes on roles, such as the 'porno bimbo character', thus emphasising perfomativity as a documentary convention and as a feature of subjectivity more broadly. While her subjectivity is equally troubled by materiality, she rejects a 'classy' sexuality and, through the use of humour and the investigation of alternative sexual discourses, Sprinkle overtly contests the dominant order. Nevertheless as a 'post-porn goddess', she may contribute to a proliferation of sexual discourses in the public sphere, but her work remains less influential than the representations that adhere to the reclamation of sexual objectification as agency.

For McNair,

> [t]here have been significant and positive changes in the way the media represent sex, sexuality and gender. The 'relentless parade of insults', the 'invisibility and demeaning stereotypes' to which women and gays have traditionally been subjected has been replaced [...] by an altogether more complex and satisfying representational diversity.
>
> (*Striptease* 205)

This is certainly the case to some degree, but the new representational practices McNair refers to cannot be wholly isolated from the entrenched conditions that structure desire of the past. Erotic representations are well established in long-standing regimes of pleasure that pertain to how they are activated within particular vehicles of vision and knowledge such as pornography and documentary. It is in alignment with these regimes that subjecthood coheres within the affect worlds of the social imaginary. While a more complex representational diversity may exist (and the figure of Sprinkle demonstrates this), a dominant ordering of sexuality prevails. I have argued that the emotions of pleasure and desire formulate a multiform popular arena in which the pornography documentary enters into a dialogue with the viewer. Despite the proliferating sexual landscape that would seem to offer greater capacity for the elevation of female sexuality, the emotions that organise a reading of the female other also make this a conditional and difficult undertaking in the pornography documentary.

Part II Pain and the Other

3
Injury, Identity and Recognition: *Rize* and *Fix: The Story of an Addicted City*

One of the early innovations that Grierson is credited with emerged as he attempted to bring to the screen the faces and bodies of the working class. He sought to portray them not as objects of ridicule, but as social agents in their own environments and with their own voices. This undertaking incorporated new sound technologies that allowed film-makers to convey the image and the voice of this subject in ways that supported Grierson's social and aesthetic agenda. In 1934 he stated: 'If we are showing workmen at work, we get the workmen to do their own commentary, with idiom and accent complete. It makes for intimacy and authenticity, and nothing we could do would be half as good' (quoted in Winston, 'The Tradition' 39). From this time on, the victimised and the stoic worker, as speaking subjects, become a key feature of the representation of the social world in realist documentary.

So far, in discussing the role of the emotions in documentary, I have emphasised the importance of pleasure and desire. I have understood the text as an object of pleasure and considered the subject of pleasure in the text – the female porn star – while acknowledging how aversive emotions, such as disgust, are also mobilised in documentary. The two chapters that follow present an examination of an aversive emotion that prevails in traditions of political documentary practice – pain. Here I explore the genre's preoccupation with individuals caught by social conditions that have caused or exacerbated experiences of frustration and anguish. The documentaries in question offer acknowledgement to the suffering of the individual in order to draw attention to broader social disparity or exploitation.

This chapter focuses on the emotion of pain and examines how documentary narratives harness this emotion as an expression of social injury. More specifically, at stake here is a certain rhetorical strategy in documentary that is informed by a discourse of pain and hurt. The perceived social injustices that serve to exploit, exclude or misrepresent certain sectors of the community are articulated as an injury. This injury results from impaired access to the social fruits of prosperous, liberal, consumerist cultures. Two recent documentaries, *Fix: The Story of an Addicted City* (2002) and *Rize* (2005), form the basis of this analysis. The two documentaries offer an avenue for investigating the figure of the injured subject; the distress, anger or anguish that arises out of social marginalisation is central to the performance of the self in these examples. Key to my discussion in this chapter is Wendy Brown's notion of 'wounded attachments' and the propensity for identity narratives to be caught in a loop of painful recrimination at the expense of an effective social agenda.

As David Morgan observes, the suffering that is embedded in social, political and economic processes is 'marginalised by the somatized language of pain' (315) because 'pain' is more frequently associated with the physical realm. Yet it is the social world, and the way this world is experienced, that these documentaries seek to convey. Pain, as a signifier, demonstrates a number of ambivalences as it frequently blurs the boundary between the physical and the psychological. It is not unusual for a slippage to occur between bodily and emotional forms of injury as significant physical hurt is almost always accompanied by a change in the psyche. This is complicated when both forms of pain are known second hand, through representation and observation. In the documentaries in question, suffering becomes visible in the course of representing social injustice. This suffering works to provoke the empathy of the viewer, an emotion that is further tied to questions of desire and the tendency to covet knowledge about the other.

Of the scholarship that explores the relationship between painful states of feeling and cinema, a large portion theorises the experience of trauma, with the Holocaust as a key problematic in these investigations.[1] I am examining a specific kind of thematic that needs to be distinguished from the scholarship and documentaries concerned with trauma. The documentary subjects I am focusing on are those for whom identity is articulated through a sense of exclusion from the established social order. In his study of injury and the politics of race, Carl Gutierrez-Jones makes a useful distinction between trauma (which is often the effect of extreme injury) and ways of addressing the experience of loss and hurt. In the case of the latter, 'injury helps contextualise a larger rhetorical economy based on perpetrator/ victim interplay' (25). Thus, injury can be identified more specifically as a term couched in a discourse of legality. As Gutierrez-Jones also notes, 'like the verb form "to injure", injury marks an act against "jure", against the law, rights, and accepted privilege' (24). In this sense, one may be injured not only by an illegal act, but also acts, or an ongoing series of acts, which assault a widely held socio-political value.

Brown describes how politicised identities emerged through historical interactions that occurred within late modern democratic discourses; she considers 'politicised identity as both a production *and* contestation of the political terms of liberalism, disciplinary-bureaucratic regimes, certain forces of global capitalism, and the demographic flows of postcoloniality [...]' (54). In this sense, the emancipatory project of identity politics materialises under the values of liberalism. Yet it is the hegemony of this same order, democratic liberalism, which is attacked by activists and others who are gaining recognition under this social order. It is attacked for systemic problems such as racism, sexism and homophobia.

Brown's work offers a context against which it is possible to chart the relationship between minoritarian discourses and their repre-sen-tation in documentary. At the same time as diversity finds its voice in the critique of racial, sexual and gender privilege, a prolif-eration and a renewed tenor is apparent in politically committed documentary. This is particularly the case where film-makers were embedded in the social movements of the 1960s and 70s, such as the women's movement, Left wing and civil rights movements.[2] Such histories of progressive liberal and radical consciousness can be seen reflected in documentary texts in a number of respects.[3] Documentaries that seek recognition for the plight of individuals caught in circumstances over which they have little or no control is one example of this. As noted above, such individuals have long been the focus of the documentarist and an early precursor of minoritarian social injury in documentary can be seen in the 'victim documentary'. *Housing Problems* (1935), directed by Edgar Anstey and Arthur Elton, is, as Winston notes, one of the first non-fiction films to demonstrate this thematic. In *Housing Problems*, on-site sound recording is used to offer the inhabitants of the slums depicted an opportunity to speak directly to the camera about their own experiences, in their own environment. This is an early technical development that also sets the scene for the use of personal testimony, a device that was to become fundamental to constructing subjectivity in documentary.

While the victim documentary and the politicised identity documentary both centre on a social problem and address an empathising viewer, the way subjectivity is figured differs. This later articulation of subjectivity extends the victim mode, but infuses it with the identity politic heralded by changes in Western culture that are indicated by increased globalisation and migration, multiculturalism and, as I have noted, countercultural movements. This subjectivity is one that arises from what Stuart Hall refers to as 'all those historically specific developments and practices which have disturbed the relatively "settled" character of many populations and cultures, above all in relation to the processes of globalisation which I would argue are coterminous with modernity' ('Introduction' 4). Identities, for Hall, emerge within specific modalities of power, at particular historical junctures.

The representation of identity and injury Brown refers to can be seen in both fiction and non-fiction forms. However, it is documentary that offers a particularly fruitful site for the exploration of the filmic narrativisation of this pain. There are a number of reasons for this. It is this genre that is most consistently employed to draw attention to issues of social justice, many of which pertain to the exclusion of marginalised individuals. Whether because of the documentary form's persuasive efficacy, or because of the relative budget required when compared with fiction film, it is historically the mode most used in the service of political advocacy, education and organisation. While documentary realism is unable to offer access to 'the real' of the historical world, the faith the viewer invests in documentary credits individuals in the narrative with the status of historical agents rather than imagined characters. Frequently, documentary texts, as is the case with *Fix* and *Rize*, are organised in such a way as to situate these agents' experiential narratives and their injuries in the context of the broader democratic public sphere. It is such an understanding – that a documentary seeks recognition for actual subjects and communities of subjects in the same world the viewer inhabits – that is integral for documentaries with a social agenda.[4]

Wounded attachments in documentary

Rize and *Fix* are both North American productions (one is Canadian and one was produced in the US) and both explore the experiences of people in under-class communities. *Fix* focuses on the plight of drug users in Vancouver, many of whom are also homeless. *Rize* is concerned with the dance phenomenon, krumping, which emerged out of African American neighbourhoods in Los Angeles.[5] It is because documentaries contribute to the range of voices that compose the moral conversation of the public sphere that Brown's notion of wounded attachments provides a fruitful way to rethink the rhetorical work that documentary undertakes. Brown is not concerned with issues of representation, such as those pertaining to cinema, but rather the logic that underpins how political claims are formulated and thus, the articulation of identity within these political discourses.

Specifically, she works from Nietzsche's notion of *ressentiment* to understand that identity, 'in locating a site for of blame for its powerlessness over its past – a past of injury, a past as a hurt will – and locating a "reason" for the "unendurable pain" of social powerlessness in the present, [it] converts this reasoning into an ethicising politics, a politics of recrimination that seeks to avenge the hurt even while it reaffirms it, discursively codifies it' (74). This produces a mode of self-identity that emphasises a wounded attachment to its own exclusion and subordination, attached to a history and a future of restating pain as a form of politics. Through this process, the self, framed through minoritarian identity politics, forgoes any possibility of effecting a change in the status quo that is the source of their oppression. For the purposes of this discussion, the documentary performance of minoritarian claims and critiques may then, paradoxically, re-articulate generic neutralised injured identities while endeavouring to enable social change.

Fix: The Story of an Addicted City by veteran Canadian film-maker Nettie Wild is set in the downtown eastside area of Vancouver. This is an area well known for its concentration of heroin and crack cocaine users and many of these, as *Fix* shows, are impoverished, living on the streets of Vancouver and unable to access effective treatment for their addiction. The narrative follows the dialogue between the different social agents and institutions interested in lobbying for harm-reduction measures, such as supervised safe injecting rooms and a resource centre. The characters in the documentary are diverse in range: a sympathetic mayor a world-weary police sergeant, the inhabitants of nearby Chinatown, a local businessman who opposes any services for drug users and the drug users themselves. However, the camera is largely focused on the lives of two activists, Dean Wilson and Ann Livingston, who have become committed to advocating for users. The documentary follows the events in the city and the lives of the different characters over a two-year period.

Wilson is himself working throughout the documentary to end a three-decade-long addiction to heroin. Livingston is a single mother who, while not a drug user, is a strong supporter of the community and also works to agitate for social change. Both are central organisers with the Vancouver Area Network of Drug Users (VANDU). The individuals that feature in *Fix* seem, at first, to fit awkwardly within the language of an identity politics that is often monopolised by a matrix of race, class, gender or sexuality. Yet the overall argumentative impetus of the documentary suggests that substance abuse is localised in this geographical area in ways that tie it to poverty and other forms of social dispossession. This is borne out in Wilson's observation in the documentary that the area of Vancouver in question represents the 'poorest postal code in all of Canada'. This points to a systemic problem rather than a personal failing. Thus Wild attempts to shift popular perceptions in ways that challenge the cultural construction of drug users as maleficent, delinquent and undeserving of public welfare resources and, as a result, unworthy of acceptance by the body politic. This stereotyping plays a role in perpetuating socio-economic neglect. It also maintains material and ideological exclusion that injures the drug user and becomes the source of social, and, at times physical, pain.

In a scene early in the documentary, a group of protesters, including Wilson, walk into a city council meeting to voice their position. In this context, Wilson addresses the meeting and states that on average one user per day is dying in Vancouver. In another scene,

Wild's camera observes an interview with Livingston conducted by a journalist. Livingston responds to a question about treatment for addiction by referring to the fact that 97 percent of those leaving current programmes return to using almost immediately. She goes on to describe the value of safe injecting sites: 'It lets them know in a very thorough and subtle way, it lets them know that people care if they remain alive to stop using drugs one day'. Livingston's points testify to the structural inequality that locates these users outside the norms and values that pertain to the collective, such as morality and governance, which ensure the welfare of the citizenry.

While *Fix* undoubtedly offers a representation of social injury, it avoids representing a straightforward attachment to restating this pain as *ressentiment* and as a substitute for political action. The documentary formulates characters and represents social claims in ways that avoid simple repetition. The central and most compelling character in the documentary, Wilson, develops through the narrative and the viewer is offered more and more insight into Wilson's life and experience as the documentary progresses. Through his long period as an addict, he spent time in prison but was also a highly successful computer salesman and, at the time of shooting, is the extremely articulate spokesperson for VANDU. In later scenes, he describes the emotional complexity of addiction and treatment for the addiction. Wilson is figured in the documentary not by a re-inscription of pain in the face of social powerlessness, but rather he is framed by his abilities and determination to work on behalf of the community and lobby those in power.

In relation to this, for Brown there is a way to break out of the cycle of wounded attachments. If the subject moves away from statements predicated in 'being' to those based on 'wanting', an aspiration for futurity and action is emphasised rather than the repetition of the pain of exclusion. The different perspectives represented in *Fix* are structured into an account of the situation in the city that calls for resources for drug users. The call is repeated in different forms throughout the documentary in meetings and in interviews with characters such as Wilson, Livingston, the mayor and healthcare volunteers. This is an account that seeks to shift viewer perceptions away from the stigma of heroin and crack cocaine addiction and reconfigures the problem of substance abuse as one pertaining to healthcare rather than crime. The documentary is not calling for the alleviation of drug abuse and addiction in the first instance. Rather, the narrative draws attention to the need for material healthcare resources and thus a means to address the individuals' exclusion from the social order and the welfare state. On these terms, the documentary enunciates a movement towards transformation and emphasises the possibility of a different future.

Rize, by director David LaChappelle, offers quite a different example for consideration. Set in the poor neighbourhoods of greater Los Angeles, this documentary is concerned with the local subcultural phenomenon of 'clowning' or 'krumping'. This dance form took hold among African American youth in the aftermath of the 1992 Rodney King riots. A central figure in the documentary is Tom Johnson (Tommy the Clown) who is credited with beginning the movement. As he endeavoured to turn his life around after serving time in prison for a drug conviction, he began hip-hop dancing at children's parties in a clown costume. It was from this that the fast-paced, frenetic style of krumping evolved. *Rize* draws from the formal elements of the dance film or the music video with long dance sequences recorded in homes, competition stadiums and on the streets of Los Angeles. Although these sequences are accompanied by interviews and verite scenes exploring the lives and perspectives of dancers and their families, *Rize* forgoes the in-depth portrayal of characters that is seen in *Fix*.

The narrative implicitly draws connections between class disadvantage and the way krumping has emerged among African American youth. The documentary opens with archival footage of the Watts riots in Los Angeles in 1965 that is then juxtaposed with footage from the riots of 1992. An inter-title then brings us to the same city in 2005 and a voiceover states: 'This is our neighbourhood, this is where we grew up. We were just kids back then when all this happened, but we managed to grow from these ashes and this is where we still live.' At a later point in the documentary, one of the interview subjects, Dragon, says in his description of groups of krumpers coming together: 'There is a spirit that's there – a lot of people think they are just a bunch of rowdy [sic], they're heathens they're thugs. No. No, what we are is oppressed.' The form of injury that *Rize* represents is located at the historical intersection of race and class. This juncture is understood by Patricia Williams when she writes that 'groupings of race and class intersect in such a way that race increasingly defines class, and such that the property interests of large numbers of white individuals are understood to be in irreconcilable tension with the collective dispossession of large numbers of people of colour' (191). Racialised and classed subjectivity is frequently posed in discourse in ways that are conjoined.

Many of the interviewees refer to the way krumping was taken up as an alternative to the cycle of gangs, drugs and crime that had become symptomatic of a culture of dispossession. A number also emphasise the absence of organised activities for youth, beyond football and basketball, as are found in the more affluent neighbourhoods, such as after-school programmes or performing arts schools. The pain present in *Rize* is one that stems from an injurious exclusion from the fruits of late capitalism. They are denied the possibility of a life lived in safety, protected from crime, and they lack the social resources that offer opportunities to aspire socially and economically.

Rize offers a portrait of a racially specific subculture[6] that has resisted appropriation by the dominant culture while functioning to inspire self-expression and common purpose in the face of hopelessness. Comments made by characters in *Rize* distinguish krumping from the now commodified culture of hip hop. Despite advocating a resistance to the commodification of krumping, the articulation of politicised identity in the documentary reiterates and remains invested in the wound of marginalisation. The call to rise above adversity that recurs in the narrative is focused on the alleviation of pain, yet it also re-inscribes the injury. Without putting forward a reconfiguration of the discourses through which this identity is enacted, the text is unable to shift the terms through which domination and subordination are produced.

In the opening scenes of *Rize*, Dragon, who offers some of the most consciously politicised commentary in the documentary, addresses the camera: 'if you are drowning and there's nothing around to help but a board floating there, you're going to reach out for that board, and this is our board [...]. We are going to sail into the dance world, the art world, were going to take it by storm. Because this is our belief.' This framing evidences the rhetoric in the documentary more broadly that, while suggesting a degree of futurity, does not move from a position of 'being' to 'wanting' because it remains attached to the history that produced the powerlessness. While a history of oppression should not be elided, in this case identity is defined by past hurt without a foreseeable transformation of that wounded attachment.

Exploring the statements that construct injured subjectivities in documentaries such as *Rize* and *Fix* offers an avenue through which to understand how the rhetorical moves made by the documentary frame subjectivity. While in both cases individuals are presented through their strong associations with emotional pain as an outcome of social disadvantage, the two documentaries offer different ways of perceiving the potential for transformation. While *Rize* is focused on the terms of systemic oppression and how they have led to the current circumstances experienced by the krumpers, *Fix* is more concerned with the dialogue between different parties in the city and what can be done to change conditions for drug users. As speech acts, the two documentaries are positioned in contrasting ways with regard to the logic of wounded attachments. Yet Brown's theory can only provide a partial understanding of how pain shapes subjectivities within documentary. In the next section, I consider how subjective expressions of injury position the viewer and orient desire, with documentary aesthetics playing a key role in determining how these subjects circulate as objects of empathy.

Consuming injured identities

The documentary form produces not only documentary subjects, such as those in *Fix* and *Rize*, but it also interpellates documentary viewers. As I have noted in Chapter 1, documentary is most effective when it can engage the sensibilities of the viewer to offer an affective *and* a social experience. This combined function is also central to Renov's notion of 'pleasurable learning' (*Theorising* 35). The poetics of documentary, as Renov notes, offer pleasure *in* knowledge and knowledge *as* pleasure. In the representation of pain, the expression of distress, anger or anguish that arises out of social marginalisation becomes a performance to be consumed by the viewer. The pleasurable learning Renov refers to, translates into a viewing experience that is focused on empathising with the other and their predicament.

In other words, documentaries that focus on politicised identities provoke empathy with the other's injury, and thus a desire to gain knowledge about the particularity of the other's experience.

Empathy is an intersubjective function. It is the capacity to be aware of the other's perspective, or more specifically, it is the ability to state: 'I can perceive as you perceive' and 'I can feel as you feel'. The most appropriate – but not the only viewer-position – to experience this empathy is one that inhabits the same liberal democratic sphere in which the injury has been perpetrated. In regard to *Fix*, Wild herself notes that the documentary, 'through art, created a space without recrimination for the voiceless to be heard' (NFB 51). The film seeks a reframing of the stereotypes of drug users and to this end, Wild notes that her aim was 'to get people speaking about the unspoken and feeling what it would be like to be in someone else's shoes' (NFB 51).

This goal is bound up with the documentary's address, which was primarily aimed at the citizenry of Vancouver, and beyond this, at the Canadian public sphere, prior to local council elections in Vancouver. *Fix* gained theatrical release in Canada's major cities and was accompanied by the film-maker and cast at screenings in regional centres with forums organised to generate discussion among interested parties, such as AIDS and user advocate groups.[7] In the wake of the release of the film, a council was elected who subsequently authorised North America's first safe injection site. Geoff Pevere refers to these events in his review of *Fix*:

> It's possible none of this would have happened, at least not in the same way, without the help of Wild's film, which played for weeks last year at a cinema just minutes away from the very streets where junkies were dying, Wilson was cleaning up discarded needles and Owen was trying to convince people there was a better way.
>
> (Pevere)

The impact of *Fix* demonstrates the capacity for documentary to strategically intervene in and shift the terms of public debate around particular issues. The documentary argument seeks to recruit the allegiances of the broader community. Yet this is most effective in the instances when it speaks to an audience already open to comprehending the plight of the other.

The sign of the 'victim' has been a consistent magnet for the empathy of the audience in documentary and *Fix* necessarily references this tradition. The victim documentary features significantly in the dominant narrative of documentary history and, as I have argued, exerts a strong influence on the representation of politicised identity. Winston contends that the production of this subjectivity in documentary resulted from the conscious combination of Robert Flaherty's emphasis on the romanticism of the individual in his work and Grierson's concern with social responsibility. This produced characters defined by a movement 'from the heroic to the alienated' (Winston, 'The Tradition' 38) and an effective rallying of empathy in the audience for the purpose of initiating a changed social consciousness. For Winston, the victim as documentary subject established a convention that was to continue through to television journalism and the innovations of the direct cinema movement of the 1960s. Yet critiquing the ethical relationship between documentarist and victim, Winston focuses little on the process of spectatorial engagement and the question of empathy. This is a consideration that is central to how the figure of the victim works as a documentary device and, more saliently for the concerns of this discussion, as an object of emotion.

In *Fix*, the character of Wilson is important in this respect. He is the persuasive locus of the text as he stands as the entry point for the viewer to gain knowledge about the experience of drug users. The documentary casts him as a multifaceted subject through which the cultural assumptions around substance addiction might be destabilised for the viewer. Yet his otherness is also highlighted – Wilson's experiences are far removed from the lives of much of the audience that are asked to empathise with his predicament. Elizabeth Spelman foresees the potential for appropriation when empathy is one-sided: 'empathy does not necessarily reflect or encourage knowledge; having it does not require recognising another as separate, nor hearing what they may have to say about the empathetic gesture or about what is claimed to be understood' (130). In other words, a non-dialogic relation between audience and the object of empathy can entail the consumption of the representation of pain without any significant (or political) acknowledgement of the other. In this way, the specificity, or uniqueness, of the other is negated.

Further, in documentary, the object of empathy is necessarily aestheticised as it is formalised in representation. As E. Ann Kaplan and Ban Wang observe, the 'aestheticisation of the other does not simply render traumatic history into images, but in its obsession with violence and trauma, it flattens difference, history, memory, and the body into an abstract, pleasing mold' (11). This function of trauma also holds for the painful effects of other types of injury. Pleasurable learning, or knowledge proffered in the interests of empathy, translates here into a potential for these texts to present pain as the reductive authentication of otherness. This effectively again fossilises the subject's identity in the moment of perceived pain and eclipses the cogency of their political claims.

In this sense, while the desire of Wild, the film-maker, may be to engender politicised recognition of pain and injury, or a sense of being 'in someone else's shoes', this pain may equally construct a viewing subject encouraged to perceive the character on screen in a manner that re-incorporates them into political stasis. The compulsion here is to be drawn to the moment when the rhythm of the editing, the framing of the image, and the pacing and content of the dialogue indicate the putative origin of the wound. In the case of *Fix*, this is the personal hardship and horror that have led to, and characterised, the wound of the drug user. This is the desire to experience what the text presents as an unambiguous feeling, or what Dyer terms 'intensity'. In this sense, the victim is coded in ways that bind an empathetic engagement to an explanatory vision.

In the opening scenes of the documentary, Wilson's first comments to the camera refer, in an almost offhand way, to the time in his life when he worked as a computer salesman with IBM, which is followed by a scene in which he goes through the ritual of injecting heroin. Nevertheless it is not until much later in the documentary that more significant information is given about Wilson's past experiences. *Fix* is organised in a way that constructs Wilson as testifying to his turbulent past without pinpointing in the narrative the defining moment that exists at the heart of, and sparked his life of, addiction and crime. There is one central sequence in which this occurs. As the camera observes Wilson, framed by an open door, Livingston states in voiceover: 'It's almost as if he does drugs because he's got this terrible defect of personality, this something so terrible has happened to him that its unbearable to be Dean without being high.' The doorframe places the audience at one remove, as if they are observing Winston through the eyes of the narrator, Livingston, thus enhancing his status as object.

Following this, Wilson himself speaks to the camera in medium close-up, lucid but visibly influenced by the drug. Thus, the sequence shifts to place him as speaking subject. Yet the expected revelation as to why Wilson began using drugs is never fully realised in this address to camera. He describes going to prison when he was 17 but when Wild asks him, from off-screen, how long he was there he states only that it was 'a long time'. He says that he was imprisoned for smuggling and then refers to the unavoidable racism of the social hierarchy in prison. Despite these references to his past, the audience is denied access to the authenticating moment that encapsulates the other's pain.[8]

Significantly, in addition to the psychical pain of the drug user, *Fix* includes images that corporeally mark the intravenous drug user and offer evidence of their drug use. As I have noted, in the opening scenes of the film, Wilson is shown performing the process of injecting heroin as he speaks about the dangers and effects of the drug. Later in the documentary, Wild and her camera are present as a young woman lies down in an alley in order for a companion to find a vein in her neck that is viable for an injection of heroin. These two scenes offer a spectacle that, albeit in a very different way, rivals the dance sequences in *Rize*. The ritualistic self-harm represented in these scenes, which may indeed be physically painful, works to resist any sanitisation of the lives of the individuals in *Fix*. In no way are they depicted as insulated from the physical hardships of addiction. Yet these scenes, this time in a wholly visual way, also present evidence that authenticates the identity of the user and fulfils any audience desire for this substantiation. As spectacular evidence of the other's otherness, these images potentially eclipse subjectivity, especially in the case of the young woman who remains a peripheral, undeveloped figure throughout the narrative.[9] Nevertheless if these scenes can act as a confirmation of otherness, they still do not locate the origin of the suffering of the user.

In *Rize*, the nature of the subjective suffering is differently formulated and seeks a different address to the audience than does *Fix*. While the film is focused on politicised identity, its rhetoric is not organised in a way that mobilises activism around a particular issue, such as that of racialised disadvantage. The narrative of the film is more oriented towards presenting the pleasure of the spectacle of krumping and contextualising this dance movement through reference to the injury of African American oppression than towards using the documentary form as a persuasive device. *Rize* gained a much broader distribution than *Fix*, with wide theatrical release in the US and a commercial DVD distribution. Part of this success is owed to LaChappelle's notoriety among music and music video fans through his direction of video clips for artists such as Christina Aguilera and Britney Spears. Moreover, the striking stylised image of two dancers that was used to market the documentary, and its appeal to a music video and music documentary audience, indicates an avenue of consumption that privileges the spectacle of the film above the interview-based narrative that presents the social background and experiential aspect of krumping (Figure 3.1). One reviewer suggests this facet of the documentary's address when he writes: 'On the whole, though, this is a fashion photographer capturing his subjects in a flattering way. It's beautiful [...]. The music

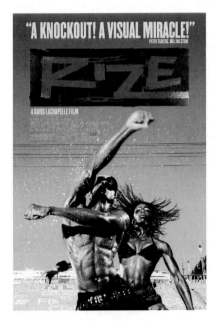

Figure 3.1 Rize (David Lachappelle 2005). Courtesy of David Lachapelle Studios/Hsi/Darkfibre Ent/The Kobal Collection

is the main attraction, and dialogue is clear when it needs to be' (Cullum).

This aspect of marketing and the spectacular audio and visual editing of the documentary may overshadow the politicised narrative, but the latter remains integral to its overall reception, as interviews, observational segments and dance sequences are interwoven throughout. In this way, the documentary oscillates between the exoticisation of the black bodies through music and dance, and the appeal to an empathetic identification with the pain of the injured, minority identity. Yet as in the case of Wilson in *Fix*, the explanatory narrative moment is elusive. The pain experienced by these individuals is the product of racist and economic oppression present over a number of generations; because of this, there can be no single personalised wound, only the repeated hurtful manifestations of this history.

Nevertheless it is still the case that in the depictions of the lives of those who practice krumping, the worst of this pain might be sought as, again, authentication. The central incident in *Rize* that lends itself to this appropriation of pain concerns the violence that plagues these Los Angeles neighbourhoods. During the making of the film, a 15-year-old dancer, Quinesha Dunford, is tragically killed when she is randomly targeted and shot by gang members while on her way to a corner shop. This event is attended to only briefly in the documentary, despite the fact that the film is dedicated to her memory. Presaged by comments from interviewees describing the dangers of living in the neighbourhood, Johnson, in clown costume, is shown entering the Dunford's living room where a group is watching a video of Quinesha dancing at a competition. This cuts to footage of a television news segment that reports the 15-year-old's murder. Although images of the funeral and a brief interview with a woman, who may be Quinesha's mother, follow this, the text resists delving, in an extended way, into the loss and its consequences for the characters. Rather than maintain and thus fully realise this aesthetic of pain through images of lament or violence, the scene shifts to the funeral casket salesman whose thriving shop is surrounded by deserted businesses. Shot inside his shop, the salesman speaks jovially to one of the male dancers: 'Better clown right, or you'll end up here with me.' This shift away from interior, personal experience nullifies the potential for the revelation of subjective pain.

This authenticating explanation of pain is slightly different to Brown's social injury in that it is a moment of dialogue, between viewer and text, rather than an identity repeated in discourse. But both, when perceived to eclipse subjectivity, concern the problematic collapsing of complex cultural histories of marginalisation into non-politics. Similarly, the empathy that is meant to resonate with the viewer cannot guarantee that they will recognise the specific and unique aspects of the other's predicament or their status as a multifaceted social subject. The subject can too easily be read as only a manifestation of pain.

Indeed, while *Rize* and *Fix* do not present, in sound and image, the moment that verifies the other's otherness, the representation of pain poses generic problems for documentary's address more broadly. The perceived authenticity of any performance or event in documentary is reliant, in part, on the aesthetic conventions of documentary. Realist documentary conventions signify authenticity. Thus reality does not simply reside in the text – verification of authenticity occurs in the activity of viewing. What this suggests is that the text alone can never authenticate the explanatory wound. This is a necessary limitation in the language of documentary. This question of authenticity does not pertain only to a filmic language. Elaine Scarry observes that pain is something that, simultaneously, cannot be denied, yet cannot be confirmed. It is unsharable and 'it ensures this unsharability through its resistance to language' (4). This would indicate that, regardless of the particular documentary, the pain of the other would always remain beyond total capture.

Cultural theorists have debated the prospects for the appropriation, disavowal or suppression of painful emotional narratives in the social realm at length.[10] Moreover, while the object of pain and empathy can be presented in a text, ways of reading or responding to this object are not fixed. Responses to these representations are conditional and potentially multiple. As a way of focusing this issue of interpretation, a question can be posed: 'is to rethink the victim documentary as a political documentary also to ask what form of political response the documentary seeks?' Returning to Brown, in regard to the problematic of minoritarian pain she argues that 'all that such pain may long for – more than revenge – is the chance to be heard into a certain release, recognised into self-overcoming, incited into possibilities for triumphing over, and hence, losing itself' (75). This need for a recognition of pain is echoed by Ahmed who writes that the 'solitariness of pain is intimately tied up with its implication in relationship with others' (29). Thus, pain requires acknowledgement – if it is witnessed it can be granted 'the status of an event, a happening in the world' (Ahmed 29). There exists a paradox, then, between what Scarry describes as the unsharability of pain and the necessity for an intersubjective awareness of pain. This paradox points to the importance of seeking and examining ways to represent political pain, so it might be witnessed and vanquished, despite the difficulty of this project.

Wounded attachments are not a rhetorical phenomenon restricted to documentary. They exist as a symptom of the movements of late modernity more broadly. Yet one manifestation of political documentary practice is governed by a certain enunciation of subjectivity that lends itself to the stasis of repeating the injury of exclusion while seeking recognition for this same marginalisation. This rhetorical phenomenon is distinct from, and also indebted to, a historical repetition of the figure of the victim in documentary. While these documentaries function as political instruments that draw attention to social injustice, and are thus valuable, the limitations and complexities of documentary minoritarian pain must also be recognised. The pain expressed in *Fix* and *Rize* is the result of an injury inflicted on an identity and on a collectivity of subjects. Despite the difficulties its witnessing and articulation might present, it is necessary for this pain to be acknowledged by another collective – an audience. A politics of injury and pain must formulate an address to the audience that emphasises the relationship between pain and systems of power. Such an address must also attempt to circumvent representations that feed into a desire to consume pain, a desire that seeks out the familiar and the pleasurable. Where the expression of injured identities is concerned, documentary plays a small but important part in presenting avenues for imagining future possibilities in the historical world that further public debate, think towards social transformation and offer clear alternatives for re-working the conceptualisation of social others.

4
Women, Pain and the Documentaries of Kim Longinotto

Despite a long and prolific career in which she has produced a significant body of work committed to a distinct set of thematic concerns, Kim Longinotto's documentaries remain under-theorised by film scholars. She has been producing films in the UK since the 1970s,[1] however, Longinotto is most well known for the feature-length documentaries made in Japan, Iran and in parts of Africa. This chapter focuses on four of these works: *Divorce Iranian Style* (1998) and *Runaway* (2001), both made in Tehran and co-directed with Ziba Mir-Hosseini, *The Day I Will Never Forget* (2002) made in Kenya, and *Sisters in Law* (2005), co-directed with Florence Ayisi in Cameroon.[2] Longinotto's filmic subjects are almost always outsiders or the disenfranchised, principally women and children, and in this sense they share much with the marginalised identities of the previous chapter. While they may reference the tradition of the victim documentary, the rhetoric evident in Longinotto's documentaries is markedly different from those discussed in Chapter 3. In this case, pain is not tied to a static self-subversion. This is, in part, due to the way Longinotto's largely observational camera seeks out sites in which social change is already underway – the individuals in her documentaries are firmly posed as the subjects of politics. The pain represented here accompanies social antagonism and the endeavour to break with existing regimes. Women, specifically, are the subjects of this pain and their performances in the documentaries invoke this emotion in different ways. Yet they are also objects of pain, and thus objects of empathy, as these are frequently the emotions that shape the relationship between the viewer and suffering depicted in the worlds of the documentaries. Longinotto is an important film-maker to focus on in this respect because her work is consistently interested in questions of marginalisation *and* agency. Moreover, the additional problems posed by making films in non-Western contexts for primarily Western audiences are also brought into view by these documentaries.

In all her documentaries set in non-English-speaking cultures, Longinotto consistently confronts the epistemological problematic of producing meaning around subjects who might be defined as the cultural other. Yet her work sits in contrast with ethnographic documentary approaches that codify their subjects so that, as Nichols points out: 'They occupy a time and a space which "we" must recreate, stage, or represent' (*Blurred Boundaries* 67). In this codification, the time and space of modernity, and European-derived humanism, is opposed to that of the pre-modern or the primitive, in this case Iran and Africa, respectively. In Longinotto's film-making practices, the terms insider/outsider, modern/pre-modern, agency/ passivity and the knowable and unknowable are constantly in play. The investigations and characterisations in her work frequently begin from the point at which these oppositions are thrown into question.

Such a destabilising of cultural discourse is most often sought in the documentary genre through the formal devices of self-reflexive or essayist styles, yet Longinotto's documentary objectives are realised by way of realist conventions, chiefly an observational style. It is through these conventions that Longinotto orients the narratives towards collusion with particular individuals and a shared political agenda between filmic subjects and co-directors. In her discussion of feminist documentary practice in the 1970s and 1980s, Julia Lesage cites the effectiveness of 'traditional "realist" documentary structure' (223); while Longinotto's work can be located in relation to a lineage of feminist non-fiction film, it is quite distinct from the consciousness-raising documentary to which Lesage is referring. Constituting a more contemporary phase of feminist practice, her work employs the conventions of realist documentary to seek a renewed understanding of the structuring of social relations, the dynamics of transformation and the different ways that women across cultures are finding to function in this dynamic.

The outsiders on whom Longinotto's camera focuses in these four documentaries are grappling not only with personal crises but also with ways of negotiating the intersection of modernity and traditional or religious law. As I will explore, this struggle is framed by Longinotto's camera, across cultures, in a manner that locates the cultural 'other' as not outside of, but entrenched in, the complex paradigms of modernity. Moreover, in her attempt to represent female subjectivity and social transformation, Longinotto necessarily renders the emotional and physical pain of marginality and individual agency, posing a relationship between pain (and its representation) and political struggle.

This set of documentaries engages with imperialist discourses that inform the hierarchical relation between the West and the non-West. In the case of Iran, this is a historical discourse that orientalises and exoticises the other. The African other is constituted through neocolonial notions of primitivism and paternalism. While these are different discourses, they are related in ways that contribute to my reasons for selecting these particular documentaries from Longinotto's extensive body of work; not only are these documentaries produced almost sequentially, but their political contexts also offer a different complex of modernity than does Longinotto's Japanese work. These are predominantly Islamic cultures that have been repeatedly posited as opposed to European modernity, as timeless and governed by mysticism rather than reason and 'progress'. Spectatorial pleasures are conditioned by these inflections. Rey Chow identifies an idealising opposition to modernity, a desiring 'recourse to the archaic, authentic *past* of other cultures, in the assumption that somehow such past is closer to the original essence of humanity than Western culture' (194). With the figure of 'woman' further aligned with the underside of reason, civilisation and progress, the feminised cultural 'other' exemplifies the negative value in relation to the masculine ideal of enlightenment humanism.[3] What occurs in these four documentaries when Longinotto, a British film-maker, turns her camera to images of female subjectivity in Iranian and African cultures – images that are already so saturated with meaning and desire?

My inquiry is framed through Chow's argument for an acknowledgement of the coevalness of cultures and their power structures.

In order for cultural translation to occur, Chow argues, a reductive notion of 'primitive others' must be replaced by a perception of the way these cultures are 'equally caught up in the generalised atmosphere of unequal power distribution and are actively (re)producing *within themselves* the structures of domination that are as typical of non-European cultural histories as they are of European imperialism' (195). Longinotto's films set in Iran, Kenya and Cameroon recast cultures that have become familiar to Western audiences through their demonisation or primitivisation, and depict them as 'themselves transforming and translating into the present' and as cultures that 'are equally engaged in the contradictions of modernity' (196). Because Longinotto is always concerned with exploring, through representation, hierarchies of value, her documentaries narrativise the contradictions and conflicts that permeate cultures as hegemonies shift and reform.

More specifically, these documentaries explore the paradoxes of gendered subjectivity and modernity. These paradoxes are revealed at the points at which Longinotto's films present women as the subjects and agents of change. In Chapter 2, I looked at the problem of female agency in terms of issues of pleasure, desire and taste with regard to the female porn star. This discussion furthers this examination, but the aesthetic issues and the formations of power within and against which the subject is formulated contrast greatly with those of the pornography documentary. Longinotto's women are responding to or working within civil and state institutions; thus, they are more explicitly depicted as engaged in changing those institutions. Thus, the documentaries are marked by what Nichols refers to as an 'intentionalization towards the future' ('Historical' 157) and an address to the viewer that establishes the filmic possibility for an ethical approach to the other. Although Iran and Africa provide very different cultural contexts, Longinotto and her collaborators' documentaries present women in both regions who are struggling with the interrelationship between long-standing custom, either in regard to Islam and its laws or in regard to traditional, tribal law, and the Westernised legal system of the nation-state. These documentary explorations of female agency are couched in the context of the family, its regulation by the rule of law, and its function as a technology of gender and culture.

Divorce Iranian Style and Runaway

Divorce Iranian Style presents the microcosm of a family court in Tehran presided over by the cleric Judge Deldar. The women who feature in *Divorce Iranian Style* utilise all their resources to resolve issues to do with their divorces. In her published commentary on *Divorce Iranian Style*, co-director and anthropologist Mir-Hosseini writes: 'I saw women in Iran not as victims but as pioneers in a legal system caught between religious tradition and modernity' (196). It becomes clear in the documentary that these women's claims and requests must be made in ways that are recognised within Shari'a law and its inscription in a formal legal system, as well as within the expectations of post-revolutionary Iranian culture.[4] There are few avenues through which women can petition for divorce and the women's statements are limited to those that might be recognised by the prevailing order. Legitimately, women can only seek to end a marriage on the basis of their husband's inability to father a child, insanity and deception.

As Lindsay Moore notes in her discussion of the documentary, the narrative's 'informing discourse' is suggested through the 'juxtaposition of court scenes with those in the mosque at prayer time and with shots outside, in which the late Ayatollah Khomeini's portrait looms large on a billboard, thus linking religion, politics, the law, and patriarchal dominance' (24). This network of associations not only frames the narrative, but also indicates the conditions under which female subjectivity can be articulated within the order established by the law courts. Yet *Divorce Iranian Style* is interested in revealing the impossible totality of this order. Longinotto focuses her camera on a specific site of disciplinary power in which subject-formation is articulated not only in terms of traditional Muslim law and its placement of women, but is also informed by what Wendy Brown refers to as the 'fiction of the autonomous, willing, reasoning, rights-bearing subject convened by modernity' (Brown, *Politics* 10) an individual who is structured through discourses of the fulfilment of the self.[5]

In *Divorce Iranian Style*, Longinotto's observational approach is accompanied by an intermittent female voiceover. This voiceover is in English, contrasting with the Farsi that features in the rest of the documentary. The voiceover offers information about the legal procedures in the court and the backgrounds of the individuals who appear in the film. Much of the on-screen action takes place in Judge Deldar's courtroom and the offices and waiting rooms around the court. In the courtroom, Longinotto's camera is set up next to his desk, and the women who are brought before him frequently look at and make statements directed to the camera.[6] One woman who appears early in the film, Massi, tells the camera and the judge that she and her husband are incompatible because of differences in class status: 'We couldn't live together, our ideas were very different.' But Massi must seek a divorce on the grounds that, after five years, the couple has not been able have a child. In the courtroom, she is determined but also visibly anxious. She makes a great deal of his 'sexual problems' and the court rules that he must undergo a medical test. In another case, Ziba, who was married at 14 to a man 22 years her senior, is now, one year later, seeking to divorce and return to her studies. The voiceover states that Ziba has no acceptable reasons for divorce and the camera observes her desperate search for excuses. While standing before the judge with her husband, she asserts that he should undergo an insanity test, that he initially lied to her about his age, that he has a violent temper and stays out until unreasonably late at night. When the divorce is not granted, Ziba takes out a petition against her husband to force him to negotiate, alleging that he was physically abusive and threatened to set her on fire. Following this, the two again appear before Judge Deldar to address her complaint, and Ziba, looking from the judge to the camera, whispers, 'I'll withdraw my complaint, just say you agree to divorce by mutual consent.' Eventually, after much haranguing, he agrees.

The courtroom represented in *Divorce Iranian Style* is an arena in which women tell the stories of their marriages and perform subjectivity in ways that abide by religious law. Yet in this context, they also articulate a right to strive for personal fulfilment beyond the primacy of the family unit. As one woman states while speaking to the camera, almost in a soliloquy style as events continue to unfold around her: 'If I respect him, he should respect me [...] Aren't I a person too, don't I want a life?' But if these women become agents of change in ways that draw on the discourses of modernity, including feminism and gender equality, this does not entail a straightforward alignment of Islam with the pre-modern and the West with modernity. Rather, Longinotto depicts female subjects who are finding ways to negotiate within the complexities of post-revolutionary Iran.

This is a society that saw significant modernisation under the Shah and rapid change after 1979 under the rule of political Islam. Azadeh Kian-Thiebaut describes women's social struggle within the Islamic regime:

> [There are many women in Iran who] emphasise their activity in the public realm and impose their own interpretations of Islamic laws and traditions to initiate legal reforms and modify traditional cultural perceptions of women. In doing so, they form an identity which is no longer founded on traditions. The result is that they now perceive themselves as women/individuals rather than as exclusively mothers and wives.
>
> (141)

This negotiation also signals the paradoxes of perceiving these women as agents in the terms set by discourses of modernity. While, on the one hand, enlightenment humanism inaugurates the rights-bearing subject, on the other it brings the symbolic violence through which, as I have noted, otherness is constituted through a process of sexualisation and racialisation in ways that have facilitated Western imperialism. Thus, a performance of the self that works at the intersection of a discourse of rights and 'interpretations of Islamic law' may also be enacting forms of Iranian cultural identity that seek a selective and strategic fit between tradition and change in contemporary Iranian society.[7]

In *Runaway*, Longinotto's second film in Iran and with Mir-Hosseini as co-director, women are again represented seeking a fit between cultural tradition and the self as rights-bearing individual. Also set in Tehran, this documentary explores life in a shelter for girls and young women who have fled from mistreatment by their families. Rather than a religious male judge, women run the shelter, working as counsellors and mediators for the girls and their families. In *Runaway*, Longinotto moves away from the conception of women as singularly determined to manipulate Islamic law seen in *Divorce*. The women and girls in this second documentary are more complexly rendered: as individuals, they are differently caught in the dynamic of modernity and the desire for autonomy.

The complexities are particularly evident in the example of Atena, who explains that after returning to the family home to escape an abusive husband, her stepfather attempted to rape her. Atena's mother returned home while this was happening and doused her in gasoline with the intention of setting her on fire. Atena took flight before this occurred. The mother, whose husband has since left, is shown visiting the shelter, but she refuses to take Atena back, believing that her husband will soon return, and she asserts that Atena acted immodestly at home. Although the women at the shelter offer to find Atena a job and support her in the interim, and they counsel her to reduce contact with her mother and to 'put herself first', Atena states in reference to her family 'if I don't see them, I'll be sick'. In another instance, Setareh, a 20-year-old woman, sits with Mrs Amoozad, a shelter worker, and tearfully retells fragments of her life in which her father facilitated her abuse and that of her sister and mother at the hands of other men. In a later scene, she is found a job and lodgings by those working at the shelter.

Central to the image in many scenes is the large desk at which Mrs Amoozad and the other staff in the shelter sit to interview those seeking refuge and to settle conflicts within families. While the inhabitants of the shelter usually do not sit formally across the desk but to the side of it, the desk nevertheless signifies authority, and the calm and reasoned approach of the counsellors locates them as figures that hold sway within the walls of the shelter, if not Iranian society more broadly. The film shows the viewer instances in which the women work to intervene in family affairs and either return women to their families or offer them the resources to make their own lives. In a number of cases there is not an exact match between what the shelter workers advocate, and what their charges are able to realistically achieve given their circumstances. Thus, there is a tension emphasised in the documentary between the aspiration for autonomy – often sought by the shelter workers – and the circumstances in which women must live according to familial and cultural pressure.

The context of *Runaway* differs from that of *Divorce Iranian Style*, in that while both present women in untenable situations, there are fewer visible examples of manoeuvring within the dictates of Islamic law in *Runaway*, as the women who run the shelter work subtly within the expectations of Shari'a law and other social structures to facilitate options for their charges. While assuming very different roles, the shelter workers and their wards are both cast as 'rights-bearing subjects' with the potential to take action within their respective situations. Yet the filmic subjects necessarily also operate under the sign of the paternal authority of the state, and this is reiterated in the mise en scène with large images of Ayatollah Khomeini again shown hanging in the hallways of the shelter.[8] In differing respects, *Divorce Iranian Style* and *Runaway* both emphasise the personal experiences and effects of cultural expectation. The documentaries do not represent the composition of power in a detailed way and, instead, formulate a critique through focusing on how female subjects work within economies of power. The women must operate within the existing Islamic political regime in ways that acknowledge the authority of the state and religious tradition, and yet they are not fully determined by this authority as they engage a broader process of self-fashioning.

Mir-Hosseini says that in *Divorce Iranian Style*, 'we wanted to let women speak, to show them as individuals going through a difficult phase in their lives and to communicate the pain – and the humor – involved in the breakdown of a marriage' ('Negotiating' 191). But the emotionalism of the documentary performances, in ways that echo Chong's mannered performances noted in Chapter 2, fit awkwardly with the naturalism expected of documentary subjects. In their desire to influence proceedings, the women in *Divorce Iranian Style* deploy heightened emotions of pain, suffering, desperation and relief. This presentation of the self is most evident in the character of Maryam. If Ziba presents a tearful and distressed face in her proceedings in the courtroom, Maryam's pain is even more marked. After remarrying, she loses custody of her two small children, who must legally be returned to her ex-husband. After managing to delay this return, Maryam goes back to court but repeatedly refuses to give up her four-year-old girl. She has no choice but to go before the judge and plead with him to ask her husband for consent for custody. Her distress is physically apparent in her tears, shaking voice and hands. In a comparable scene of threatened mother–daughter separation in *Runaway*, Atena, her mother, and Mrs Amoozad meet to discuss what should be done about Atena's future. Determined to return home despite her mother's resistance, Atena becomes distraught and tearfully pleads with her mother, her body contorted around Mrs Amoozad's desk. In both cases, it is at the intersection of culture and individuation that this pain and anguish becomes visible as performance.

In these moments, individual performances are so saturated by emotions that they push against the bounds of documentary realism. At points, *Runaway* and *Divorce Iranian Style* share something with the themes and conventions of the fictional genre of melodrama. Both present the emotionalism of family drama and social and personal conflicts from a female point of view. For Linda Williams, melodrama, pornography and horror are 'body genres', all marked by the female embodiment, on-screen, of particular emotions. Williams writes 'melodrama can encompass a broad range of films marked by "lapses" in realism, by "excesses" of spectacle and displays of primal, even infantile emotions' ('Film Bodies' 3). For audiences reading across cultures, this effect of exceeding documentary realism is doubled. I, for one, cannot pinpoint the exact nature of the dialogue between 'authentic' pain, a performance for the judge or counsellor and the film camera.

Longinotto does not clearly direct this interpretation in the text, nor does she seem to direct the character's performance. Her observational technique facilitates what Sara Cooper refers to as the failure of ethnography to assimilate the cultural other: 'the ethnographer learns to know what s/he fails to know of those s/he studies' (45). For Cooper, this failure enables the documentary subject to evade filmic capture. Longinotto seeks to portray the operation of female subjectivity, but in *Runaway* and *Divorce Iranian Style* the performances blur the boundary between the authentic and inauthentic in a manner that defies the possibility to fully position the women in the narrative. The processes through which agency is enabled (the performance of the self) cannot be fully apprehended by the viewer or the documentary camera. The film-making process and the cultural or legal system are subordinated to the women's aims as they explore the possibilities of self-creation.

Sisters in Law and The Day I Will Never Forget

The Day I Will Never Forget and *Sisters in Law*, two of Longinotto's African films,[9] differ greatly in their use of pathos from the ones shot in Iran. Rather than the performance of emotion, these examples offer a different documentary reference point for Linda Williams's notion of body genres. Instead of a performance of excessive emotion, these documentaries have at their centre the affect of physical pain. *The Day I Will Never Forget* is set in Kenya, partly in Nairobi and partly in rural areas and villages. The documentary is concerned with the practice of female genital cutting (FGC) or female genital mutilation (FGM), also referred to in the film as circumcision,[10] usually conducted on girls entering puberty. Throughout the documentary, Longinotto works closely with Fardhosa Ali Mohamed, a nurse who tells the camera that she herself has undergone FGC and who works to change attitudes towards the practice in Kenya. The film again employs observational techniques interspersed with interviews and accompanied by minimal voiceover. The documentary opens with a number of women, including Fardhosa, preparing a Somali woman for her wedding. The issue of the woman's cutting is discussed in the context of the difficulties that may occur on the wedding night. Fardhosa urges the woman to come and see her beforehand for a surgical procedure that will alleviate the risk of pain and infection.

FGC has been the object of wide transnational debate. Opposition to the practice has drawn on a discourse of universal human rights and critiques of patriarchal violence against women, as well as advocacy of women's health and sexuality. In some instances, arguments against FGC have been buttressed by explicitly or implicitly opposing the 'barbarism' and primitivism of African cultures, especially Islamic cultures, with the 'civilised' West. Cultural relativists have resisted condemning the practice, arguing that FGC can only be understood within the system of meanings specific to a cultural group. Complicating these positions is the fact that FGC has also been taken on as an issue of cultural maintenance – as a tribal or Islamic practice it asserts traditional culture as a way to challenge the pervasiveness of neocolonial influence and for this reason there has been a resurgence of FGC in some areas. In *The Day I Will Never Forget*, these debates are not explicitly referenced. Rather, the cultural complexity of the practice is suggested as women voice differing perceptions of FGC, most notably by the female elders who carry out the practice.

Longinotto orients the narrative towards dispelling the assertion that girls consent unconditionally to undergo FGC through focusing on the cultural pressure exerted on the girls. In one scene, older women have visited to teach a group of village girls about their tribal customs. The group is told that FGC is voluntary. Girls who have recently undergone FGC are also present. In reference to the custom of a man having multiple wives, a woman states: 'You got circumcised so that you'll stay with one husband. Only with him. A man is meant to have as many women as he pleases.' In another scene, the practice is misrepresented to other girls who are about to undergo FGC: they are told that it is not painful and that it will be a good experience.

Yet while many of the women in *The Day I Will Never Forget* are depicted as struggling with the weight of cultural expectation and the authority of family and tradition, these women are juxtaposed with women like Fardhosa who work within the confines of culture to effect change. *The Day I Will Never Forget* brings to light the misinformation and attitudes that perpetuate FGC. This casts some subjects, such as the female elders who perform the practice, as simplistic and perhaps even ignorant of the trauma they inflict and why they inflict it. In stark contrast, Fardhosa is associated with the discourses of medicine and science. In this respect, in *The Day I Will Never Forget* the criticism of traditional practices is more evident than in the previous films. Yet rather than an absolute opposition between the terms of modern and pre-modern, the documentary presents the intersection between these discourses and, thus, the realities of Kenyan modernity and its contradictions. Longinotto includes only local informants in this and indeed all of the films discussed here. This contributes to the manner in which, within the texts, those confronting and negotiating with pre-modern and/or traditional masculine authority are women who are also subjected to this same discursive authority.

In a scene that functions as the nexus of the documentary, two young sisters are shown undergoing the procedure. Fardhosa, who had been negotiating with the parents around the girl's welfare, is also present. This sequence is highly charged; as the second girl hears her sister's screams she pleads not to undergo the ritual but is forced by her parents to have it performed. Although the request is not made known in the documentary, Fardhosa had instructed Longinotto not to intervene, as it would jeopardise her work in the community. In an interview Longinotto recollects:

She'd been working in that community for a couple of years and she'd convinced that particular man [the father] to let the

circumciser do it the easy way, not the complete thing with the
stitching [...]. She'd been trying to stop it in that area and couldn't
get the family not to do it. So she'd got that concession.

(Fowler 104)

The documentary also shows the girls the day after the ordeal. They
are subdued and enjoying gifts given to them to celebrate the event.
When questioned by Fardhosa, one of the girls claims they had both
wanted the procedure. In addition to the problem of consent, the
question of intervention and action reoccurs throughout *The Day
I Will Never Forget*. If the film itself represents Longinotto's own
intervention, the multiple voices and experiences rendered in the
narrative present differing forms of action possible within Kenyan
society. Fardhosa works within the structures of modernity *and* tradition, other girls defy their parents and run away, and some struggle
with living with the effects of FGC as adults. Following the scene
featuring the two sisters, the second half of the documentary is
more concerned with the initiative of young women themselves. In
an unprecedented move, a group of perhaps 15 girls from surrounding villages join forces and engage a lawyer, filing a case to prevent
their parents from carrying out FGC against their will. While parents,
and more specifically fathers, are interviewed outside the courtroom
and assert anger at their daughters' 'disobedience', thus attempting
to subject the girls to the ideology of traditional culture, the documentary emphasises and thus validates their affiliation with the legal
system and individual rights.[11] The case is successful and the girls'
request for protection and individual sovereignty are fully recognised
by the law.

The role of the Westernised legal system in Africa is a central feature
of Longinotto's next film, *Sisters in Law*, co-directed with Florence
Aiysi. Set in the town of Kumba in West Cameroon, *Sisters in Law*
focuses on a small number of cases with female plaintiffs that come
before the law courts. Yet unlike in *Divorce Iranian Style*, women have
authority in the court system, notably State Prosecutor Vera Ngassa
and Court President Beatrice Ntuba. Framed as subjects enabled by
a Westernised legal system, these women are unequivocally operating
under the sign of modernity as they administer both customary
and Western law.[12] The documentary moves between their offices,
the courtroom, and the streets and homes of the village. The work

these women do brings us full circle from *Divorce Iranian Style*: the apparently female-dominated justice system in Kumba presents an inversion of Judge Deldar's Shari'a court. Yet in the cases they adjudicate, women and young girls are again struggling within the tension between custom and modernity.

The context of these trials is particularly complex due to the historical influences on the regime of law in this part of Africa, where jurisprudence is an admixture of customary law, Islamic law and British colonial law. Family law bears the mark of this hybrid approach, with both statutory and customary marriage regulations in play.[13] In the opening scenes, the fusion of legal systems is suggested when a woman and her husband, from whom she is separated, come to Ngassa's office. Her father has given their child to her husband, and the woman is seeking to have the child returned. Questioning them about the process by which they were married under customary law, Ngassa deems that their union was not conducted in the correct way under the dictates of this law and that their marriage is void. She chastises the woman's father, who is also present, for facilitating the marriage against the woman's will:

> Your daughter has become merchandise. The way you people play in the villages. The way you play with women and children. That's what makes her his wife? Eighty pounds and a pig? [...] That's what you men do. You just harvest children all over the place. Without marrying the mothers.

Ngassa's character is marked by both anger and resolve to engage in the step-by-step process of justice as she confronts perpetrators.

In one of the central cases in the documentary, Amina seeks a divorce from her husband due to his constant physical and sexual abuse. She must confront a community that is against her decision and witnesses who discredit her claims. Her constant refrain, as others in the community try to cajole her into returning to her marriage, is 'I'm not going back.' With the encouragement of the female lawyers, she maintains her determination. One lawyer visits Amina's home: 'You're a human being like him. Why does he think he has the right to beat you, just because he feeds you?' Following court proceedings, Judge Ntuba grants her a divorce.[14] The viewer learns at the end of the documentary, as Ngassa addresses a classroom of women accompanied by Amina and Ladi, another woman who has successfully filed for divorce, that previous to their victories it had been 17 years since a case of spousal abuse had been successfully tried in the district. Leaving this revelation until the end of the film, Longinotto places a final emphasis on the changes inaugurated by the female officials and their work to enfranchise women and children.

The action in *Sisters in Law* is constituted not only by the rulings made in the court, but also by the recounting of events as complaints are heard and evidence provided. Other cases in the documentary focus on nine-year-old Sonita, who has accused her neighbour of rape, and six-year-old Manka, who is found, covered in welts and scars, in a church after fleeing her abusive aunt. These cases are brought to trial, and their perpetrators, including a female assailant, Manka's aunt, ruled guilty and sentenced. Adults repeatedly view the wounds inflicted by a coat hanger that are evident on Manka's back and legs, and Sonita is at least twice asked to specify the details of the rape she experienced and to gesture to relevant parts on her body. This testimony is a process for the subject of the injury to achieve closure and redress, but it is also an avenue through which others in the community and in the court can come to terms with the violence that has occurred. As Dori Laub writes, 'the emergence of the narrative which is being listened to – and heard – is, therefore, the process and the place wherein the cognisance, the "knowing" of the event is given birth to. The listener therefore is party to the creation of knowledge *de novo*' (57). However, knowledge of the event is registered in one way for those present and in another way for the viewer.

The film reaffirms that an event occurred by fixing the testimony and/or other evidence in sound and image. It also interpellates the viewer into the process of 'knowing' in ways that position the viewer as the subject of knowledge. This is particularly the case where observational documentary is concerned. Within the established canon of documentary conventions, observational techniques attempt to offer the greatest approximation of the viewer's own gaze. The contract between viewer and text promises a sense of discovery.[15] The viewer will encounter places and characters at the same time the camera does and each event will be known anew in the process of viewing. In a way that extends Laub's formulation, the event is seen, heard and discovered by the viewer in contexts well beyond the initial telling. This is the case with not only *Sisters in Law*, but also *The Day I Will Never Forget*, *Divorce Iranian Style* and *Runaway*, which are also interested in the way the court, or counsellor, and/or the documentary viewer, function as witnesses to accounts and fears of physical and emotional pain. These testimonies are not offered directly to the camera as interviews, but instead are spoken in a social context as stories told to counsellors, judges, lawyers or social workers, maintaining the observing gaze of the viewer.

For Cowie, the placement of the viewing subject as the subject of knowledge allows for an identification with the social actors which in turn contributes to the pleasurable experience documentary affords (30–2). Yet *The Day I Will Never Forget* stands as an example that, in some scenes, extinguishes the possibility of knowing an event and the desire for this knowledge. I am referring to the physical and psychical pain the viewer is asked to witness, pain that is attributable to what Felman and Laub term an 'extreme limit experience' (xvi).[16] The film presents women narrating their own experience, elders describing how girls are restrained during FGC, practitioners explaining in detail what is done and a scene of Fardhosa attempting to defibulate a young bride. The key examination of pain occurs during the scene described above involving two sisters undergoing the procedure. In this excruciating scene, the camera focuses on one girl's face as she observes her sister's ordeal and hears her screams. The viewer observes both the sister's fearful response and the unfolding of events as the girl is restrained. The camera does not show the actual cutting.

Regardless, this scene and, to a lesser extent, the descriptions, obliterate the desire to know and with it the documentary pleasure in discovery or identification. This depiction of corporeality becomes formally excessive to the documentary (albeit very differently than does the performance of emotion in the other documentaries), and competes with the overriding formal and narrative principles of the genre. In documentary, these principles endeavour to position a viewer through desire for actuality as knowledge. This excess is comparable to that found in Williams' body genres as the viewer is drawn into an 'involuntary mimicry' ('Film Bodies' 4) of the sensations presented on screen. However, unlike the genres Williams refers to, excess is not bound up with the generic system. The pain depicted and the sensations the viewer may experience are specific to this film and effect a suspension of the pleasure documentary ordinarily offers.

If the viewer's desire to assume the position of the subject of knowledge is impaired, the weaving together of layers of knowing throughout the text may be eclipsed. Although Longinotto renders the complexity of FGC as a cultural practice – acknowledging the paradoxes, disjunctures and pressures that characterise all cultures – the representation of extreme physical pain may overshadow these nuances. Scarry argues that the failure to express pain and to 'objectify its attributes' will 'always work to allow its appropriation and conflation with debased forms of power; conversely, the successful expression of pain will always work to expose and make impossible that appropriation' (14). Scarry's approach has multiple implications for *The Day I Will Never Forget*. Longinotto has discussed the scene in the documentary in regard to the 'taboo' of showing the reality of the practice and how doing so on film nullifies its power over women (Fowler 105). At the same time, however, pain is expressed through the film, but it remains impossible to *know* it through representation. This a problem shared with the representation of social injury explored in the previous chapter. In both instances, it cannot be appropriated by any discourse, including religion and traditional culture, both of which in this case function as 'debased' forms of power that have brutalising effects. The only response to the representation of the affliction of extreme physical injury is aversion. The structured testimonies of pain are central to Longinotto's endeavour in *The Day I Will Never Forget*, but the narrative representation of these experiences remains a necessary impossibility. *Divorce Iranian Style* and *Runaway* are organised in a way that thwarts total assimilation of the female subject, while in *The Day I Will Never Forget* the central object of knowledge, FGC, is also unassimilable.

These four documentaries focus on the performance of female subjectivity within specific and interconnected regulatory regimes – the institutions of the state or civil society and tribal or Islamic culture. They seek out the experiences and processes that position women as agents of social change. The relationships of antagonism in which these female subjects are embedded bring to light the pain and injury that are, in some cases, part of their experience within these formations and, in others, the effects of the conflict that are produced by working against these regimes. Indeed, as the only representation offered is by way of the observation of the camera, these documentaries almost exclusively locate female subjectivity within the confines of the discourses and environments I have discussed. Thus, the women are presented as subjects who strive for an agency that is constituted through ideals of individual sovereignty and enlightenment humanism, principally by way of a Westernised legal or welfare system.

This is the case whether it is female subjects who are administering the law or attempting to transform their lives through appealing to the courts. This focus eclipses other cultural forces that may be a factor for these individuals such as popular culture, education, class and so forth. Within her focus, Longinotto is attentive to the particularity of diverse cultural contexts, historical influences and the importance of localised solidarity between women in each documentary. As Patricia White observes with regard to *Sisters in Law*, at times the reception of these films by critics and reviewers has collapsed this particularity in ways that 'universalise' (125–7) the representations of female success and deny the systemic and political problems faced by these women. While narratives of humanist individualism provide an entry point for Longinotto's film-making practice, they are not constitutive of female subjectivity in the documentaries. More accurately, this subjectivity is situated within a web of social and historical influences that impact on the women's experiences and contribute to localised feminist practices.

A cinema of translation: Documentary, collaboration and futurity

In *Divorce Iranian Style, Runaway, Sisters in Law* and *The Day I Will Never Forget*, the terms upon which agency, political struggle and pain are represented are tied to Longinotto's consistencies in style, thematic focus and approach to production. The subject matter on which she focuses her camera and her consultative and collaborative approaches to film-making foreground Longinotto's practice as one that entails constant reflection on processes of translation. In the four films discussed here, there is a movement of meaning between spectator and text, but also between social agents within the context of production, such as co-directors, and for characters within the narrative. In the case of women on screen, the self is often presented as a translation between and across ideological claims such as those offered by discourses of tradition or humanism and rights. In these documentaries, the filmic constructions of political subjects seem to necessitate the presentation of physical and psychical pain, as characters press against personal and social frontiers, narrating the hardship they have experienced. It is these experiences that Longinotto's camera seeks out.

Social transformation in some cases produces pain, as in the example of Maryam in *Divorce Iranian Style*, who is determined to stay with her new husband but also keep her children, or it is made visible in the process of confronting exploitation, as cases of abuse are articulated and brought to court in *Sisters in Law*. In both cases, subjectivity becomes a site of pain. Yet far from equating female subjectivity with the emotions and their corporeal expression, Longinotto's documentaries narrativise the political arena in a way that registers the mutuality of the political and the emotions,[17] thus depicting change without insulating political action and social antagonism from the conflict and pain that accompanies it. Longinotto has registered her interest in women's potential: 'The most hopeful change seems to be happening from women, and the people that need change the most are definitely women' (Smaill 178). The kind of performative subjects that are constructed through her documentaries are women negotiating the effects of power that produce pain and suffering, effects which in turn are inseparable from the capacity to act. Whether it is Ngassa's indignation in the face of the treatment of those without power or Atena's anguish at the prospect of being alienated from her family, passion is concomitant with power and our experience of the political.

I have noted that these films, in focusing on the plight of marginalised individuals, share something with the tradition of the victim documentary that I described in Chapter 3. Alexandra Juhasz critiques the conventions of the victim documentary as a form of film-making that typically re-inscribes the power of the film-maker to exploit the suffering of the other and to 'judge another's pain through his controlling vision and voiceover' (78). In light of this, Juhasz discusses the possibilities offered by collaborative feminist video practice and the problem of representing experiences of pain and struggle. She explores the alternatives for presenting women's victimisation in documentaries in ways that do not necessarily re-enact that victimisation. In one sense, Longinotto's camera necessarily 'judges' the pain of the other through the choices she makes in framing her subjects. Yet the film-maker/filmed relation constructs the filmic subject as self-determining rather than unconditional victim, complicating the designation of active/passive. Longinotto's authorship is thus marked as a documentary practice of reciprocity in a way that encompasses not only her work with co-directors, but also often her relationship with women in front of the camera.

This is not to say that the women in her films completely evade capture by the film-maker/filmed hierarchy of documentary representation, but rather that this uneven distribution of power is deployed in the interests of a relationship of collusion. In *Divorce Iranian Style*, Maryam is accused by her husband of tearing up a court order outside of the courtroom, a punishable offence. Maryam confidentially tells the camera that, despite her denials, she is guilty of the offence; but when Judge Deldar asks Mir-Hosseini if she and Longinotto saw this happen, they reply that they did not. The film-makers did not witness Maryam's actions so are not, in effect, lying to the judge. This interaction, including the film-makers' omission, is clearly shown in the documentary and exists as an example of explicit collaboration between subject and film-makers. The moment in *The Day I Will Never Forget* when the two sisters undergo FGC stands as an exceptional instance when the film-maker witnesses the events while collaborating with the subject, Fardhosa. Longinotto describes how the second girl clutched Longinotto's leg as she held the camera: 'Emotionally, I'm thinking, I've got to save her; she doesn't want it done, and she's fighting. I had thoughts of grabbing her and taking her parents to court to stop them doing it; it was a complete battle' (Fowler 104). In this case, the collaboration requires that she *not* act despite her own conflicted feelings. An additional force compelling Longinotto's inaction is the constantly negotiated role of the documentarian who endeavours to maintain the camera's observational viewpoint.[18]

In another example, Longinotto notes that, throughout the production of *Sisters in Law*, Ngassa facilitated the camera's access, as a co-director might (Smaill 180). This relationship points to Longinotto's most obvious expression of collaboration. Given her profile and experience as a director, Longinotto could easily produce work in ways that would not necessitate co-direction roles, yet she consistently shares co-direction credits with the women with whom she works. Decades ago, Claire Johnston deemed that 'it is idealist mystification to believe that "truth" can be captured by the camera or that the conditions of a film's production (e.g., a film made collectively by women) can *of itself* reflect the conditions of its production ... new meaning has to *be manufactured* within the text of the film' (28). Yet more recently, Juhasz speculates that if the production process 'feels non-hierarchical, multicultural, feminist, or collective, could this create some of that feeling ... in the viewer?' (92) Another approach is offered by Janet Staiger's elaboration of authorship as a 'technique of the self' that acknowledges the film-maker as a product of discourse. Rather than lauded as possessing an originary personality or creative agency, the author is thus considered in terms of the repetition of performative speech acts; 'the message is produced from circumstances in which the individual conceives a self as able to act' (Staiger 50). The circumstances of production that are specific to Longinotto's collaborative project might then produce new selves able to act in cooperative ways. Statements of collaboration and reciprocity circulate through and around the texts to redistribute agency between authors.

Longinotto's collaborative practice is a particular kind of citation or series of statements that positions her auteur status in the field of documentary as a non-normative one. These projects consistently bear the marks of a strong consultative process that seeks input from not only co-directors, but also women already working in the environments depicted. This expression of collaboration and its attendant reciprocity entails a translation of meaning between authoring subjects, frequently in the interests of a mutual social agenda. In addition to the notion of collaboration, Longinotto's authorship is marked by her consistent interest in working with subjects in different cultural contexts. *Divorce Iranian Style*, *Runaway*, *Sisters in Law* and *The Day I Will Never Forget* received funding from British television, Channel Four or the BBC, and are made primarily for an English-speaking audience. They have also achieved significant success on the festival circuit.[19] Longinotto's stated aim is 'to allow the audience to make a sort of leap where they can feel what the person in the film is feeling, through cultures' (Smaill 181). Her comments suggest that the texts organise an empathetic engagement that might engender political action or consciousness. But this dialogue between audience and the object of empathy is, as demonstrated in reference to Nettie Wild's documentary, *Fix*, a utopian prospect given the potential for appropriation when empathy is one-sided. It too easily negates the particularity of the other and denies any differentiation between objects of empathy.

Yet an empathetic address is secondary in Longinotto's work to what I argue is the central narrative thread that weaves across these four documentaries. It is the representation of female political subjects as they 'translate into the present' (196), to borrow Chow's phrase, within particular cultural contexts that is the object of her work, rather than the pain and suffering of the 'other' in difficult situations. This project surpasses any operation of empathy to initiate an ethical acknowledgement of the other in her specificity. Extending Chow's formulation, I would assert that the coevalness of the subjects achieved in terms of film form and practice generates an historical consciousness specific to documentary.

Perceiving a temporal relation between text and spectator, Nichols argues, in the course of his discussion of *Who Killed Vincent Chin?*, that film 'may construct a dialectical "will to transform" as an intentionalization toward the future' ('Historical' 57). He speaks of a consciousness of the future as 'that time in which we act upon what we learn now. It is the ceaseless dialectic of past, present and future that sustains historical consciousness for the historical actor as well as the historical spectator' ('Historical' 56). The 'will to transform' is at the forefront of Longinotto's work, as the difficulties faced by her characters are always accompanied by a movement towards individual, and sometimes collective, enfranchisement. This movement is coupled with the potential for subjects to act. Nichols's understanding of futurity centres on the critique of history and the multiple interpretations offered by the formal juxtapositions of the collage style deployed in the documentary he discusses. The realism that explores pain has a different way of portraying the crisis of meaning in the representation of the historical world. In Longinotto's work, this crisis coalesces around documentary performances of pain that confound verification by the viewer, as in *Divorce Iranian Style* and *Runaway*, or the representational impossibility of physical pain in *The Day I Will Never Forget*.

The two chapters in this section have explored the representation of experiences of frustration and suffering, the subject in pain. In the previous chapter I argued for the need to find ways of representing pain so that it might be witnessed and acknowledged by an audience without invoking a fetishising mode of empathy. The documentaries discussed in this chapter realise this opportunity clearly as the focus on female subjects of change directs the narrative towards the future and away from an empathetic identification. The social potential of her work has also been recognised by groups working for material change in the communities represented. Longinotto's work has been screened not only in the West, but also in the cultures in which it has been made; for example, *Divorce Iranian Style* has circulated through informal means of distribution in Iran, and *The Day I Will Never Forget* has been taken up by aid groups in Kenya.[20] Thus, the documentaries potentially participate in the transactions between political groups within these cultures. Like her cinema of translation, this activism is a shared project. In many instances throughout the production and narratives of these films, co-directors and subjects collude and reciprocate in the interests of bringing into representation the links between subaltern suffering and political action.

Telling stories and presenting testimony that concerns not only women but also children, Longinotto's work importantly and implicitly implicates spectator and text in a mutual 'presentness' that extends across the West and its perceived others. Aspects of her practice approach the other by way of a cinema of translation. Such a cinema observes Gayatri Chakravorty Spivak's maxim that '[i]n every possible sense, translation is necessary but impossible' (13). While all documentary functions as an imperfect translation of the historical world into sound and image, Longinotto's films offer multiple dimensions of translation. The focal point of her documentary realism is the translation between systems of law or between discourses of tradition and of individualism that are concomitant with a movement through modernity. Chow argues that cultural translation can no longer be thought of as only linguistic or a conversion from an original to a derivative; it also encompasses the multi-directional translation of meaning. She understands translation 'as the co-temporal exchange between different social groups deploying different sign systems that may not be synthesizable to one particular model of language or representation' (197).

Thus translation occurs not only across cultural borders, but also between and within social groups, genders, religions and classes. Collectives are never homogenous. Their heterogeneity inevitably sparks antagonism and conflict as the hierarchies within collectives are negotiated. Longinotto's four films, through focusing on this transformation, place pain at the centre of the documentary representation of the subject.

Part III The Labour of Authorship: Caring and Mourning

5
Loss and Care: Asian Australian Documentary

In the case of socially or politically oriented documentaries, it is easy to assume that the ideologies of the film and the ideologies of the film-maker are one and the same. Reading formations frequently infer a link between the social or political intentions of the film-maker and those of the documentary, a notion I discussed in Chapter 4 in regard to Kim Longinotto's 'cinema of translation'. The aim of this chapter and the next is to look more closely at the author as a site, and indeed a product, of the emotions – emotions that tie individuals to social issues.

Here I perceive the documentary author through a mode of self-hood in which performative speech acts, such as the films themselves, express the subjective emotional attachments of the film-maker. In the documentaries that I discuss, frequently the object of care is the social collective represented in and/or addressed by the documentary. These authors are framed as agents who intend, through their film-making, that the collective will become the object of the viewers care. In this sense, emotion plays a potentially binding role; emotion circulates with the documentaries and binds viewers, film-makers and the social collective. In this chapter, the Asian Australian author-subject is posed as a site of mourning *and* care; emotions that coalesce around these diasporic individuals as they engage in and are produced through social and textual relations. In these cases, the documentaries' aesthetic qualities reinforce and mirror the different functions of the emotions, accentuating the production of authorship as a site of the emotions.

The potential for documentary to play a role in the process of mourning, whether the process is undertaken by film-makers or particular communities and audiences, has been well established through a number of different notable examples. These range from prominent films such as Claude Lanzmann's *Shoah* (1985) or *Last Days* (1998) to works as varied as *Tongues Untied* (Marlon Riggs 1989) or *Blue* (Derek Jarman 1994). These films frequently offer a meta-discourse of mourning in ways that make grief and emotional anguish representable and contribute to the process of unburdening or detaching from those who have been lost. My focus in this chapter is, in some small part, concerned with this documentary meta-discourse as a way of accommodating loss. Yet much more central to this analysis is the *effect* of the struggle over the representability of loss. The grouping of films that motivates this enquiry expresses mourning as a dimension of diasporic authorship. Examining a cluster of four films, this chapter understands a caring Asian Australian authorship to emerge as a consequence of a process of mourning.

These documentary narratives are propelled by the activity of mourning for that which has been lost or is unfulfilled. Yet as I discuss, this is not simply mourning that exists as an end unto itself; this mourning informs relations between subjects and operates in conjunction with a caring attachment to particular communities. The first two documentaries I discuss, *Chinese Takeaway* (Mitzi Goldman 2002) and *Sadness: A Monologue by William Yang* (Tony Ayres 1999), feature a strongly biographical central narrative which is spoken, and at times performed by a single narrator who is the locus around which Asian Australian subjectivity is formulated in the documentaries. The second two, *The Finished People* (Khoa Do 2003) and *Letters to Ali* (Clara Law 2004) are films that are directed by Asian Australian film-makers, but take as their object of enquiry the broader field of the Australian public sphere. Although *The Finished People* was a film marketed as a drama, its generic coding is ambiguous and, as I will argue, there are a number of ways in which it can be fruitfully understood as a documentary work. In many respects, this grouping of films offers an avenue to question straightforward categorisations of authorship. All the films suggest a strongly collaborative production process and, as I will discuss, in the first two documentaries, the Asian Australian subjects are in fact co-authors, positioned alongside the credited director.

This is a 'messy' collection of films to discuss in relation to documentary and Asian Australian authorship. Not all are specifically engaged in the interrogation of Asian Australian identity. Moreover, all favour, to differing degrees, more experimental modes of documentary narrative and as a group they exhibit a diverse and uneven range of approaches to documentary aesthetics. Despite these inconsistencies, the films all present a strong authoring personality. This personality is expressed through stories of loss and care. Significantly, these emotions not only engage the viewer in the stories and events represented, they also work to unsettle the formal qualities of documentary representation itself.

This discussion builds on Renov's theorisation of death and mourning in contemporary documentary. Renov usefully expands mourning beyond familial sorrow to look at the greater potential for identificatory practices to work as an 'intrapsychic activity' (*The Subject* 125). He explores the way death opens up a gap in the (Lacanian) Real. This void might then be confronted by words and images, signifiers that contribute to the process of mourning. In keeping with the concerns of this book, my notion of mourning, as well as loss and care, is an expanded one that requires a different set of theoretical tools than those put forward by Renov. This is a conception of mourning that includes not only the unbearable experience of another's death, but also the losses that are bound to the movements of modernity, such as the lost fullness which is the promise of diaspora, the failure or absence of universal citizenship and the lack of safety in life lived in advanced capitalism. These questions and the documentary subject at hand, the diasporic author, will be explored in relation to documentary works that specifically reference Australia and an Australian cultural imaginary.

While the cultural diversity of Australia's population is frequently acknowledged in popular discourse, the breadth and specificity of this diversity is spoken of less frequently. Post-war immigration policies have produced an Australian citizenry that, proportionally, constitutes one of the largest immigrant nations in the world, second only to Israel. This cultural diversity exists in tandem with the continued linguistic and political dominance of a British settler derived culture and the disenfranchisement of Aboriginal peoples. The preceding decade has seen a new shift in perceptions of otherness and nationhood in the Australian public sphere. The state-sponsored multiculturalism that was in place from the late 1970s until the mid-1990s gave way to an increased currency of a language of singular nationalism and a refutation of cultural pluralism. This anxious, exclusionary shift was fuelled at the level of public debate and policy by over a decade of conservative government (1996–2007) that emphasised national 'unity' and minimised references to diversity and cultural particularity. Tseen Khoo describes this as a 'new dynamics of exclusion in contemporary Australia in the wake of the "re-territorialising" of Australian boundaries, MV *Tampa* events,[1] and ongoing global anti-terrorist rhetoric and legislation' (3). As she also notes, for Asian Australian communities this dynamic echoes a century of exclusionary cultural politics first formalised by the Immigration Restriction Act in 1901.[2]

This exclusion, and the ethno-racisms it entails, exists as an informing discourse in the four films under discussion. Produced over the course of the last decade, these documentaries, albeit in very different ways, draw attention to the struggle over recognition and hegemony from the perspective of diasporic subjectivity. However, rather than focusing on Asian Australian identity politics specifically, my emphasis here concerns how subjectivity acts as a locus for the circulation of particular emotions in the context of Australia's dominant ideologies of nation building. This is also an endeavour to theorise an alternative to conceptualisations of political identity based in an emphasis on centre/margin or the hybridisation of ethnicity and difference. Instead, a focus on the work of the emotions provides a way to rethink how diasporic subjects might contest ethnicised hierarchies.

Sadness: A Monologue by William Yang **and** Chinese Takeaway

For Freud, 'mourning is regularly the reaction to the loss of a loved person, or to the loss of some abstraction which has taken the place of one, such as one's country, liberty, an ideal, and so on' (252). Judith Butler extends the psychology of mourning beyond simply loss, to the denial of an anticipated fullness: 'In a phenomenological sense, mourning is part of any epistemological act that "intends" or "anticipates" the fullness of an object, because that end cannot be reached, and that fullness is elusive' ('Afterword' 471). Diasporic narratives are not always necessarily or exclusively about loss; many are also focused on new horizons of potential. This said, lost objects of love and other kinds of lack frequently pervade diasporic narratives. In one sense, 'the experience of immigration itself is based on a structure of mourning' (Eng and Han 352). For first generation migrants, as David L. Eng and Shinhee Han observe, what is mourned is the loss of homeland, family, language and the privilege offered to those who can assume the status of the dominant culture. Butler's observation is particularly salient in understanding other types of collective mourning, such as the unfulfilled promise of the idealised life in diaspora, as a lost fullness.

Sadness and *Chinese Takeaway* both explore Chinese diasporic experience in Australia. They also share a number of formal attributes and this similarity owes much to the way both existed as one-person stage performances prior to their filmic adaptations. The two documentaries revolve around the individual narratives of William Yang and Anna Yen, respectively. Yang's work was adapted to the film format by director Tony Ayres and Yen's by Mitzi Goldman. While these documentaries were inspired by theatre pieces, there are important differences, in both style and content, between the two cinematic versions. What is consistent, however, is the autobiographical inscription of the narrators' monologue. While neither Yang nor Yen are formally credited as directors, both are distinct expressive agents in the diegesis of the film. For this reason, they sit alongside Ayres and Goldman as authoring subjects and are the focus for my analysis of Asian Australian authorship in these documentaries.

Sadness revolves around Yang's monologue and consists of three sets of narratives which are illustrated in the mise en scène with Yang's still photography, his direct address to camera and, occasionally, staged re-enactments. The first two narratives are linked; after recounting the death of his mother, Yang's process of mourning propels him on a quest to garner information about the murder of his uncle in 1920s Queensland in Northern Australia. The third dimension of *Sadness* is composed of stories about many of Yang's friends in Sydney's gay community who died of AIDS-related illnesses in the 1990s. The narratives are woven together in ways that portray them as different dimensions of Yang's identity as gay and as Chinese Australian. While *Chinese Takeaway* does not seek to juxtapose such seemingly disparate narratives, Yen as the author-subject similarly recounts experiences in diaspora and those of the women in her family in particular. The opening scenes of the film show Yen's journey to Hong Kong to uncover her grandmother's stories about her female ancestors' lives in China, then Hong Kong and then her mother's move to Sydney in the 1960s. Not only is she the speaking subject, telling the story of her own past, but she also performs the parts of her mother, father and grandmother, among others, in the re-enactments that feature in the film. The film explores Yen's mother's experiences in Australia, the hardship of living in diaspora and Yen's own personal grief near the end of the documentary when it is revealed that Yen's mother committed suicide.

In both *Sadness* and *Chinese Takeaway*, Yang and Yen articulate the personal losses that are inseparable from familial movements between home and host culture. These are also losses that are bound up with the pressure or demand to assimilate to Anglo-Australian culture and the impossibility of meeting this demand. As Butler notes, mourning is part of an intended or expected fullness that cannot be reached. This is relevant to not only the personal stories in the documentaries, but also at the level of documentary style. *Sadness* and *Chinese Takeaway* are texts that re-present and interpret the import of what has been lost through re-enactment and this re-enactment itself brings to the fore the elusive fullness of the referent in documentary. In this respect, the affective authorship I have proposed consists of both formal *and* subjective or thematic aspects of loss.

On the one hand, these texts re-enact the stage performances that precede them and, on the other, more significantly, both re-enact events from earlier in the lives of the central biographical subjects. For Ivone Marguiles, the re-enactment film 'creates, performatively speaking, another body, place, and time. At stake is an identity that can recall the original event (through a second degree indexicality) but in doing so also re-form it' (220). The events recreated in *Chinese Takeaway* include Yen's journey to Hong Kong to speak to her grandmother and aunt, and also the experiences of her mother in Sydney when Yen herself was a child. In *Sadness*, while a handful of scenes are re-enacted in a studio setting, much of the monologue is accompanied by Yang's own still photography. In both instances, events that had occurred in the historical world are repeated in the documentary through a separate indexical register – the re-enactment.

The re-enactment can recall, but cannot bring back the experience of the original event; it is always structured through its connection to loss. Margulies describes this as 'the positive residue of a loss: the unavoidable perception that re-enactment can only produce another image and that the closer it recalls the original the more it distances itself from it' (230). This is a positive residue because, for Marguiles, the re-enactment film functions as a model for social action and a way to morally re-conceive of a 'mistaken past'.

The events in *Sadness* and *Chinese Takeaway* are re-formed, yet not in a manner that acts as warning or pedagogy. The awareness instituted is of a different order; it is one of mourning for what has been lost and rather than a mistaken past, as in Margulies' formulation, it is a past that is specific to the experiences of diasporas in Australia.[3] Thus, the function of loss is doubled as it refers to both the formal re-enactment as the realist deficit between the event and its representation, and the authorial mourning for a lost object that pervades the events themselves. The scenes in which this is most apparent are those in which the documentary signifies the re-telling of death. When *Sadness* and *Chinese Takeaway* represent the death of a lost loved one, each constructs the encounter between the viewer and the text through slightly different aesthetic approaches. Yet both draw on still photography and the image of the face. As the work of a number of scholars attests, the relationship between death and the image of the face is a particularly rich arena for screen culture and theories of the image.[4] This is no less the case in these films as the moments that focus on the face exist as principal points of revelation and sadness.

Yang's own face addressing the camera and photographs of the faces of those close to him are central to the way *Sadness* formulates an address to and encounter with the viewer. These photographs include the faces of Yang's relatives, such as that of his mother shortly before her death, as well as those of Scotty, Allan, Nicholaas and other friends who had died of AIDS. As Yang describes these people, their faces become infused with the anticipation of death, whether they are ill at the time the photograph is taken or not. In one sequence, Yang recounts the last visit with his friend, artist David McDiarmid. Yang states: 'I was leaving on a tour the next day. I didn't have a plan for my behaviour; I thought I'd take my cues from him. We said goodbye at the door as if we'd see each other again next week, although we knew this would be the last time. "This is all very strange" was his only comment; I felt it too.' Rather than a voice-over, Yang speaks directly to the camera in this sequence, his face in medium close-up against the backdrop of a red curtain.

Photographs of McDiarmid himself and images of his artworks precede the scene. In this sequence, faces are associated with the space between friends, which becomes impossible to comprehend in the anticipation of death. Yang's narration (and the accompanying images) steers a course through the incomprehensibility that surrounds the death of his friends and his mother. This navigation, and the re-telling it requires, becomes the medium of Yang's grief. Apparent, in a more abstract sense, is an ethical space of community in death that is inhabited by 'the brotherhood [sic] of individuals who possess or produce nothing in common, individuals destitute in their mortality [...]. The one becomes the brother of the other when he puts himself wholly in the place of the death that gapes open for the other' (Lingis 157). Perhaps most significantly, Alphonso Lingis understands this as a relation of alterity: 'One no longer sees oneself in the others or sees the others in oneself. One comes to see the other in an *other* place and time [...]' (Lingis 170). The documentary presents the space between the figure of the author and the face of the lost object of love as one that is constituted by mourning and a relationship of alterity.

Anna Yen, while not mourning a community of the dying, nevertheless, mourns the death of her mother who is at once the familial other, perceived in relation to the self, and also, paradoxically, becomes irreducible to the self as the other that she sees in an '*other* place and time'. The documentary becomes a process for approaching this otherness. Hence, the mourning that occurs is for the loss of her mother and also, by de facto, a mourning for that which her mother lost in the movement into diaspora. This is most acutely represented as loss of family support, agency and a lost hope in future possibility. Yen re-enacts her mother's arrival in Australia, where she intends to study, but soon discovers she has been duped by her own mother into a marriage with a wealthy businessman living in Sydney who is 20 years her senior. Consequently, Yen's mother is raped, becomes pregnant, and is obliged to remain with him in Australia, lonely and isolated from her family. While she has gained material security, the promise of, as she states, life as a 'modern woman' in diaspora, is shattered.

In the closing scenes of the film, Yen narrates her mother's suicide. As a rope is shown being attached to a beam, Yen describes a particular day when she happened to go to a friend's house after school: 'That was the day my mother died. I felt nothing for a long time.' Following this, the screen is filled with black-and-white photographs of Yen's mother when she was young, then with a baby in her arms and then an image of Yen herself as a young teenager. These faces are more fleeting than those meditated on in *Sadness*. However, they appear at the emotional height of the documentary's exploration of Yen's relationship with her mother. Because of this, the relay of faces emphasises not only the daughter's relation with her mother, but also the face of the author at the encounter with death. In *Sadness* and *Chinese Takeaway*, then, there is a relay of faces as the face of the author encounters the other and this is mirrored for the viewer who is confronted by the image of the author, an object steeped in loss.

In her discussion of ethics and documentary, Cooper writes: 'The face takes us out of the very relation it simultaneously creates: the Other always exceeds the idea I have of it, escapes my grasp, and thus breaks with the spatial symmetry that would equate my position with its own' (18).[5] The face of the other presented in these sequences is, for the most part, that of the Asian Australian other. But less relevant in this case is the ethnic particularity of the face than the specificity of the encounter – an encounter with the face at the scene of mourning. This specific meeting with the other is what differentiates the other; it is the face at the scene of mourning that becomes not the other of the self but an autonomous other akin to Cooper's theorisation. This is not to say that the particularity of individual or Asian diasporic experience is denied, but that Yang and Yen's autobiographical narratives become meaningful via emotions of loss. Hence, the encounter is one that potentially confronts the established codes by which the 'ethnic' other enters representation.

In these documentaries, mourning delineates moments of encounter between viewer and author. Rather than an attachment to a particular notion of Asian Australianness, this is a relation that seeks to exceed preconceived ethnicised hierarchies. Loss, by way of the documentary re-enactment, engenders a kind of productive failure that disrupts the illusion of full access to the referent that is central to documentary aesthetics. Further, they may perform the pain specific to diasporic experiences, but Yang and Yen are not determined by this subjectivity. Instead, the combination of loss in the documentary re-enactment and the effect of mourning seek an ethical engagement beyond these categorisations.

The Finished People and *Letters to Ali*

Khoa Do's *The Finished People* and Clara Law's *Letters to Ali* present slightly different kinds of author-subjects but again they disrupt easily categorisable notions of Asian Australian authorship. Firstly, this is due to the way the texts explore an expanded notion of diaspora and displacement. In contrast with the autobiographical emphasis of the previous two films, *The Finished People* and *Letters to Ali* implicitly take as their object the sphere of the national and the political realm of liberal democracy. These film-makers are positioned as authors either within the documentary, as in *Letters to Ali*, or in the extra textual discourses that have been integral to the reception of the film, as in *The Finished People*. Their subjectivity is located transnationally, across national borders, and yet the films are also entrenched in the dialogue of the Australian public sphere. Again, lost objects underpin these documentary endeavours. However, in this case, rather than lost loved ones, it is an ethico-political loss that motivates the filmic investigation. Moreover, the narrative of loss again informs the stylistic presentation of the texts.

The Finished People is a film that confuses the categories of fiction and documentary. The film grew out of a project at a community welfare centre and was scripted by the director/producer, Khoa Do, in collaboration with a number of non-professional actors who make up the cast. While the screenplay is fiction, it draws on the experiences of the writers. These experiences have generated, in *The Finished People*, narratives dealing with homelessness, poverty and drug abuse. Centrally, it is the lives and desperate decisions made by three young men living in the Sydney suburb, Cabramatta, which make up the three unconnected storylines. While none of the group were themselves homeless, they worked with Do in creating characters and a script that reflected the environment that exists in and around Cabramatta. The unprofessional origins of the film offer it a kind of documentary realism, largely due to the formal signifiers of cinema verite, voice-over and digital video technology, while the events on screen are, in actuality, scripted. It is these aspects of documentary representation that interest me most because they appeal to a viewership through the discourses of actuality; rather than existing in a fictional world, the aesthetic concerns of the film orient these characters towards the actual world of contemporary Australian society.

This orientation is evident from the opening scenes of the film when one of the three central protagonists, Des, references the Australian prime minister of the time. Homeless, Des is taking refuge in a doorway with his girlfriend. In voice-over he states: 'If I had one day to live, three things I would do. I would try as hard as I can to shoot John Howard[6] [...]. Another thing I'd like to do is I'd like to thank everybody who ever cared for me, ever actually showed they did care.' This also begins to suggest some of the absences that this film mourns through its process of re-presentation. These include deficient political responsibility in the form of the welfare state and modernity's promise of egalitarianism and safety under the matrices of liberal democracy. 'They think we're finished people' is a phrase that appears as an inter-title on screen at the opening of the film and signifies, for the characters, the loss of a particular kind of narrative of the self that centres on personal fulfilment and the way a broader collective acknowledges the value of that self. In this sense, the disenfranchisement experienced by these individuals is defined by a personal loss of hope in the future. This is expressed in one instance by 20-year-old Van, a character who is depicted as living in a car park atop a Cabramatta building. He speaks in voice-over about his dreams and the process of abandoning those dreams as his optimism about the future diminishes: 'they would just get dropped one after another'. The cast represents actors of Italian, Maltese and Aboriginal descent. It also reflects Cabramatta as home to a sizeable population of Indo-Chinese heritage, and significant within this is the Vietnamese diasporic community, including Van. Echoing Yen's mother's experiences in *Chinese Takeaway*, for the diasporic subjects in *The Finished People* what is additionally mourned is a lost fullness or the fulfilment of the promise of diaspora.

Not only is there an implicit focus on diasporic experience within the film, but also the publicised details of the production process emphasise the Vietnamese Australian background of Khoa Do.

The Finished People screened for only a short time on general release in Australian cinemas. Despite this, due to a significant video and DVD release, its success at international film festivals and favourable attention from film critics, the film's notoriety intensified over a period of time. During this period, the unconventional production conditions were highlighted in reviews and other publicity. Alongside this extra textual material, Do's public profile and his personal history, including his journey form Vietnam at a young age, have circulated in the public sphere along with the film text.[7] The narratives of mourning in *The Finished People* have then folded into the formulation of Do's diasporic authorship. Associated with the figure of Do is the hardship and difficulty linked to the movement to the host culture as well as the hope that accompanies the discourse of the 'successful migrant' who overcomes adversity to succeed in diaspora.

Director Clara Law is known as one of Australia's foremost diasporic fiction film-makers. She is prominent in the on-screen events in *Letters to Ali* and this presence firmly establishes her subjectivity as author of the film. *Letters to Ali* begins with Law describing her own movement from Hong Kong to Australia. In this sense, it shares something with the autobiographical narratives previously discussed. However, rather than an on-screen, embodied narrator or a voice-over, Law's subjective voice is represented in the documentary through the consistent use of written text on the screen. While Law's authorial positioning is located in the opening scenes and she is present as a character throughout the narrative, it is not the film-maker's experience of diaspora, but rather others' hardships endured through moving between cultures that are central to the documentary events, as is the case with *The Finished People*. After reading an article in the newspaper about Trish Kerbi, a woman who had been exchanging letters with 'Ali',[8] an unaccompanied 15-year-old Afghani interned in a detention centre for asylum seekers, Law decides to contact her. The ensuing narrative follows Kerbi and her family, including three children, as they attempt to help Ali secure a visa. The documentary also follows the family on the 8000-km road journey from Melbourne to visit Ali in Port Hedland, Western Australia.

This personal narrative is intertwined in the film with an exploration of a history of Australian government policy in relation to asylum seekers.[9] At one point in the documentary, Law provides

Kerbi and Ali with a list of words and asks them to speak about what they associate with these terms. Ali's responses are again relayed in inter-titles and when the term 'suffering' is suggested these read: 'to be imprisoned for months in the detention centre, not knowing if his family is alive or dead, to be unsure if he will be deported tomorrow, to have no home, no country, no future'. While what is articulated here is a loss of hope, this is compounded by a loss of status as well, the effective suspension of the category of 'citizen'. This suspension is characteristic of the non-place that is the detention centre. As Suvendrini Perera writes: 'The refugee or "stateless" figure represents that which cannot be contained within the nation-state because of anxieties over "national security", and is therefore relegated to a new space, "the camp", within state boundaries, and yet outside.' Through focusing on the particularity of Ali's plight, this film expresses a perceived lack of care on the part of the nation-state, reiterating statements made in *The Finished People*.

Asian Australian authorship functions as a set of statements that circulate alongside these texts, or is signified within them, and in conjunction with an ethical desire to combat the perceived losses of the imagined community. *Letters to Ali* and *The Finished People* present a different notion of the ethical to the previous films; rather than the ethic of the encounter with the other, it is an ethico-political recognition that these films seek. This is, for Chantal Mouffe, an enterprise that values pluralism and 'that concerns the specific values that can be realized in the realm of politics through collective action' (151). Thus, these films attempt to engender a more collective scene of mourning that implicates the broader social realm. This mourning circulates with the film in a way that involves a recognition of the forms of interaction that mark some others as deficient or inferior. Following this, the films seek a revaluing of the other, a process that saturates the other with mourning.

This attempt is mirrored in a formal experimentation that again draws attention to the documentary expression of this absence. Here, it becomes evident in the texts as a troubling residue, the loss of certainty in the verisimilitude of the documentary text. This is due to an awkwardness that permeates the poetics of these films.[10] I have noted the interface between fiction and non-fiction that characterises *The Finished People* and this brings with it an uncomfortable formal quality constituted by unpolished acting styles and edited storylines that resist a conventional flow. These aspects produce an uneasy relation to both fiction and non-fiction as the film can secure neither adequately. Similarly, while *Letters to Ali* employs observational modes and is more categorically a documentary, the stylised use of text on screen brings an awkwardness to the documentary realism as its representation neither purports documentary objectivity nor a fully essayist style of subjective representation.

In both cases, there is a distancing from the filmic subject that results from the lack of clear generic codes. A formal indeterminacy mediates the viewer's encounter with Law, Kerbi and her family and Ali, or Van and Des. It highlights, for the viewer, the construction of the text and the impossibility for the other to be fully present within this. In the case of scenes featuring Ali, the problem of the face-to-face encounter is heightened. In order to maintain his anonymity, Ali's face has been blurred with computer-generated effect while the rest of his body remains in focus. This foregrounds the distance between subject and viewer while also placing an emphasis on the mode of encounter, the text.

This function is similar to what Nichols refers to as a 'troubled and troubling text' (241). These texts open out that which is 'beyond the ideology of unity or wholeness by intensifying the very antinomies, the logical scandals, inherent in narrative' (241). When fissures appear in the conventions of genre, there results a loss of intimacy and agreement between text and spectator. For the representation of otherness, be it the Asian other, the disenfranchised other or the foreigner in the shape of the asylum seeker, this textual loss aids a movement beyond the dialectic of self and other. The social political loss is articulated in conjunction with Asian Australian authorship in such a way that the mourning becomes expressively tied to the formally troubled text. Indeed, in all four films narratives shaped by loss produce difficult textuality, whether formally troubled or impossible documentary knowledge of the ethnicised other in the face of death. Moreover, the attachments that shape both text and author locate the author's agency in the Australian public sphere. This is not simply or only diasporic subjectivity that is attached to a Vietnamese or a Chinese homeland, an elsewhere, but rather is an ethico-political investment in recognising the de-valuing of social subjects more broadly.

Collectivity and care

In Hamid Naficy's discussion of exile and diasporic cinema, what he terms 'accented cinema', he notes that the formal concerns of postmodernism that characterise much of this cinema are suspended when the homeland is referenced: 'The referent homeland is too powerfully real, even sacred, to be played with and signified upon. It is this powerful hold, that of the homeland, that imbues the accented structures of feeling with such sadness and sense of terminal loss' (27). The films under discussion here differ from those discussed by Naficy.[11] As I have noted, the experience of diaspora is central to these documentaries, but homeland is not the site of intense feeling that Naficy describes. Losses connected to displacement do feature in the films, but it is the confluence of subsequent losses in diaspora that are more pertinent. Thus, the documentaries are entrenched in what Naficy, drawing on Raymond Williams's well-known phrase, describes as a 'structure of feeling' that encompasses more than a longing for homeland. In other words, while I have discussed the way this mode of authorship works more broadly to fold together social, political and aesthetic loss, mourning also frequently seeks out the acknowledgement of a collective, much in the way I described in Chapter 3. However, at stake here is a broader appeal to the emotions in which the potential to influence communities of care exists alongside the work of mourning.

Butler puts forward the possibility that loss can also underpin belonging:

> Loss becomes condition and necessity for a certain sense of community, where community does not overcome the loss without losing the very sense of itself as community. And if we say this second truth about the place where belonging is possible, then pathos is not negated but it turns out to be oddly fecund, paradoxically productive.
>
> ('Afterword' 468)

For Freud, mourning will decrease as the subject detaches from the lost object. It is only in the pathology of melancholia that affect persists as a kind of stasis. When a common sense of loss persists, this must inevitably depart from Freud's distinctions between melancholia and mourning for an ongoing, but productive, identification with loss. Following Butler, the Asian Australian authors discussed here present a possibility for enabling a community, much like that posed by Lingis, as a ground for action. This can occur in the way that emotions work in the maintenance of boundaries between subjects, to produce a distinct collective, and also intersubjectively, binding a collective together.

If there are two modes of ethical encounter engendered in these documentaries, both seek to make visible cultures of difference within the Australian public sphere in ways that recognise the complexity and value of that diversity. This translates into an authorship that seeks out particular interpretive communities that share a feeling of care. This is the case whether it is the recognition of the value of disenfranchised individuals in *The Finished People* and *Letters to Ali*, or the complex and unassimilable otherness in the biographical narratives of *Sadness* and *Chinese Takeaway*. Ghassan Hage's reading of the affective dimensions of belonging and citizenship is important in this respect. I wish now to turn from mourning to caring emotions. Care, or a deficit of care, can characterise the boundaries between groups of individuals. For example, there are communities who care about a particular issue or group and communities who are represented as uncaring. Hage refers to the mobilisation of care for the national institutions of the host culture and participation in the political process. Specifically, the characterisation of 'migrant care' in popular debate oscillates between a portrayal of 'people who are too "home-oriented" and thus not participating enough, or as phantasmatically imagined people who are participating too much – so much they are feared to be "taking over"' (Hage 1). In both instances, these characterisations act as exclusionary tactics that suggest that migrant care is actually concerned with participation *without* adequate affective attachment to the polis.

This polis for Hage is the Australian national culture, which has been overwhelmingly influenced, particularly under the conservative rule of the last decade, by political debate that has fostered a 'paranoid nationalism'. The concern over migrant participation sits within this as part of nationalist expression of 'worrying about one's nation' (22). This culture of national worrying is a response to a fear for the fate of the nation in the face of perceived threats. This 'pathological' fear is for Hage a result of a lack of care on the part of the nation-state itself in the contemporary era. If this care *by* the nation existed, 'worrying' would be replaced by a reciprocated care *for* the nation based more in enjoyment of a good life, rather than a protective and paranoid 'defence of a good life they cannot access' (30).

Film-makers can be understood to exist alongside and as an effect of their films in ways that make apparent their attachments to the social world. These four documentaries present an affective Asian Australian authorship with very specific attachments. In the absence of a caring nation, they seek to act as loci for rallying care, and thus belonging, based on an acknowledgement of difference in many manifestations – Asian Australian difference, queerness, asylum seekers and the impoverished. The films ask that a national community of viewers reciprocate this care and also become the object of care. *The Finished People* and *Letters to Ali* resonate most powerfully as vehicles that link the emotional investments in social justice issues with the call for the citizen to question the effectiveness of the institutions of the state. Thus, the sphere addressed by this care might be the viewing nation, but it also might be any viewership that recognises the ethical appeal organised by the films. This is a care for life lived in the Asian diaspora and for otherness more broadly. In this vein, Hage writes that 'care essentially generates an inter-subjective and reciprocal ethics that is intrinsic to its nature: there is no caring without caring back' (29). These documentary subjects, through their personal and social forms of mourning, become potent sites for energising a caring reciprocity. This function is inseparable from their designation as diasporic, and specifically Asian Australian, subjects.

Moreover, the documentaries confront what Trinh Minh-ha describes as the 'totalising quest for the referent, the true referent that lies out there in nature, in the dark, waiting patiently to be unveiled and deciphered correctly. To be redeemed' (50). If the texts play a role in dismantling this illusion of the true referent, they do so in ways that rethink the formal qualities of non-fiction film as the losses of the authors and characters weave into the text's self-conscious failure to access the referent. Asian Australian subjectivity, in the four documenters under discussion, is produced as an effect of care and mourning. In turn, this mourning produces ethical forms of caring and, thus, seeks out a reciprocal caring relationship with the Australian audience and also, necessarily, with the nation.

6
Civic Love and Contemporary Dissent Documentary

In her recent review of the terrain of documentary culture, B. Ruby Rich offers the contemporary interest in documentary a historical context when she writes that the 'landscape for documentary production, history, and theory is richer than it has been in the United States at any time since, perhaps, the last explosion: the direct cinema or cinema verite movement of the early 1960s [...]' (109). This richness is marked not only by renewed audience interest in documentary, but also, as Rich infers, by a proliferation of styles in and approaches to the production of documentary. This formal diversity has not occurred suddenly but, rather, has emerged over decades as audience expectation and documentary aesthetics have succumbed to the influences of a changing media landscape. In formal terms, the terrain of contemporary documentary is exceptionally diverse.

My focus is on a particularly visible trend within this recent revival, a grouping of examples that share both stylistic and political agendas. These documentaries demonstrate an overt crafting of the text in a way that, I argue, foregrounds the labour of the film-maker, the author. In this sense, my focus is on the reflexivity of these documentaries. My use of the term contrasts with Bill Nichols's formulation of the 'reflexive mode' in his taxonomy of modes. Documentary production often throws up a confluence of modes in a single text, frequently eschewing straightforward divisions. While the documentaries under discussion here often employ, at some point or another, observational or expository and voice-of-god techniques, in sum they postulate an experience for the viewer that moves decisively beyond the regimes of vision associated with these long-standing conventions.

Posing these works as reflexive documentaries locates them in a relationship with what Linda Williams described, in the early nineties, as a new breed of documentaries. In her essay, 'Mirrors without Memories: Truth, History and the New Documentary', Williams puts forward an analysis of documentaries inflected by postmodern concerns, most specifically *The Thin Blue Line* and *Shoah* and, to a lesser extent, *Who Killed Vincent Chin?* and *Roger and Me*. Whether it is the detail of the Holocaust, as in *Shoah*, or an erroneous murder conviction, as with *The Thin Blue Line*, these films seek to re-conceptualise the construction of reality in documentary in order to cast new light on an event in the historical world. Williams observes a cultural moment when audiences' hunger for images of documentary reality coincided with an increasing acknowledgement that the camera cannot reflect a priori, objective truths ('Mirrors without Memories' 10).

As in the films discussed by Williams, a significant portion of recent theatrical release documentary employs a self-reflexive stylisation, simultaneously drawing attention to the conditionality of documentary truth and to the problematic nature of a particular social situation or set of assumptions. Importantly, the staging and temporal manipulation in films such as *The Thin Blue Line*, for Williams, offers a self-reflexivity that signals the presence of the doco-auteur: 'in place of the self-obscuring voyeur of verite realism, we encounter, in these and other films, a new presence in the persona of the documentarian' (12). The subsequent documentary of the late 1990s and early 2000s is equally concerned with an authorial presence, whether the film-maker appears in the diegesis or is seen to overtly craft the image or narrative trajectory. The popular success much of this work has enjoyed would give further credence to Williams's observation that proposed oppositions between verite and blind faith in documentary truth in one instance, and the 'fictional manipulation' (14) and cynicism of the documentary project in another, do not accurately reflect the audience's experiences of the formal codes of the genre.

Yet the recent documentaries, which I will term 'dissent documentaries', differ from the earlier reflexive films in agenda and sensibility. They are not concerned with the problem of truth and objectivity that was a prominent feature of 1980s cultural and critical practices. However, the reflexivity in the films carries the traces of this influential documentary moment. Similarly, the recent documentaries do not take up verite or expository principles of recording and revealing in order to achieve forms of social intervention, as in an earlier phase of political film-making,[1] but there is an aspect of this political agenda present in the documentaries as well. What kind of doco-auteur is summoned by these newer documentaries and how, then, does this figure reflect the cultural sensibilities of the present? There is a new mode of reflexivity evident here that, I contend, borrows from both these previous traditions while presenting a fresh voice.

This is a doco-auteur who is aligned with and produced by both the overt, performative crafting of the documentary argument and the ethos of political intervention that signals an investment in the well-being of the collective. Specifically, this author is produced through a mode of authorial care that takes the form of Socratic questioning. This questioning is linked to a notion of civic 'love'. Rather than actual love, this is a form of civic devotion and loyalty to the social collective that is exemplified by the figure of Socrates, his methods of critique and his conception of citizenship. As I will argue, these documentaries, and the attendant mode of reflexive authorship, are contemporised through their associations with the sensibilities of irony and subversion in contemporary social justice movements. In the previous chapter, I explored how documentaries can stage or present the subjective emotional attachments of the film-maker. In this chapter, I look again at the figure of the caring author and the way evidence of his/her attachment to an object of care, the social collective, is offered in the aesthetic and thematic preoccupations of particular types of documentary.

Reflexivity in contemporary dissent documentary

Instead of emphasising vision and verisimilitude, these documentaries are much more engaged in performance, as they present arguments using sound and image in ways that seek to convey disjuncture, irony and contradiction. Bruzzi argues, as mentioned in the introduction, that all documentary exhibits a 'performative' aspect. She notes that since 2000 there has been a marginalisation of observational approaches in favour of the drama offered by historical reconstruction, more explicit forms of image manipulation and performative aspects that are moulded for dramatic effect. But Bruzzi also argues that all 'documentaries are performative acts, inherently fluid and unstable and informed by issues of performance and performativity' (1). Rather than invalidating documentary's relationship to reality, and thus the events and individuals represented, understanding films as 'performative' provides a way to more adequately grasp the changing nature of the genre and the diverse examples that make up the category of documentary. In marrying Williams's aesthetics of reflexivity and Bruzzi's observations around documentary's increasing focus on drama and performativity, I argue that the dissent documentary presents a particular manifestation of performativity – one that foregrounds the labour and attachments of the film-maker.

The three examples I focus on here – *The Corporation* (2003), *Enron: The Smartest Guys in the Room* (2005) and *Supersize Me* (2004) – offer slightly different models of reflexivity. In the first two, while a number of documentary modes may be featured, the documentary spectacle and rhetoric is driven by the use of graphics, re-enactments, archive or found footage, popular music and animation. Arguments in these works are structured through metaphor and allusions, thus marking a conscious break with observational cinema by explicitly extending the argument along the trajectory chosen by the author and highlighting a type of reflexivity. Other examples of documentaries with these features are those that owe much to *The Thin Blue Line*, and which include *Mc Libel* (2005), *Outfoxed* (2004) or *A Crude Awakening: The Oil Crash* (2006).

The Corporation, directed by Mark Achbar and Jennifer Abbott, uses a single metaphor as a structuring impulse across the whole documentary. Achbar and Abbott examine the corporation through posing it as a person (as it is instituted in the law) and extend this anthropomorphism to ask: 'What kind of person is it?' The film is then ordered into segments exploring the 'psychology' of the corporation. Titles of segments include *Case Histories*, *The Pathologies of Commerce* and *Boundary Issues*. Overwhelmingly, the central mechanism in the documentary for the delivery of knowledge is the interview format. Interviews with individuals with a wide range of associations with the corporation are featured, including academic experts, public Left-wing figures such as film-makers and writers, whistle-blowers, members of business institutes and CEOs from various companies. A female narrator also provides commentary.

In addition, the documentary is marked by the use of a varied array of images and sequences taken from other sources, such as fiction films, news footage, newsreels, graphics and advertising (Figure 6.1).

The directors establish their own position in the opening scenes when they observe how the metaphor of the 'bad apple' had been used by politicians and expert media commentators to describe high-level corporate corruption. This is done through a montage compiled from news reporting that is then juxtaposed with a sequence showing an apple-picking device. The voice-over then asks: 'What's wrong with this picture? Can't we pick a better metaphor to describe the dominant institution of our time?' It goes on to state: 'We present the corporation as a paradox, an institution that creates great wealth but causes enormous and often hidden harms'. After presenting a number of possible metaphors articulated by interviewees, some with positive inflections and some neutral, they present the 'psychopath' as the chosen point of comparison. Following this, the documentary presents a broad range of examples, historical references and abstracted ideological points to support this analogy and structure multidimensional knowledge about the corporation. The presence of the authoring subject and their location in regards to documentary truth is clearly established in the form of a questioning doco-auteur.

Also employing a range of production techniques, *Enron: The Smartest Guys in the Room* directed by Alex Gibney, explores the reasons behind the financial collapse of the Enron Corporation in 2001. While the events leading up to the collapse were widely publicised

Figure 6.1   The Corporation (Jennifer Abbott and Mark Achbar 2003). Courtesy of Big Pictures Media Corporation/The Kobal Collection

before the documentary was released, the film frames these details through a focus on the personalities of key executives, Kenneth Lay, Jeffrey Skilling and Andrew Fastow. The narrative is compiled from a significant number of interviews with legal experts, former employees including traders and high-ranking executives, politicians and journalists. It also features footage of the court proceedings following the collapse and a male voice-over narration. Adding to these familiar documentary devices are re-enactments, graphics and a collage of images drawn from other films and stock footage. Perhaps the most distinctive reflexive moments, however, are produced by the use of music and lyrics to offer ironic meaning to the statements and images represented. For example, Frank Sinatra's *Black Magic* is played in the soundtrack under a commentary about Enron's fraudulent accounting practices. This music and descriptions put forward by interviewees often provide the inter-titles that segment the themes presented. These titles include *Guys With Spikes*, *Love for Sale* or *The Sorcerer's Apprentice*. The juxtapositions and associations produced through these devices revolve around offering an account of Enron's downfall as an outcome of the personalities and actions of individuals. These devices also testify to the documentary's status as an outcome of authorial crafting.

In a different way, *Supersize Me* is structured around an authoring personality who features as a narrative protagonist and narrator. This strategy of authorship most obviously follows on from Moore's film *Roger and Me*, but it also dates back to films such as *Far From Poland* (1984), *Sherman's March* (1985) and even Dziga Vertov's *Man With a Movie Camera* (1929). *Super Size Me*, which Rich terms a 'stunt' film, follows film-maker Morgan Spurlock as he consumes only McDonalds food for an entire month. This is an orchestrated event that aims to test the health claims made by McDonalds about its food. A number of experts, such as doctors and other health care professionals, lawyers and academics, offer testimony throughout the documentary. While the lawyers and academics provide information about the sociological, economic and ethical ramifications of McDonalds' industrial and public relations practices, the medical practitioners serve to buttress the evidence provided by Spurlock's physical transformation as the narrative progresses. Here it is the body of the film-maker, as an on-screen corporeal presence, that is the focus of the film. The body also functions as the documentary spectacle. As Spurlock gains weight and his declining health is documented by doctors and described by Spurlock himself, the event and its impact on his body provide visible evidence and contribute to the argumentative logic of the film. While the documentary is performative in the sense that the author is an embodied narrator, this performativity is intensified by the way that this narrator is not simply following a series of random events but is, instead, manufacturing a highly orchestrated and rule-governed 'stunt' that works to highlight the labour of authorship.

Reading authorial attachment: Socratic dissent

The figure of the doco-auteur is central to the address of these documentaries, whether or not they appear on screen. The perform-ance of an argument about the historical world is anchored, for the viewer, in the film's signification of a political agenda. This agenda can only be attributed to the work done by the documentarian. For Grosz, the signature of the author is 'an effect of the text's mode of materiality, the fact that as a product the text is an effect of a labour, a work on and with signs, a collaborative, (even if hostile) labour of writing and reading' (*Space, Time* 20). While all texts offer evidence of the labour of a putative author, the codes and conven-tions of the documentaries under discussion offer an author who is firmly located in relation to an ideological subjectivity in the social realm. As I have suggested, these works all take up the polemic of Left wing movements. However, in ways that can be aligned with the groundswell of contemporary political activism in the current era, these works are primarily concerned with structures of corporate capitalism and its impact on the media, environment, government, labour rights or consumer culture.

Accounts of committed documentary on the Left show that the film-maker consistently takes up a position that is not looking on from outside political movements, but one that is actively engaged in engendering change. Indeed, this participation is at the very heart of Waugh's definition of committed documentary. Rabinowitz echoes this in her description of those reporting on the labour strikes in the 1930s in the USA. This history of journalism inflects the Left film-making that appears in the decades to follow and, for Rabinowitz, those who take up the tools of representation necessarily also must forge an allegiance to either side of the battle lines. She aptly describes this as a 'sentimental contract': 'an either-or situation demands that both reporter and reader must choose sides within a dichotomous class structure. In reportage, documenters serve not only to witness but to intervene' ('Sentimental' 43). The sentimental authorial contract differs somewhat in the works I address here. The form of intervention suggested by Rabinowitz and Waugh is best understood as an involvement in revealing and confronting material exploitation and oppression, and this activity can result in a documentary, a product, which also functions as an organising instrument. The authorial performance in the dissent documentaries is more one that is constructed, as I have noted, through metaphor or spectacle, in ways that often signal a form of conceptual *and* political intervention. In contrast with Depression-era politics, the terrain of Left movements is now increasingly fractured. In the absence of clear pre-established dichotomies, film-makers cast their allegiances through representation, often defining how power functions in a given situation in the process. As I have demonstrated throughout this book, social allegiances and social subjectivities are inseparable from the affect worlds of public spheres and thus sentiments, to continue with Rabinowitz's term, can work to bind subjects to one another and to communities.

This said, dissent documentary's author is constituted through an attachment to a social cause (and thus to the community who are stakeholders in that cause) and the expression of that allegiance in the text. Jennifer Abbott, who co-directed *The Corporation*, responds to an interview question regarding what she hoped the documentary would achieve:

> I think that as a filmmaker, I think that one of my goals is to make the familiar appear strange, to shift perspectives, to get people to ask questions that aren't being asked, and this issue in particular, without question is the most pressing issue of our day, corporate dominance of people and the earth literally could change life as we know it. So my motivation is to try to contribute, even in a very small way, to shifting that future, which possibly could be very bleak. So, if viewers walk away from the film asking questions about society that for the most part aren't being asked in mainstream media, finding their answers and acting on those, that's very gratifying for me.
>
> (Hart)

Significant in this statement is not only a language of the emotions in terms of Abbott's sense of 'gratification', but also her desire to initiate, in the reception of the documentary, a questioning that is concerned with the welfare and futurity of the collective. This is a desire that is bound up with a particular manifestation of care for that same collective, and thus it resonates with my discussion of Asian Australian authorship. Yet in this case there is also a specific kind of rhetoric in play that seeks to activate a questioning public, an audience. This is a subjectivity that affirms an attachment to the collective more broadly.

I argue that this can be perceived as a form of political 'love' that shares much with a Socratic love relation with the polis, the object of politics. Notoriously giving his life for his convictions, Socrates re-conceived of the meaning of citizenship and the relation between the moral role of the individual, political authority and the citizenry. He embodies the traits that these documentary film-makers also seek to articulate – criticism and dissent. Most notably, in the *Apology* Socrates conveys a commitment to the avoidance of injustice over and above prescribed duties of citizenship. The passionate intensity that characterised Socrates mission was, as Dana Villa writes, dedicated to the moral progress of his fellow citizens and 'moral progress – the process of perfecting one's soul – consists in the increasingly consistent and self-conscious avoidance of injustice' (25). In this sense, the practice of a 'true political art' is 'an activity which applies to everyone and is potentially open to everyone. The "false political art" is what passes for statesmanship and political leadership, namely the ability to "flatter" the demos and gain popular support for particular policies' (27). These values represent a desire to incite others to question all articulations of power, including that which seems to have become beyond question.[2]

Wendy Brown outlines the way the argument in the *Apology* establishes that 'dissent from existing practices, even wholesale critique of the regime, is not merely compatible with love and loyalty to a political community but rather is the supreme form of such love and loyalty' (*Edgework* 21). In this sense, intellectual critique and the cultivation of thoughtfulness is the highest form of loyalty and Brown identifies this as love, as a civic devotion; it is a 'love of one's fellow citizens as the index of civic loyalty and [...] devotion to improving citizen virtue as the index of this love' (*Edgework* 23).

This is an attachment not simply to educating a collective about a given state of affairs in the interest of engaging them on the political stage, but is rather a commitment to seeking a morally literate, questioning and virtuous collective across the spectrum of political public life.

It would seem that the paradigmatic documentary parallel for this questioning or thoughtfulness is the reflexive mode. Reflexive strategies in documentary endeavour to undermine realism itself and heighten the viewer's awareness of his or her relationship to the text and the world the text represents.[3] The formal aspects of the reflexive mode are a political correlate in that they also are understood to dispute assumptions and interpretations that dominate at a given historical moment. As Nichols notes, this mode 'attempts to emphasise epistemological doubt' (61). The model for such destabilisations is often, as I have noted, *The Thin Blue Line*, a film that poses a problematising of empirical evidence or entrenched assumptions that can, in some respects, be aligned with a Socratic tradition. The films I am pointing to here, as a group, differ from *The Thin Blue Line* in that they much more explicitly pose questions around political problems in the socio-historical landscape, such as the shortcomings of particular government administrations or the inconsistent actions and exploitative nature of corporations, singularly or collectively.

Stylistically, these documentaries present reflexive aesthetics. They are concerned with a particular form of (caring civic) intervention in which they navigate a social field of competing discourses and advocate a position within that field, thus emphasising a tradition of reflexive film-making and the sentimental contract of Left film-making. In combination these attributes testify to the labour of the film-maker. However, do the documentaries construct an author-subject who is bound to the collective through a civic love that has the capacity to produce a Socratic mode of dissent? This would require that film-makers and texts address an audience for the purposes of reproducing a subject-citizen who becomes more adept at questioning the basis of political regimes or hegemony. The documentaries would seek to interpellate a literate and questioning viewer, rather than simply instruct on a given issue or situation, and thus foster a dissent that is underpinned by an authorial devotion to the continued virtue of the social collective.[4] In other words, what is the performativity and visual spectacle that I have identified in these films achieving in the address to the viewer?

The Corporation offers the clearest manifestation of the Socratic project. This is a documentary that, through its reflexive style, constructs an authorship interested in rethinking the interrelationship between the exploiter and the exploited in ways that question the opposition of these terms. Thus, it examines the collective's complex relation with the corporation. Largely composed of interviews, the argument is compiled from different examples charting the rise and the function of the corporation. As I have noted, these threads are drawn together by aligning the symptoms of a psychopath with the actions of corporations through history. The narrative works towards stating the negative impact of corporations in the societies in which they operate. However, there is also a clear endeavour to present the conditions under which corporations themselves are perpetuated. In part, this is achieved through representing the voices of a diverse range of individuals who work within or support the corporate system. In addition to interviews with public figures who put forward cogent critiques of corporate capitalism, such as Noam Chomsky, Vandana Shiva, Naomi Klein and Michael Moore, the film-makers feature interviews with Sam Gibara, the CEO of Goodyear Tyres; Ray Anderson, the CEO of Interface, the world's largest carpet manufacturer; Nobel Prize-winning economist Milton Friedman and other experts in business and finance as well as stock traders. These interviews combine to present the corporation as less a product of personal misconduct than a symptom of the ideological field – one in which profit outweighs moral concerns. The mode of questioning and argumentation suggests the complexity of morality, and 'moral progress', as both sides of the debate present ways of 'caring' for the collective.

All interviews are recorded against the same plain black backdrop. This effectively removes any markers that would otherwise serve to embellish the identity and authority of the speaker. To a degree, the audience must infer meaning from the speakers through the spoken commentary. Yet this equivalence across speakers exists in tandem with other strategies, such as the ironic juxtaposition of images or conflicting statements. For example, in one sequence individuals on different streetscapes address the camera directly and offer names of corporations and how they would characterise these corporations if they were people. One woman says: 'General Electric is a kind old man with lots of stories'. A couple state: 'Nike – young, energetic'. A man says: 'Monsanto – immaculately dressed'. Statements from interviewees against the plain background follow this. They comment on the way corporations might or might not act as good citizens, caring for the community. The voice-over then notes:

> All publicly traded corporations have been structured through a series of legal decisions to have a peculiar and disturbing characteristic. They are required by law to place the financial interests of their owners above competing interests. In fact, the corporation is legally bound to put its bottom line ahead of everything else even the public good.

In sum, the range of statements works to denaturalise the corporation's role in society. They understand the corporation as a particular historical product that has evolved in line with a distinct ideological agenda. This approach works to shift the perception of corporations as benevolent, or at least benign, institutions that service society. In this way a set of complex rhetorical strategies is crafted for the audience in order to extend and/or question what they already understand about the discourse of corporate culture.

Enron takes an approach that is less straightforward in its questioning of hegemonic relations. As I have noted, much of the reflexivity in the documentary works to build character portraits of three of the Enron executives, thus casting the collapse of the company as an outcome of a cult of personality. While the focus of the documentary is the singular example of Enron rather than corporate culture as a system, the documentary does utilise the techniques of reflexivity to trigger a broader set of questions, albeit to a much lesser extent than *The Corporation*. *Enron* offers a counterpoint to the image of the corporation as a robust, monolithic, infallible and largely secure institution in society through examining the personalities at the top of the internal hierarchy and the inside workings of the company. The viewer is encouraged to question the representation of Enron and these individuals in the press and in the company's public relations material.

Among the collage of images that are interspersed with talking heads there is an emphasis on architecture and how this was used by the company to project an image of itself to employees and to the public. The towering Enron building in Houston, shot from a low angle, is a consistent motif that is often returned to in the film. The empty trading floor, flanked by two elaborate staircases that lead to the offices of Enron executives who were, as the voice-over states, referred to by employees as 'the smartest guys in the room' and 'captains of a ship too powerful to ever go down', also appears early in the documentary. Further, in the sequences that represent Skilling and Lay, there is repeated use of images of these executives as they appeared in the press and in marketing material, proclaiming the success of Enron. These images are glossy, highly coloured, also often shot from a low angle and, thus, promote a highly stylised and idealised impression of the men. They are framed ironically in the documentary as the voice-over and interviews highlight the fallibility and failure of Lay and Skilling (Figure 6.2). This juxtaposition serves to frame these signs as unreliable and, in doing so, also operates reflexively to undermine the claims of certainty that pervade the representation of the corporation.

Figure 6.2   Enron: The Smartest Guys In The Room (Alex Gibney 2005). Courtesy of HDNet Films/Jigsaw/The Kobal Collection

While in these examples and others the documentary encourages a questioning of the public representation of Enron specifically, and the personalisation at the heart of the narrative reinforces this, Socratic questioning would encourage the tools for a more systematic critique of the function of corporate culture. While the documentary is explicitly concerned with Enron as an exception, rather than offering an understanding of broadly held ideologies and methods that facilitated the crisis, there are moments in the film that enable doubt in the broader moral imperatives of corporations. In the sequence titled *Love Me, Love Me* interviewees discuss the preoccupation fostered among all employees with the price of the company's shares. An interviewee states that Enron was 'fixated on the stock price and fixated on a massive public relations campaign to convince the investment community that they were new, different, innovative, almost heralding a new era of corporate enterprise'. This is preceded by sequences taken from financial news reports, presumably from the late nineties, observing stock market highs. Enron executives' actions are contextualised within the confidence that came with an over-inflated US stock market. Another interviewee notes that the Enron collapse should not be thought of as an aberration or that 'something like this can't happen anywhere else. It's all about the rationalisation that they're not doing anything wrong'. She goes on to note that other powerful institutions such as banks and global accounting firms legitimised this rationalisation.

Early in the film, the narrator sets the tone for the investigation with the question: 'Was Enron the work of a few bad men or the dark side of the American Dream?' Both alternatives in this question seem to be posed as contributing to the Enron crisis in the film to follow. Lay, Skilling and Fastow are rendered as arrogant and excessive in their quest for success, as personally flawed and also, as the narrator states in an essentialising proposition, indicating something of the 'dark side of human behaviour'. All of these aspects contribute to a narrative that focuses most clearly on Enron as a particular extreme, with broader systemic concerns underpinning this. The reflexivity featured in *Enron* is thus employed to ironically render human fallibility and its impact on those who must suffer the consequences. There is less a sense of questioning the fundamental structure of the system as does *The Corporation*, than the capacity of the regime to allow individuals to abuse the system. This is the key thesis for the film's dissent.

Like *Enron, Supersize Me* focuses on one corporation within its critique. However, *Supersize Me*, I argue, departs significantly from the previous two examples and offers a unique approach to the dissent documentary: it is the body that is put forward as the site for a questioning intervention. In this documentary, character exploration is again important to the way audiences are asked to engage with the narrative, but here it is the personality, and body, of the film-maker that offers a compelling point of identification. Spurlock's embodied presence dominates the documentary, either through his voice-over or his presence in front of the camera (Figure 6.3). This presence contributes to two interwoven threads that make up the film's argument. The first is Spurlock's consumption of McDonalds food for 30 days and its documentation. Included in this are the regular encounters with the nutritionist and three doctors, the representation of his private life and conversations with his domestic partner and his mother, and his attempts to secure an interview with McDonalds public relations personnel. The second thread is composed of a broader investigation into aspects of the social order that maintain, largely through commercial power, fast food culture. Within this, experts such as public policy advocates and commercial lobbyists are interviewed. Spurlock also visits a number of schools in an examination of the school lunch programme in the US, which is dominated by low-cost food with little nutritional value. As noted, the performative aspects of the documentary are most

Figure 6.3   Morgan Spurlock in *Super Size Me* (Morgan Spurlock 2004). Courtesy of Roadside/Goldwyn/The Kobal Collection

spectacularly concerned with the orchestration of the event and its unanticipated negative impact on Spurlock's body. This emphasises the health effects of McDonald's food and, as a result, places a greater focus on effects rather than the expansion of a discourse of norms and values that underpin the hegemony of McDonalds and other fast food corporations.

In this respect, *Supersize Me* does less to offer an argumentative logic that has a questioning impetus in a Socratic sense. The reflexivity in the documentary is focused principally on the representation of effects, seeking to educate the viewer about the health consequences of fast food, almost in a didactic (and affective) way, rather than on provoking a moral, critical understanding. In many ways, the segments of the documentary that employ conventions, such as the interview format, the voice-over and observational camera, work most unequivocally to interrogate the ways in which the power of the institution is maintained. For example, Spurlock interviews Marion Nestle, the Chair of Nutrition and Food Studies at NYU and she is one of a number of experts in the sequence who describes the power of the food industry and their influence over government legislation. Nestle states then that the government is under significant pressure not to pass unfavourable laws that would restrict fast food sales. Similarly, advertising aimed at children is discussed, and a nutrition expert states: 'the average American child sees ten thousand food advertisements per year on television. Ninety-five percent of these are for sugared cereals, fast foods, soft drinks or candy'. He goes on to surmise that the ubiquity of advertising and the promotional tactics at the disposal of the food industries far outweigh parental influence on children's attitudes to food.

These statements and sequences in which Spurlock expands on the values and tactics that normalise the regular consumption of fast food work more effectively to interpellate a critically engaged viewer. Nevertheless the documentary's popular success is based in the overt expression of authorship that positions Spurlock as both an object of pleasure, due to his likable character, and as physically grotesque. However, the 30-day event functions less to provoke a rethinking of existing assumptions, and more as a demonstration that offers an extreme account of what is already widely known about fast food.

While all three documentaries present a strong authoring presence in ways that are distinctly performative, they differ in their realisation of this new mode of reflexivity and the fostering of a literate, questioning viewership. Despite this, the authors are consistently defined through their aspiration to intervene, politically and conceptually, in a given socio-political situation. This approach to the discourses that underpin the production of authorship also, then, brings to the fore a notion of the 'care of the self'. In this regard, I am posing a notion of politics that is combined with ethics. For Foucault, this type of ethics refers to a form of selfhood that is also associated with Greek antiquity. Far from a kind of self-love, this care is central to the practice of freedom: 'Care of the self is, of course, knowledge [*connaissance*] of the self – this is the Socratic–Platonic aspect – but also knowledge of a number of rules of acceptable conduct or of principles that are both truths and prescriptions. To take care of the self is to equip oneself with these truths' (Foucault 285). This care of the self, then, also often entails or is followed by care for others. One who engages in the recognition of the self is then more likely to 'conduct himself properly in relation to others and for others' (Foucault 287). Creative productivity, individual enterprise and participation in public matters are bound up with civic loyalty. Foucault's notion firmly positions the author-subject in relation to the collective as the object of care and responsibility.

This references, then, not simply an oppositional subject position and an authorship that voices the concerns of a sector of the Left or fears about the environment. It is also one that is infused by a way of being – a care of the self and an emotional attachment that construct it as an ideal of ethical authorship. From this perspective, the doco-auteur necessarily also becomes an object, and I would argue, an object of hope and desire. Yet how the author is cast in relation to specific constituencies of viewers is significant. In what remains of this chapter, I wish to look more closely at the cultures of dissent, and the media landscape, that these films emerge out of and feed into.

Constituencies of viewers and the contemporary media sphere

While the documentaries under discussion can be understood in relation to traditions of documentary film-making, they express ideals and aesthetics that can also be found in contemporary activist movements – irony and the carnivalesque in particular. In this respect, the films are well suited to the cultural sensibilities of particular audiences in the current period. With increased access to digital media, grass-roots global activist movements (such as anti-capitalist and anti-globalisation networks) have devised ways to intervene in and subvert the mass media apparatus, albeit in very localised ways. Jim McGuigan has described these cultural and political practices as a radical subversive stance within the political public sphere: 'such radicalism places special emphasis on symbolic contest, acting out various forms of carnivalesque subversion in order to disrupt, for example, the City of London in June 1999 and the meeting of the World Trade Organisation in Seattle' (437). One aspect of this 'symbolic contest' deploys physical protests as spectacles that utilise sophisticated semiotic play, mixing clowning and dancing with the occupation and transformation of public, and sometimes private, space.[5] It also includes the DIY (Do It Yourself) ethos of 'culture jamming', or the practice of reversing and transgressing the codes of advertising and other dominant media messages in ways that create new media artefacts. The internet has become a primary site for the exchange and circulation of such artefacts.[6] Seeking to change political perspectives and build communities and activist networks from below, much of this radical subversion is targeted at corporate and state interests.

Although there are clear differences between this culture, and the counter publics from which it emanates, and the documentaries, there exist clear points of comparison. Both endeavour to enter into a dialogue with the viewer/consumer that will engender recognition or action in the same world that social problems are articulated. Both attempt to do this through the use of parody, humour, the play of signifiers, creative authorship, and a focus on spectacle in a way that highlights the contradictions inherent in a given order. Each also exhibits a certain reflexive approach to the medium they employ, often encouraging a disarticulation of formal qualities and ideology simultaneously. Working in this way, the documentaries align themselves with the desires and attachments of these subcultural constituencies, many of whom may also be the audience for these films.

Importantly, with a wide international distribution, the documentaries have a more significant audience beyond these counter publics.

As noted in Chapter 1, documentary has become a global commodity over the last decade. This indicates some of the paradoxes in play here. While aligned with the new aesthetics of grass-roots movements, they still adhere to the expectations of 'old' mass media. The revival in documentary is marked by the films' financial success and achievement within the mass media economy.[7] Although they take their critiques of corporate culture to a broader audience, often this must be achieved through avenues of production and distribution associated with the social conditions they seek to criticise. Yet here I am concerned less with this particular paradox, and more interested in the central mode of address in this culture of subversion, irony and how it functions to engage the audience.

In her discussion of Socratic love, Brown poses the question: 'If critique could be expressly tendered as an act of love, if it could be offered in a Socratic spirit, might it be received differently? [...] It might then inhabit the dignified and authoritative voice of belonging, rather than the moral screech of exclusion' (35). In this instance, Brown is concerned with the question of tone and the terms of inclusion – the inclusivity of particular speech acts. Yet if the caring author seeks a mode of questioning based in ironic statements, the form of the message offers only conditional inclusivity. This owes much to the associations between irony and Socratic dialogue. Broadly, irony works through saying that which is contrary to what is meant, or through saying one thing and meaning another in a way that entails a 'playing off the stated against the instated' (*Irony's Edge* Hutcheon 37). While irony and love may appear to be strange bedfellows, Socrates used irony as a method in his quest to challenge dominant wisdom and educate the polis. Statements of irony can be seen, in particular, in *The Corporation* and *Enron* as sound and image are used, at times, to associate multiple signifiers in order to produce a further unspoken meaning. In this way, they exhibit moments of irony, conveyed through narration and formal devices, to produce inferred meaning.

Although demonstrating an attachment to a community through challenging assumptions and advocating higher ideals, the intention of the ironist is based in an elitist viewpoint positioned above that same community and above ordinary speech.[8] This would then pose a distance between film-maker or ironist and the viewer and a detachment rather than attachment to the public sphere or the interpretive community. There is an affective relationship implied here. There is both the cynical superiority and lack of affect seemingly posed by the ironist, and also the emotive process of interpreting irony. As Hutcheon writes, 'interpreters do not always agree with the attitudes they infer: irritation and distancing are just as likely affective responses as feelings of intimacy and cohesion' (*Irony's Edge* 55).

For these reasons, irony functions ambivalently as a way of directing the attachments of the audience, and thus works only conditionally as a political tool when compared with other rhetorical forms. There is no straightforward way of reading the possible effects of irony. Interpretation can range from intellectual satisfaction and pleasure in sorting through paradox and ambiguity, to exasperation, confusion and irritation. Irony can foster reconsideration or transgression of received norms, as these dissent documentaries attempt to achieve, or it can function to exclude a given interpretive community. Hutcheon notes that some critiques of irony propose that no utterance is ironic in and of itself but that 'it must be possible to imagine some other group taking it quite literally' (*Irony's Edge* 43) in order to produce the space for ironic play. This gets to the ways that irony can be easily experienced or felt as exclusionary and yet can also bring a sense of collusion and intimacy. While the documentaries may only register moments of irony, there is a tone to their overall dynamic that oscillates between addressing an already knowing audience and seeking to engage an audience not already exposed to the contradictions of capitalism and other related concerns. Irony is central to the way the viewer is positioned to interpret the particular construction of truth in a given film. Yet irony is also necessarily accompanied by indeterminacy. The intimate community of ideal viewers may only be those who share the concerns of counter-cultural movements, with many others frustrated by the distanced, even condescending tone of the documentary, or a broader questioning public may be compelled by the spectacle of actuality offered and its potential for subversion.

If Bruzzi recognises that performativity has become a more widespread feature of contemporary documentary, this performativity, or the documentary as a performative act, is tied to the subjective and the agentic. In other words, it must be read as expressive and as the outcome of intention, particularly in the case of political or dissent documentary. Consequently, this intention then takes a particular form, with particular social attachments. The practices of representation evidenced here produce a specific figuration of authorship. The work of the film-maker is evident in the mechanics of representation such as graphics, music, image manipulation, found footage, expressive editing, re-enactments or the on-screen presence of the film-maker. In turn, these different forms of crafting produce metaphor, irony, parody and other forms of playful narrative construction in the service of composing an explicit argument or argumentative position, a position that demonstrates civic love and loyalty to the collective.

There exists the potential for documentary author-subjects to further generate and extend the moral conversation between political actors, rather than take part in, as Brown notes, the shouting of competing ideology. In a way that echoes the documentaries in the previous chapter, the spirit of the dissent documentary intends reciprocity. Yet, specifically, they intend a relation with the viewer in which questioning is returned and furthered in emulation of the ideal caring author. In a number of respects, the documentarian's symbolic performance of the care of the self and civic loyalty in dissent documentary has contributed to the popular revival of non-fiction film. This has occurred at a time when the internet and digital video technology have allowed for an exponential increase in the number and range of voices to be heard in the political arena. As is now well established, this has expanded the notion of the public sphere and enacted a different phase of dialogic democracy. Broadly understood, various expressions of authorship present the image of a new and caring subjective compass within what presents as an increasingly fractured mediatised public sphere.

In these two chapters that are concerned with the labour of authorship, I have argued that particular groupings of films construct a caring documentary author as their perspective on the body politic is communicated by the texts. All films that have political aims or that attempt to tap into a social consciousness infer a caring creator. However, they are not all associated with the same modality of authorship. The Asian Australian authors will have a different relevance for different audiences within a different, more national, public sphere. They are formulated through different speech acts (the specific thematic and aesthetic coding of the text) and each enables a distinct mode of reciprocity. Moreover, the two types of authorship engender caring attachments to collectives in the face of different threats; in one case it is exclusion from the body politic and in another it is the effects of exploitative corporate capitalism. While neither body of documentaries explicitly presents caring as affective content in the text, they pose a documentary subjectivity – the author – in such a way as to emphasise the presence of emotional and ideological investments in the public sphere.

Part IV Past, Present and Future: Hope and Nostalgia

7
Children, Futurity and Hope: *Born into Brothels*

The figure of the child-subject is perhaps the most difficult mode of personhood to bring into analytical focus. This is, in part, because representations of children have, over the last century, become saturated with emotive meanings. The experience of being a child has been displaced in public culture by the burden of hyperbole and pathos; the 'child' often becomes the discursive screen onto which a society's fears and hopes are projected. These are fantasies that present childhood as innocent, vulnerable, pure and at risk. Conversely, children can also be threatening, untamed and unruly. In the name of these fantasies, children become objects of desire to be protected, nurtured and coveted. The child has come to symbolise numerous emotional attachments that frequently serve to sentimentalise rather than seek out the actuality of child experience and subjectivity.

This chapter considers these projections of the child other in order to apprehend how documentary might reframe representations of childhood and childhood experiences. I attend to the actuality of child experience at the point it enters representation; the documentaries I am interested in here are those that present children as they perform for the camera. Documentary expresses the transitional state of childhood in unique ways. Non-fiction representations frequently co-opt the child into a politics of hopefulness and futurity. As I explore, this occurs through an interplay between the objectification of children and the rendering of child subjectivity. In particular, I assess the representation of childhood in *Born into Brothels: Calcutta's Red Light Kids*, a recent award-winning American documentary focused on impoverished children in Kolkata. In the next two chapters, I focus on how objects of the emotions, whether children or the performances in reality television, encourage distinctly temporal imaginaries. In both chapters I question how modes of selfhood, which are located at intersections of past, present and future, are figured in ways that might subvert the social orders to which they are bound.

Hope is not a first-order emotion, like pleasure or pain, but rather it is an affective configuration of other emotions such as optimism and joy. My aim here is to understand hope in relation to the question of the future. The future is often posed contingently, betraying the interests of the questioner. In this sense, hope circulates alongside uncertainty and the figure of the child is an important site for the exploration of this emotion. Children are objects of hope; they are cast as representative of the collective's future hopes, new life and progress, often through gestures that anthropomorphise the historical evolution of the nation or society. Images of suffering children are consistently universalised to emphasise human vulnerability and frequently they also suggest that not only a subjective, but also a collective future is in jeopardy. Less often, children are also subjects of hope, performing aspiration and narrating experiences and perceptions that are underway and intended towards that which has not yet been realised.

James Dodd, describing the phenomenon of hope, writes that hoping is often posed between two extremes: 'on the one hand, it is an effort to bring oneself out of a today into a tomorrow, which is sustained by a temporal brush with the goodness of what is anticipated; or it is the attempt to avoid at all costs the consciousness of what today has become, by fervently believing in a fiction that has been set up as an alternative mode of being' (119–20). Also posing hope in relation to futurity and an anticipatory consciousness, Ernst Bloch, in his extensive work *The Principle of Hope*, takes hope as integral to external reality: 'expectation, hope, intention towards possibility that has still not become: this is not only a basic feature of human consciousness but, concretely, corrected and grasped, a basic determination within objective reality as a whole' (7). Bloch's project centres on a utopian reality principle[1] that combines wish and knowledge, affect and cognition in such a way that anticipates that which has not yet been realised. In effect, for Bloch, there is no uncertainty about the future, or the not-yet, as the future is already there and we must discover how to approach it. Hope then is both an emotion (the opposite of fear) and a 'directing act of a cognitive kind' (12). In Bloch's work, an emphasis on social and political possibility conceives of hope as a kind of subjective resource that can activate, simultaneously, knowledge and emotion. In this sense, he eschews the uncertainty, fear of the future or escapism that representations of children can signify.

A recent special issue of *Screen* takes up the task of investigating the important relationship between film and television and children. In the introduction to this issue, Karen Lury discusses the mythology and ideological symbolism that consistently stand in for the figure of the child in discourse and how these conceptualisations cannot ever fully encompass the child and childhood. She describes the contributions to the issue as interested in how child 'agency – the disruptive, impossible, unintelligible aspects of childhood and the child – is imagined, portrayed and performed in film and television' (308). Representations of the child frequently resist containment and constantly reformulate and challenge expectations around how childhood should be signified. This is a way of understanding how children are perceived to act, their identity, and thus how they can be manifest as social agents. There are a number of considerations that make apprehending the child agent a difficult task for film scholarship and documentary studies in particular. As discussed in earlier chapters, documentary (as a text and as a production process), complicates individual self-determination because performances are necessarily ambiguous – they present the individual as autonomous but performances are also assimilated to the demands of filmic representation, not least of which is the film-maker/filmed hierarchy. In addition to this, and more fundamentally, social conditions and discursive regimes play a part in shaping self-narration and the way subjects might conceive of themselves and their ability to act.[2]

Yet there is a further sociological dimension to the representation of children. In many cultures, children lack a clear social status as they exist beyond the tenets of citizenship and self-determination, but are protected by a discourse of rights (James and James 37). Adulthood and childhood are often posed as dualisms and they are reliant on one another for definition, but the actual line between the two is almost impossible to distinguish. Children represent an unclear social, cultural and political zone. Moreover, the products of childhood expression and imagination are largely absent from the public sphere. The experience of childhood, from the perspective of children, is seldom narrated outside the domestic realm. The narrative richness described by Lury is, I argue, enhanced by this ambiguity and by the filmic possibilities entailed by the navigation between the child as object and the child as difficult subject-agent. Lury is, for the most part, referring to fictionalised and metaphorical representations of children. While documentary is also concerned with imagining the child as agent, the different expressive qualities of the genre produce a special relationship between non-fiction and the child.

Documentary and children

The documentary camera has frequently focused on children, but this has not always been done in the interests of exploring the child as speaking subject. In the Greirsonian tradition, *Children at School* (1937), *Housing Problems* and *Enough to Eat* (1937) feature children and while they are integral to rousing sentiment around social and national problems, such as poor education, slum housing and malnutrition among the working class, children are represented in ways that position them as objects acted upon by social and political forces. Similarly, the later film *Children of the City* (1944) by Bridget Cooper presents the social causes of child delinquency in ways that represent children at risk, exposed to poor social welfare. In another respect, experimental autobiography, with examples such as *Daughter Rite* (1980), *Sink or Swim* (1990), *Tarnation* (2003) or *History and Memory: For Akiko and Takashige* (1992), has strong associations with childhood. This is childhood remembered from the adult filmmaker's point of view, often visually recalled through home movies, photographs or re-enactments. These representations seek ways of narrating present experience through the lens of formative events facilitated by childhood relationships. While all of these examples are strongly suggestive of temporal concerns pertaining to childhood, whether it is a quest for social change that may secure the children's future or the relationships between experimental pasts, presents and futures, my focus here is on the performance of childhood and the temporal coding of documentary's address. Some of the documentaries that are encompassed within this category include *Seven Up* (1964), *7 Plus Seven* (1970), *High School* (1968), *Poto and Cabengo* (1979), *Hoop Dreams* (1994), *Spellbound* (2002), *To Be and to Have* (2002), *Hold Me Tight Let Me Go* (2007) and *The Boys of Baraka* (2005).

In the second edition of her book, *New Documentary*, Bruzzi discusses *Seven Up*, *Hoop Dreams* and, to a lesser extent, *Spellbound* as documentary journeys. They are works made over extended periods of time and follow a collection of individuals. Michael J. Shapiro reads *Hoop Dreams* through a notion of an 'obligation to mobility' (28–9) that functions both in terms of the movement of sporting (black) bodies and social aspiration. Yet neither Bruzzi nor Shapiro draw attention to how each of these journeys also rely on the signifying potential of childhood. The central premise in each documentary is the transition between childhood and adulthood or the exploration of adult aspirations embodied in the child. *Hoop Dreams* follows two African American students, William Gates and Arthur Agee, as both follow their ambition to become professional basketball players. The documentary begins when both are 14 years old and depicts their lives over the course of five years as they seek to ascend out of an underclass neighbourhood in Chicago. The first instalment of the *Seven Up* series was broadcast in 1964 and a sequel appears every seven years. The same 14 British participants appear in the documentaries. A key consideration of the initial documentary was to show children at different extremes of the class system and this contrast continues as a central device for reading the subsequent instalments. While not filmed over an extended period, *Spellbound* also features a group of children who demonstrate markedly different character traits and come from diverse social backgrounds. The eight children in the film are competing in the annual National Spelling Bee in Washington, D.C. The documentary highlights not only the children's motivations and perceptions but also the labour and anxieties of their parents within this highly competitive environment.

In these kinds of documentaries, the child is a potent objectification of time passing. Change and transition in relation to children always occurs rapidly and markedly. Not only do they alter visibly as their bodies change, but the way in which child-subjects narrate their experiences and their perceptions of the world shifts significantly over increments of time. Moreover, the image of the child comes to symbolically embody this potential for rapid change; as viewers, we are constantly aware that the child featured at any point in the film captures a moment already in transition. For Bruzzi, the journey documentary is also tied to the tradition of cinema verite as the largely observational style of the film asks viewers to 'look on' as individuals change over time. The camera follows the dramatic transitions of their lives rather than prompting this drama (Bruzzi 86–7).

Linked to the representation of historical time passing is the way that children also, discursively, become a site for the exploration of aspiration and striving. Seldom focusing on single children, documentaries concerned with the performance of childhood follow a collection of subjects and their movement towards a goal and some form of hoped for success. In this sense, while not all of these documentaries are explicitly about competitions, aspiration and movement are measured through the comparisons between children and these contrasts structure the narrative. Through highlighting the way different individuals navigate life's hurdles on the road from childhood to adulthood, these documentaries seek to make sense of broader social expectation and inequality. Whether implicitly or explicitly, these documentaries explore how children are affected by and meet the demands of adult worlds. If within the narrative, children embody time passing and the movement forward towards specific goals (to win the spelling bee, to achieve a professional basketball career, to grow into adulthood and economic and personal success), documentary also confers on them a status as historicised subjects.

The experience and construction of duration is a key issue in discussions of cinematic time. Malin Wahlberg examines the specificity of performance and the passing of time in documentary:

> In documentary the poignant event of time passing often seems to result from the assumingly spontaneous performance of the social actor. For example, the drama of the testimonial act owes much to the expected authenticity of the subject and her address to the camera and a response to the interviewer off-screen. A pause for effect, a frown of irritation, and signs of intimidation or hesitation may, together with camera angles, mode of framing, and editing, result in a significant slice of time.
>
> (91)

While Wahlberg observes an important dimension of temporality and performance, I am interested in a more widely posed notion of how documentary supports a consciousness of the time of the subject rather than documentary realism's relation to perceptions of time passing. This is the subject in history or the subjective movement through history and the staging of this in the documentary. While this consciousness functions through a combination of textual time and historical time, the emphasis is on the latter and the intersubjective relationship between filmed performance and the film-maker's witnessing of the performance. Nichols describes how realist documentary conventions authenticate this relationship: they are 'a mark of authenticity, testifying to the camera, and hence the filmmaker, having "been there" and thus providing the warrant for our own "being there", viewing the historical world through the transparent amber of indexical images and realist style' (*Representing* 181). This relationship is the trace or the persistence of the event past. Representations of children, and particularly those that extend over intervals of time, invoke a heightened awareness of the subject's movement through history.

C. R. Snyder writes, 'to desire, in short, is to hope' (25). At stake here is also the question of narrative desire. If the child is posed as an object of hope within a narrative structure, this does not translate into narrative desire in a straightforward way. If there is a certain perceived formal, thematic and temporal movement associated with children in documentary, it may not be the case that the audience desires a fulfilment of childhood potential in a singular way. Desire, and in this instance narrative desire, is for movement, even if it is towards failure. This is because narrative desire can work in conflict with character desire. This is observed by Gregory Currie:

> Here the conflict in desire is not a conflict structurally like the kinds of conflicts we most commonly find in our desires concerning real events and people, for it is a conflict between desiring something for a character and desiring something for a narrative. The conflict is also notable in so far as *it is a conflict we find desirable*.[3]
>
> (emphasis in original, 144)

The social positioning and fantasies concerning childhood exist as an important site of identification, but social hope and character aspiration can be in conflict with, and perhaps even subsumed by, the desire for narrative (documentary) evidence of transition and movement. This may be success but, equally, it may also be the failure seen in tragic moments and stories. This is a desire for the successful triumph of the child in the spelling bee in *Spellbound* or, equally, the anguish of failure as a word is misspelled.

As I described in Chapter 4, the experience of pleasure in the documentary spectacle relies upon the viewer's status as the subject of knowledge. Moreover, observational techniques attempt to offer the greatest approximation of the viewer's own gaze. If the contract between viewer and text promises a sense of events unravelling or discovery, knowledge and discovery in these documentaries revolve around the uncertainty of the outcome and the equivalent possibilities of success and/or failure. While there may be some kind of identification with the children's journey, the greatest desire is to see the exaggerated change that images of children symbolically promise to deliver.

A further emphasis on movement occurs in this context when the significance of emotion is considered. Emotion can be about producing stasis, and political stasis in particular, as the example of wounded attachments in Chapter 2 demonstrates, but they are more often engaged in movement. Affect-laden representations are frequently described as 'moving'. The sense here is that emotions extend from the outside world to the internal world. Ahmed reformulates this operation to understand emotions not as something we have, but rather that emotions move and 'create the very effect of the surfaces and boundaries that allow us to distinguish an inside and an outside in the first place' (10). Further, I have demonstrated throughout this book Ahmed's proposition that it is the objects of emotion that circulate (Ahmed 11) and these objects include the subjectivities that become objects of others' feelings. Moreover, speech acts generate and maintain objects of feeling in ways that highlight the performativity of the emotions; they are reiterated and thus performed in discourse. Documentaries themselves are modes of enunciation that focus an accumulation of speech acts, but the ones I wish to foreground here in relation to children reference discourses of hope and futurity.

Significant examples of child performances in documentary such as those in *Hoop Dreams*, the *Seven Up* series, *The Boys of Baraka* and *Hold Me Tight, Let Me Go*, are all also notable as commentaries on structural social issues such as gender, class and race, recalling the British documentaries of the 1930s. Here, success and failure are not isolated as humanist concerns, away from systemic and cultural issues of social advantage and disadvantage, but rather social difference provides the terms through which agency and aspiration, and thus the documentary performance, are constituted. This performance frequently draws on the subjective desire for good life, promised by democratic principles of egalitarianism and the potential to ascend socially or to maintain and persist without falling into disadvantage. Further to this, as objects of hope these children are easily mobilised alongside hope for social change and other political desires. As I have noted, this desire works in line with the attachments of documentary filmmakers that are staples of committed film-making practice. Political documentary is motivated by hopeful attachments – an optimistic attachment to either material social change or the possibility of a change in attitudes and in the social imaginary. *Born into Brothels* is a documentary deeply entrenched in a politics of hope. It is a documentary that emphasises both the subjectivity of the film-maker and the impoverished child other as an object of hope. Yet it also seeks to position the child as subject. In the discussion that follows, I seek to identify what is at stake in this specific formulation of childhood.

Born into Brothels

Like many films that focus on children, *Born into Brothels* makes sense of the child narratively and formally in ways that keep the terms of hopefulness and futurity, success and failure in constant play. The documentary achieves this while marrying a vivid and rich visual style with themes and images of poverty and disadvantage. The film follows the work of British-born photographer, Zana Briski, as she offers photography lessons to a small group of children in Kolkata's largest red-light district, Sonagachi. The children are aged between eight and twelve at the time of filming and include five girls (Kochi, Puja, Tapasi, Suchitra and Shanti) and three boys (Manik, Avijit and

Gour). As sex workers, the children's mothers lack social mobility and are presented as unable to offer their sons and daughters a clear path out of poverty and disenfranchisement. The documentary confronts this hopelessness and uncertainty in ways that follow two narrative threads. The first is the activity of offering the children a degree of creative agency as they learn how to use still cameras and succeed as young photographers, documenting the world around them. The second also follows Briski's endeavour help the children, but in this case it is through social and educational mobility as she attempts to place them in boarding schools, thus securing their future outside the red-light district and, for the girls, beyond a life in the sex industry.

The line between Briski's undertaking and the goals of the documentary becomes blurred with the knowledge, not revealed until the credits, that Briski co-directed the film with her partner, Ross Kauffman, who is the cinematographer. The film is, thus, deeply implicated in a participatory and activist agenda though which the film-makers are actively engaged in the events they are recording. Despite this, the documentary adheres, for the most part, to an observational style with sequences showing the children learning about photographic technique from Briski, in their daily lives playing on the streets of Sonagachi and in their homes doing domestic chores. Briski's voice-over is also prominent in the soundtrack as she describes her experiences and motivations in working with the children. The children themselves frequently speak to the camera (presumably they are actually speaking to Briski via a translator), with their commentary appearing in subtitles. The photographs taken by the children also feature prominently and provide a recurring visual motif in the documentary.

The adjectives used by reviewers to describe the children's plight in the documentary range from 'sad', 'moving', 'touching' as well as 'hopeful' and 'hopeless'. One reviewer, Andrew O'Hehir, described himself as 'weeping tears of grief and gratitude' at the conclusion of the film. These characterisations locate *Born into Brothels* squarely within a history of imagery that ties the child to excessive emotionalism. In the nineteenth century, children were understood, within a romantic tradition, through a pathos that frequently idealised the child as closer to nature and the virtues lost to the adult (Cunningham). As Patricia Holland observes, the aesthetic experience of sentiment took hold in the late nineteenth century with pictures of children becoming more prevalent and greater distinctions emerging between adults and children. The pathos of these images offered an emotional avenue to make sense of the high rates of child mortality at the time (Holland 144).

In analyzing present day depictions, Holland also describes the trope of the suffering child in impoverished countries that persists in news reports and representations used by aid agencies: 'Suffering in the underdeveloped world continues to secure a sense of comfort among viewers in the "developed" nations, by assuring them that they have the power to help – in the same "natural" way that adults help children. That power is confirmed by the gaze of an appealing child' (148). Holland is describing a slippage between feeling for a vulnerable and needy child and posing a whole society as vulnerable and in need. This is a slippage that facilitates a parent–child dynamic between viewers in affluent countries and impoverished nations. Such representations, moreover, pose the society and the child as equivalent objects of sympathy and desire as suffering affirms, in a compelling way, a familiar association between object and emotion. These representations serve to maintain the child as an object of fantasy, caught in a stasis of vulnerability. Such fantasies disempower the child and exacerbate the distinction between children and adults.[4] The subjectivity of the child and their status as agent becomes erased and adult power confirmed.

In light of these powerful and pervasive narratives, *Born into Brothels'* presentation of the child agent is a paradoxical one. In the early scenes of *Born into Brothels*, a number of the children are introduced to the viewer as one girl, Puja, speaks to the camera and describes her friends' qualities and attributes. The image of Puja speaking is interspersed with both still photographs of the children (presumably taken by Briski) and moving images of the children in groups as they play in the street and use the cameras (presumably shot by Kauffman). The actual photographs taken by the children soon follow. But before this, there is another series of shots that show a number of children engaged in domestic chores and speaking of their perceptions of their own futures. Puja states: 'I keep thinking of going somewhere else – getting an education. I wonder what I could become.' Another girl, Tapasi says: 'Even though I'm poor I don't really think about it. You have to accept life as it is.' These statements are the children's but they evoke oddly adult sensibilities of hope and hopelessness, blurring the boundary between child subjectivity and the adult framing of this subjectivity in the text. In a different way, Puja's descriptions of the children seem more akin to what one would expect as she offers her impressions of her friends.

The documentary attempts to make a crucial ideological intervention in presenting the point of view of children, their creative and imaginative expression through photography. This action empowers children and foregrounds the products of child activity and learning in a way that renders them not as tropes but as individuated subjects beyond singular representations of suffering. This is a conception of childhood very seldom seen, not least with regard to poor children from Kolkata's slums. It is this interweaving of cultural otherness, poverty and the child's creative vision that constitute this as a compelling documentary for audiences and scholars.[5] Yet the children also remain the objects of particular adult fantasies that assimilate the documentary enunciation of the child into one that confirms adult, including the Anglo-American film-maker's, power in relation to the ethnic other and the child other. As I have noted above, the child subject-agent of documentary is one that easily confounds representation. Here I look more closely at the paradoxes of *Born into Brothels* and how the documentary attempts to bring child agency into representation, the deployment of the film-maker filmed hierarchy and the formal relationship between photography and moving image.

The photographs taken by the children are central to the narrative and to the visual style of the documentary. Usually, photography and children are associated by way of the family snapshot. These are intimate and evocative texts that are closely tied to family togetherness and rituals.[6] Yet *Born into Brothels* eschews the themes of domestic photography. Instead of family coherence, many of the photographs are evidence of the urban environment in which the children live, including portraits of one another and their interactions as a group. From this child's eye-view, we see not only the streets and interiors of Sonagachi but also the different styles of photographic practice that evolve across the group. The documentary draws attention to the details of this practice as Briski instructs the group and discusses the childrens' encounters as they roam the streets with their cameras. Significantly, Briski observes in the voice-over how difficult it is to film in the red-light district. The children are much less constrained. In photographing the individuals who inhabit and visit Sonagachi, the children become both voyeurs and self-ethnographers. Their scopophilia, or pleasure in looking, is relayed to the viewer who incorporates it into their own epistephilia – the desire to know that Nichols credits as central to documentary's address. For the young photographers, there is a sense of achievement as they learn to take photographs and gain the affirmation of adults. Tapasi encapsulates this in a comment: 'Today I took someone's photo and he swore at me. I didn't mind. I know you have to put up with a lot if you want to learn to do something well.' For Freud, 'looking' and 'mastering' are ego instincts that suggest a development of the ego. There is a mastery over vision and the adult world implicit in Tapasi's achievements.

In addition to the children's own statements, the photographs function as clear markers of expression and agency. Yet the way they are positioned formally and narratively works in tension with the future aspirations and hopefulness that the children, as objects and, often, as subjects convey. The photographs are either black and white or vibrantly coloured (Figure 7.1). They are presented throughout the film and edited together into montages with Indian music featured in the soundtrack, suspending the documentary narrative in terms of voice-over and images. This frames the children's products as an interruption to the movement of the narrative rather than part of its development to a resolution. In some sequences, images of the children are interspersed in these montages as slow motion moving images. One notable scene in which this occurs shows the children on their first excursion to the beach. The scene on the bus on the way home depicts the girls dancing in slow motion and highlighted in dark orange tones. Their subjectivities, and at times their bodies, are located in an elsewhere, abstracted out of the narrative and their own everyday environment as they are aestheticised through colour and rhythm. There is a disjuncture between their everyday activities as they are represented in the documentary and the beauty of the photographs.

This presents the children's experience of photography as a relief; it is an excursion from everyday life into a space of play and artfulness. The pleasure of this interruption is reflected in the photographs themselves for one reviewer: 'what the images mainly convey

Figure 7.1 Born into Brothels: Calcutta's Red Light Kids (Zana Briski & Ross Kaufmann 2004). Courtesy of HBO/Thinkfilms Inc. The Kobal Collection

may simply be the blossoming of sensibilities starved for attention and a sense of possibility. The thrill of this becomes a kind of all-pervasive joy in some images' (Smith 31). Yet it also locates their photographic agency outside the documentary narrative and thus outside the material change that is the basis for the documentary.

In voice-over, Briski refers to the predicament of the children: 'without help they are doomed'. 'Help' in the film is represented only by Briski's own efforts and takes the form of photographic work and her attempts to place the children in boarding schools. Beyond the photographic activities I have described, the children also exhibit their work in Kolkata and in New York, where it is shown and auctioned at Sotheby's. A number of the children make the trip to New York and one of the boys, Avijit, goes to Amsterdam to the World Press Photo Foundation to participate in the Children's Jury in 2002. It is stated in Briski's voice-over that the principal reason for selling the photographs is to raise money to aid the children's ascent out of the brothel and out of poverty. While these efforts have led to a number of initiatives, including the Kids With Cameras foundation[7] and similar projects in Cairo, Haiti and Israel, these initiatives and the financial success of the children's work is not detailed in the documentary.

Born into Brothels suggests an aesthetic and thematic confluence between photographic practice, the photographs themselves and the children as objects of hope and as aspirational subjects. Yet how these connections are actualised in the documentary in terms of material change remains unresolved. A smaller portion of the film focuses on their boarding school admittance and this is much more clearly linked to their future success than the photography. In closing, the documentary presents information about the progress of each child a year after filming. Out of the seven children, two remain in boarding school, five live at home, still in Sonagachi, due to either their own choice or decisions made by parents. This final account is brief and no information is given about whether or not they continued with photography. It seems that no actual change in their circumstances has occurred and thus, for the viewer, desire for the characters to succeed and narrative desire for success (or failure), are left unfulfilled.

Hope and futurity are articulated in *Born into Brothels* in ways that perform, discursively, histories of signification that constitute children as certain objects of feeling. While the documentary is 'moving' in the way it engages the sensibilities of the audience, there is no clear direction of this emotion at the conclusion of the film in relation to either hope or lost hope. The children are stuck in a temporal state similar to what Berlant refers to as 'survival time'. In her discussion of children in *La Promesse* (1996) and *Rosetta* (1999), Berlant argues that children are solicited to the 'reproduction of what we should call not the good life, but the "bad life" – that is, a life dedicated to moving towards the good life's normative/utopian zone but actually stuck in what we might call survival time, the time of struggling, drowning, holding on to the ledge, treading water, *not-stopping*' (emphasis in original, 279). The representation of survival time defies narrative desire. However, this is offset by the fantasy of difference the documentary appeals to.

The children's status as cultural and impoverished other is also important to the fantasies they direct. In discussing the popularity of *Hoop Dreams* among audiences, bell hooks writes: 'it is precisely the fact of blackness that gives this documentary its popular appeal. The lure of *Hoop Dreams* is that it affirms that those at the bottom can rise in this society, even as it is critical of the manner in which they rise. This film tells the world that the American dream works' (78). Yet she also notes that the film's popularity demonstrates 'the extent to which blackness has become commodified' (78) in American society. Similarly, *Born into Brothels* moves audiences and critics to such a degree because it is about the potential ascent of the other, the racialised, economically disenfranchised and desperate other who is marked by difference from the audience.[8]

The children are the exoticised focus of the film while also providing access to the spectacle of the environment in which they live. They do this in a way that, Frann Michael writes, the film-makers cannot:

> Perhaps the film's central paradox is its reliance on the children for access to the exotic world of Sonagachi, even as it attempts to distance and remove them from that world. The structure of the film – and particularly its omissions – helps position the children as both the victims of the red light district and the vehicles of an aestheticising vision of it.
>
> (53)

Moreover, the photographs' position as objects of desire and also as commodities is heightened because they are the products of poor Indian children from Sonagachi.

In her investigation of the relationship between looking, power and class-consciousness in written and photographic documentary, Rabinowitz writes:

> The photographic image reinforces bourgeois culture even when it seeks to expose its damaging effects as in the case of documentary photographs that reveal 'How the Other Half Lives.' Yet these objects, the classed, sexed and gendered bodies of visual imagery – have the power to hold the gaze of their viewers; they are produced by *and* produce the 'political unconscious' of middle class culture.
>
> (*They Must* 38)

The unspoken term in this passage is the 'racialised body' which works equally in discourse to maintain the terms of class hierarchy. Further, as I discuss below, the terms of class consciousness must now be revised to account, across cultural and national borders, for the growing attention to what it means to be poor within a globalising economy. Rabinowitz's focus is on a much earlier cultural imaginary, with her central point of reference the well-known literary and photographic work by James Agee and Walker Evans, *Let Us Now Praise Famous Men* (1936).[9] I pose a relation between the book and *Born into Brothels* because *Let Us Now Praise Famous Men* emphasises an aspect of self-narration absent in the documentary. Agee attempts to reflect on his own position as outsider and draw attention to the activity of depicting and gazing at an unfamiliar world. He attempts to 'dislodge the meaning and effects of his class and race and gender' (Rabinowitz 47) in his desperate attempts to communicate with the tenant farmers.

Yet Briski and Kauffman forgo this self-reflection and, moreover, Briski neglects to announce her presence in the film as that of the authoring subject. With no indication in the text of her position, her documentary performance centres on her own desire to help the children. I have noted in previous chapters the way political or Left-oriented film-making can involve a 'sentimental contract' or the participation of the film-maker in the political movements they record. In this manner, the documentaries can work within movements to instigate social change. *Born into Brothels* differs from many documentaries of this kind in the sense that the film is *about* the film-maker as a facilitator of social change, rather than the film prompting the viewer to engage in change. Briski herself becomes the most potent agent of change in the documentary and the appeal to the audience to be moved to 'help' in some way, aligns the audience with Briski's point of view. Yet as the agent of change, she stands in for, and effaces, the activism already operative in the red-light district. In her discussion of the film, Michael observes that *Born into Brothels* neglects to mention the activism of social workers, medical personnel and the sex workers themselves that has transformed Sonagachi over a number of years. Michael believes the film-makers would have been aware of the resources established by activists and, indeed, some of the activists themselves.[10] In this regard, Briski stands in the documentary, perhaps falsely, as the children's 'only hope', a production of the author-subject that sits in contrast with other committed documentary practice.[11]

Children and modernity

Just as the Europeanised West has been posed as equivalent to modernity, its non-Western others are consistently represented as outside the teleology of progress. As I have already discussed, this positions the other in another, authenticating, archaic time. Anthropological discourses, in particular, have exacerbated this characterisation. Fatimah Tobing Rony captures this when she describes the tendency for some cultures to be homogenised, 'conceived as remnants of the human past, and thus [they] are represented as timeless, without history' (68). This pervasive narrative is, in a number of respects, disturbed by *Born into Brothels*. As I have noted the documentary subject, and the child subject in particular, is signified as moving through history. Yet more pertinently, the children are not located within a timeless culture, but rather within the temporal and spatial flows of modernity. However, this positioning does not enable upward mobility – it accentuates and maintains the stark deficit of realisable aspirations.

Most notably, the immobility experienced by the children and their families is accentuated when cast against the film-makers' mobility. In the documentary, Briski notes that she has been living in Sonagachi 'on and off' for a number of years. As a professional photographer, her aim was to photograph the women who work in the area, but she soon turned her attention to the children. Briski's hybrid Anglo-American accent, her place of residence in New York and her ability to move across international borders with ease are evidence of her status as one of the mobile global elite. It is not made clear in the documentary how Briski is able to finance her time with the children and it appears to be leisure time rather than labour. The tourist, for Dean MacCannell, is a counterpoint to the worker in that the tourist is not restricted by systems of industrialisation, but rather has access to the vista of the modern social totality and thus can consume the 'universal drama of modernity' (7).[12] Leisure has been a facet of post-industrial modernity for the privileged classes and tourism is based in the imperative that leisure should be productive in some respect. It is an active pursuit of self-betterment. Married with a contemporary social justice agenda, Briski's tourism is productive, participatory and compassionate as she interns herself in Sonagachi and combines community activism with film-making.

If the film-maker's and narrator's mobility can be aligned with an identity produced by modernity, so can the children's immobility. While Avijit is invited to Amsterdam, the documentary highlights Briski's anxiety around securing him a passport. At another point in the film, Avijit describes his parents: 'My mum lives in the village. If she was [sic] here she'd make me get an education. My mum used to say jokingly "I'm going to send you to London to get an education." We don't have money to live let alone for studying.' The children are, as I noted above in relation to Berlant's survival time, suspended or stuck. But rather than the European post-Fordism Berlant refers to, the children are caught by a different facet of modernity.

The women who care for the children participate in an economy that pre-dates modernity, both in India and elsewhere. Yet the sex industry, and the lives of those associated with it, has changed in ways that are symptomatic of more recent historical shifts. Exploring the sex trade in Kolkata, Carolyn Sleightholme and Indrani Sinha note that Sonagachi emerged as a red-light district at a time when a number of cultural changes were occurring as a result of industri- alisation and colonialism. These shifts include the marginalisation of cottage industries that had previously supported women who subsequently turned to sex work. Another contributing factor was the influx of traders and migrant workers and the presence of British soldiers, all of whom supported the sex trade (8–9). Sleightholme and Sinha also discuss the incidence of trafficking and the ways women enter the sex industry in contemporary Sonagachi. Many of the women are cajoled with false promises or offers of help out of crisis situations while a smaller number are kidnapped (38). Moreover, Kolkata receives women from around India, Bangladesh and Nepal who come, through various channels, to work in the sex industry (Sleightholme and Sinha 40). This constitutes Sonagachi as a centre for international migration movements. While no information is given about the personal histories of the women who feature in the background in *Born into Brothels*, given Sleightholme and Sinha's study, it is likely that they are in a similar position to many who have travelled from afar, either out of desperation or deception.

The children are tied, through their relationships to family and place, to a globalising, albeit underground, economy. While they are connected to the effects of modernity and the terms of industrialisation and mass migration, unlike Briski the children and their families have an unrecognised, informal relationship to this economy. Because of this, they are located precariously, at the fringe of the increasingly stratifying movements of global capital- ism. As likely migrants, the workers of Sonagachi inhabit Zygmunt

Bauman's 'unfathomable "space of flows" where the roots of present day precariousness of the human condition are sunk' (66). If the film, and the film-maker as tourist, witnesses the drama and precariousness of modernity, the children come to exemplify a vulnerability to exploitation that stands as affectively representative of the lack of safety that is the betrayal of globalising capitalism.

At the conclusion of the documentary, the children cannot be realised properly as objects of hope; they remain without social or economic mobility. They will, undoubtedly, find some kind of social footing as they mature into adulthood, but the film suggests this will occur in the realm of unpredictable and contingent labour and thus they will remain within the provisional economy, necessitating improvised survival tactics. This 'treading water' contrasts not only with the status of the film-makers and their implied proxy, the viewer, but also with the products of their labour, the photographs. The way the photographs feature in the narrative, as I have noted, presents an interruption, the suggestion of a less grim elsewhere, away from the everyday. While they may offer this signification as narrative and formal devices, as *products* they offer a different meaning. As commodities that have demonstrable currency in the global art market, the photographs attain a mode of mobility that eludes the children. This contrast becomes increasingly evident in the documentary. They are desirable objects of beauty circulating in and signifying a different temporality to that which the children inhabit. Yet the photographs' desirability is enhanced through their association with the children's exotic subaltern stasis. This is made clear in the scenes that show the children's reception at the gallery in New York where their photographs are on show. This association may also be a key reason for the documentary's appeal. Hopefulness coalesces around the images because of their proximity with the children (the consummate objects of hope) and yet it is the children who are not viable as subjects who will realise this hope.

If children perform in documentary in ways that bring into focus the location and potential of the historical subject, the terms of advantage, disadvantage and social ascent, they are always articulated against broader social systems of desire and value. In *Born into Brothels* capitalism represents a crucial background for understanding the child-agent. In her discussion of lives lived at the bottom of class structures within contemporary capitalism, Berlant writes that 'its hard to imagine revolution, or indeed any future, if you're an informal or unofficial worker' (290). Hence, the 'sensorium' of these workers is an 'effect of the relation between capitalism's refusal of futurity in an overwhelmingly productive present and the normative process of intimacy [...]' (301). The connection to global capitalism that the children and their families in *Born into Brothels* experience is oriented towards the refusal of an imagined and, therefore, anticipated future.

Overburdened with emotion and expectations around how the child should be signified, filmic representations of children have the capacity to reformulate or to subscribe to entrenched conceptions of childhood. *Born into Brothels* forgoes this opportunity to reformulate the meaning of the child. While it emphasises child subjectivity and agency in the form of photography and creative labour, the film does not significantly shift the terms through which child subjectivity is posed. This is primarily because the photographs – the means by which the point of view and agency of the children is represented – are located beyond the representation of child experience in the narrative. Moreover, the children remain tied to the emotion that constitutes them as objects of hope without this being harnessed in any way that might intend towards the future and instrumental change. All the inhabitants of Sonagachi, the film-maker not withstanding, are suspended in survival time, denied a clear assertion of futurity. Although this usefully offers a depiction of the effects of global structural inequality, the documentary also seems to commodify, exoticise and aestheticise not only the child, but also their impoverished surroundings that are the effect of this inequality.

Born into Brothels invokes hopefulness (and its associations with futurity and children) only to imagine these connections in ways that are contradictory and present suspension and deferral rather than movement. The documentary, in posing the film-maker activist as the agent of change and the central compassionate, affective force in the lives of the children closes down the possibility that even without a clear pathway out of poverty, the children may be maintained as subjects of hope within their own communities. The mothers, grandmothers and occasional fathers in the children's lives are represented as either absent, cruel, superstitious or unconcerned about the children's future welfare. It is, in the main, only other children who are portrayed as offering a reprieve from the harshness of the surroundings. This again contrasts with Briski's resourceful, adult compassion and reinforces the notion that boarding schools, rather than parental care and guidance, are key to the children's well-being. Further, presenting the relationships between the children and their guardians as without affect forecloses on the possibilities (and a kind of psychical futurity) offered by the caring bonds between family members. At least in some cases, these must exist for the children. As Michaels notes, the fact that Shanti, for one, chooses to return to her family suggests that the boarding schools may not meet all of the children's needs or expectations (58).[13] It may be that in foreclosing on this dimension of their lives, on intersubjectivity, the documentary also misses an opportunity to explore a space of lived experience that offers a reason to persist in spite of, and in the face of, the refusal of material mobility and futurity.

8
Nostalgia, Historical Time and Reality Television: The *Idol* Series

Reality television is one of the few avowedly effective documentary forms. Its reliance on emotional discourses and registers is much more openly proclaimed than is often the case with non-fiction texts. Associations with accentuated emotionalism have cemented a place for reality programming in the domain of television because this emotionalism is wholly compatible with the medium's alignment with mass culture, commercialism and light entertainment. Critiques of reality television have consistently focused on the intensity of participant performances and its consistent preoccupation with personal lives as a way to delineate between the civic service ethos of documentary proper and the quotidian and confessional nature of reality television. Further, this delineation has been central in scholarship that emphasises reality television's role in diffusing the non-fiction form's perceived educative function. In this respect, the emotionality of this programming is seen to contrast greatly with the emotionality of the documentary discourses of sobriety.

Yet reality television's influence on non-fiction film and television is undeniable. Even with the rise in the theatrical release of feature-length documentary, the greatest changes to occur in the culture of documentary have been brought by the tidal wave of reality non-fiction programming on television in many countries around the world. This programming has irreversibly influenced much film-making practice and audience perception of non-fiction while extending television's already close associations with the production and distribution of documentary.

I now turn from questions of futurity and hopefulness, emotions that frame the child in documentary and popular discourse, to questions of historical time and the aesthetics of television. Narratives of temporality and affect are frequently intertwined in popular and scholarly perceptions of both reality programming and television's address more broadly. In this chapter, I explore how subjectivities produced in the *Idol* reality television format, and *Australian Idol* in particular, might contest or affirm these narratives. The construction of the self in this case revolves around, in one instance, affective social lives, particularly those tied to kinship histories, and in another, the function of nostalgia as it pertains specifically to popular music. This analysis emerges out of an attempt to rethink conceptualisations of reality television that cast it as a devalued form, aligned with the feminised emotionality of the personal realm and without social or historical relevance. These critiques are the focus of the next section.

Conceptualisations of history and emotion

Significantly, scholarship exploring reality programming has fixed on the function of the emotions. Anita Biressi and Heather Nunn observe that 'reality TV's lexicon of emotion, intimacy, immediacy and the everyday' (24) locates it in the category of 'light entertainment', contributes to the perceived 'dumbing down' of non-fiction and 'distances it from the Reithian ideal of public television' (24). In a slightly different way, Bruzzi understands emotion as central to the address of factual entertainment: it structures readings of authenticity and performance. In this way, Bruzzi notes:

> it is convenient to label [emotional] moments as 'authentic' moments when generic restraints and imposed artificiality are ruptured. However, these moments of extreme emotional articulation are now so predictable, even necessary, to the success of a series that they do just the opposite, signalling as opposed to masking their formal rigidity.
>
> (143)

For Bruzzi, personalities are chosen to appear on screen depending on their ability to perform emotively and, thus, provide points of identification for the audience. This produces disproportionately intense performances of emotionality (142). These performances have an ambivalent relationship with the perceived authenticity of the observational mode. While there is the potential for reality television to reinforce *documentary* authenticity (the unpredictable), Bruzzi argues that emotion re-inscribes the necessary conventions of reality television and therefore 'on demand' inauthentic emotions (the predictable) are emphasised. Such characterisations attest to the way reality television is anxiously encompassed by the category of documentary. The representation of and appeal to the emotions are taken up by critics in ways that both suppose a non-fiction taxonomy *and* foreground reality television's role in troubling the boundaries of the taxonomy.

John Corner puts forward one of the most influential formulations of the relationship between reality television and documentary traditions. Expanding on the hybridisation of television documentary, Corner describes the growth of popular factual entertainment such as reality television and docu-soap by way of 'documentary-as-diversion'. Locating this programming within a 'postdocumentary' culture of television, he notes the shift away from the 'outer world' of the social in documentary towards the 'inner world' of the micro-social: 'The documentary foreground has frequently become a highly defined narrative of localised feelings and experiences presented against what is often a merely sketchy if not entirely token background of social setting' (Corner 256). Following this, emotion is key to reality television's entertainment quotient and it marks out the commercial or exchange, as opposed to cultural or civic, value of this programming. Corner furthers this notion to again understand the role of the emotions in structuring viewer responses: spectatorial positions in regards to reality television switch rapidly between 'empathy and detachment, fondness and dislike' (Corner 257). Importantly, both Corner and Bruzzi place the performance of the self, the on-screen participant, at the centre of the emotional contract between viewer and text.

I do not dispute the characterisation of the shifting terrain of television documentary put forward by these scholars. I am interested less in thinking about the role of the emotions in redefining documentary than in examining the mode of social subjectivity that is enabled by the affective terms of reality television. Rather than further emphasising the disparities between a documentary culture of social merit and one of distraction, my aim is to explore how reality television, and the example of *Australian Idol* in particular, might function simultaneously as a good/social *and* good/commercial object. This necessitates a more deliberate collapsing of the distinctions between commercial entertainment and documentary sobriety. It requires thinking about how reality forms pose subjectivity in ways that transcend the opposition between documentary-as-diversion and documentary's traditional socio-historical concerns.

Specifically, my aim is to consider how reality television's emphasis on the affective, the personal and the 'microsocial' might be understood, in keeping with the concerns this book, to further an understanding of the relation between non-fiction and the work of emotions in public life. In their discussion of reality programming, Helen Wood and Lisa Taylor note: 'there is still much to be unearthed about the cultural politics of what audiences feel about the representational capacity of television' (148). While I am not engaging in the empirical audience research that Wood and Taylor undertake, my questions posed in relation to *Australian Idol* combine this call for understanding with Jane Roscoe's claim that popular factual television 'may yield strategies for enlivening and extending the [documentary] form' (292).

An understanding of the affective social dimensions of reality television must also confront another important narrative of value that shapes popular and critical perceptions of the form – the question of history and historical time. The early work on 'liveness' by Stephen Heath and Gillian Skirrow or Jane Feuer has been formative in the analysis of televisual aesthetics. These scholars explore how television interpellates the spectator into the medium's ideology of presence and immediacy through an overarching fantasy that perceives there to be an equivalence between the time of the event and the time of transmission. This proposition has ramifications for how the individual in the domestic realm feels bound to the imagined community. Temporal equivalence has the capacity to engender a societal co-presence that facilitates a collective consciousness as it links contemporaneous social realities and events with the domestic lives of individuals by way of viewing rituals.[1] Significantly, public service broadcasting works at the heart of this idea of co-presence, a point I will return to.

Yet this notion has also contributed to the conceptualisation of reality television, and television more broadly, as a devalued cultural form. In part this is because liveness is frequently thought to encourage forgetfulness and to eschew history due to an aesthetic emphasis on simultaneity and a perpetual present. In ways that echo the evaluation of reality television in relation to documentary, this emerges as an ethos of distraction that is posed against social merit where concepts of liveness are invoked.

Reality television has been predominantly associated with the 'presentist' bias that characterises television more broadly. Misha Kavka and Amy West observe the properties of the genre that contribute to this:

> Instead of dates and years, Reality TV counts hours, minutes and seconds, setting participants against deadlines, insisting on time in its smallest parameters. To locate oneself in the time of history goes against the power of reality programming – and of the televisual medium itself – to create intimacy and immediacy.
>
> (136)

Through a minimisation of history and a decontextualising of the past, reality television is thought to fulfil the temporal potential of the medium itself. Following this, the ahistorical realm of the personalised, intimate and immediate eclipses historical conscious-ness and knowledge of historical events.[2] One way in which this is evident in the *Idol* format is through the narrow temporality of the competition. The time of the competition dominates the progression of each week's instalment, which is centred on one of the contestants being voted out of the contest by the public. Rather than situating the on-screen events in history, *Idol* programmes are more concerned with the contemporaneous unfolding of the present and the insular and localised consequences of the competition. Serialisation in reality television reinforces this temporality as the competition defines the progression from one programme to the next.

But television *does* offer images of the past that are consistently rec-ognised by communities of viewers as 'history'. How can this be made sense of given the temporal bias in television towards presentism? The capacity for television to represent 'history' is disputed and complex. Geoffrey Nowell-Smith writes: 'television throws up a million and one images referring to or evoking multiple layers of pastness, but the sense they make is increasingly arbitrary' (170).

For Nowell-Smith, this is because television provides its own reference point for historical knowledge, decoding images of the past through its own images of 'history' with no outside point of verification. I disagree that this presents an arbitrary logic; this layering of pastness within the live address of television is a mode of temporality that viewers are increasingly adept at interpreting and making relevant to their own historical positioning in ways that compliment more authorised understandings of history. Bill Schwartz uses the term 'scrambled' to describe ways of experiencing historical time through the mediatised present of television. He concludes that 'television time may indeed be scrambled: but it is neither indeterminate nor does it function outside historical time. Just like memory, it is a critical constituent of our temporal world' (105). I contend that historical time is often formulated in reality television not outside of, but through the subjective and the particular. It is through the subjective that past and future are consistently worked over in the present.

Reality television may codify emotional performances within generic predictability and minimise the explicit appeals to civic responsibility that are a cornerstone to much documentary film-making practice. However, there are modalities of historical consciousness built into the address of reality television that are particular to the form and that are the basis for the connections between viewers and texts. Different objects of the emotions, such as those posed by popular music and personal narratives, exist beyond the straightforward articulation of de-historicised emotionality and performance in the *Idol* series. Viewer connections to these dimensions of the programme rely on an awareness of and access to shared pasts and these play a role in making sense of the collective experience of the everyday. Television frequently necessitates a kind of mirroring of our own location as historicised subjectivities in a manner that enjoins a collective viewing experience. There are modes of selfhood engendered here that are more socially inscribed and more proximate to the socio-political than seem immediately apparent. There are two central mechanisms in play here that I would like to explore – the performance of the self, a performance that evokes multicultural, transnational histories and the recycling of popular music – a function that encourages a nostalgic recognition of popular national pasts. Both these are tied to the manner in which the *Idol* format is particularised in different national contexts.

Subjective histories and affective public life

The *Australian Idol* series contributes to a format that has seen success in different manifestations around the world over the last decade. Su Holmes charts the expansion of reality pop series' from the first recognisable manifestation in New Zealand in 2000 and Australia in 2001 with *Popstars* (which was taken up across European television industries), through to the more successful *Pop Idol* in the UK and *American Idol: Search for a Superstar* in 2002. The first season of *Australian Idol* aired in 2003 on the Ten network. This proliferation evidences how the reality pop competition series, in the *Idol* incarnation, functions as a global television format. It is now well established that this mode of programming emerges within, and contributes to, a rapidly changing television market that is increasingly globalised and yet also aimed at niche, localised audiences. With more differentiated content required to fulfil expanding television industry needs, a logic of adaptation, transfer and recycling has become a significant strategy for media industries.[3] The case of the *Idol* format, which has been exported around the globe, exemplifies this ethos in the way that it remains true to the original recipe and yet local personalities and themes anchor the text and ensure that it is sufficiently 'indigenised' to resonate with local audiences. Thus, there are a number of cultural nuances that accompany the industrial and commercial impetus of adaptation.

The shape this localisation might take differs across types of reality television, yet there is agreement that formats will be made culturally specific to the local context.[4] Graeme Turner asserts this clearly in relation to national identity in stating 'narratives produced for a local audience are always going to operate in some relation to established discourses of local or national cultural identities' (417). In the case of the *Idol* format, local comprehensibility is focused around subjective expressions of personal traits and experience. The personalities of the contestants and their lives outside the competition are given as much airtime as their vocal talent. Over the course of different seasons, the judges have included Ian Dickson, Mark Holden, Kyle Sandilands and Marcia Hines, with Hines the only judge to appear every year. With the exception of Dickson, these individuals were celebrities before their association with *Australian Idol*, largely through different kinds of work in the Australian music industry. The presenters, James Matheson and Andrew G have a long running association with Channel V, a cable TV music channel. The notoriety of all these individuals in the Australian media sphere has increased significantly since appearing on *Australian Idol*.

These aspects, and the representation of the contestants and their lives in particular, offer a point of connection for the viewer that functions through both affinity and attraction. As a number of scholars have noted, celebrity and stardom are central components of reality television, and the game-doc in particular. The performance of the self is integral to this and as Su Holmes observes, the *Idol* mode of stardom works at the interface between the ordinary and the extraordinary. The ordinariness of the contestants is central to the appeal of the audience: 'The emphasis on the ordinariness of the contestants contributes to a deliberate blurring of boundaries between contestant and viewer and as a result, a potential invocation of the audience's own aspirations (or fantasies) of success and stardom' (Holmes 156). Key to fostering this affinity are the segments of the programme, often appearing before contestants go on stage or as they are voted off the programme, that offer montages of the individual's background, their domestic life and their self-narration in voice-over. These sequences present a notion of 'performance' that is more aligned with documentary performance than the 'on stage' competencies that the contestants are formally judged on. The 'off-stage' performance is equally important to viewer responses and, for the concerns of this analysis, is equally implicated in the signification of cultural subjectivity.

Turner suggests that 'cultural visibility and interest' is important to the way these series' become 'water cooler' formats – they actively feed into and maintain conversation and gossip. This is a mechanism for building audiences that encourages 'a highly reflective relationship between the programme's trajectory and the viewer's interests and preferences' (Turner 421). This is extended into other media, such as magazines and the internet, as gossip, and the relationships it fuels, are given further material to work through across commercial media platforms. This works particularly efficiently, Turner notes, as narratives extend over time and build audience knowledge of serialised narratives. Through this response at the level of the everyday, a localised sense of shared cultural meaning is fostered. Looking further at this notion of shared cultural meaning and Turner's 'reflective relationship', it is possible to understand this interaction as a mode of publicness based in fantasy and affinity, shared life-worlds and a recognition of personal attributes. Holmes and Turner suggest forms of spectatorial engagement that are distinct from the psychoanalytic paradigms of cinema studies. However, their approaches retain an emphasis on the psyche and intimate forms of awareness and belonging.

When discussing a notion of publicness and *Australian Idol*, the diversity of the group of contestants must be a key consideration. My focus is on the sixth season of *Australian Idol* that went on air in 2008 and, as with the seasons that preceded this, the make up of the final 12 contestants that compete over the largest section of the series is highly diverse. The 12 include a Maori woman from Aotearoa/New Zealand, contestants of Italian, Sri Lankan and Vietnamese descent, and within this are contestants from urban and rural parts of Australia. Other seasons have also featured contestants from Malaysian, Indonesian, Aboriginal, Irish and Pacific Island backgrounds. This is a pluralism seldom seen in any single instance on free-to-air Australian commercial television. The demands of the competition and the programme, the quest for singing talent and a diverse range of musical personalities, produces a group of individuals who, collectively, foreground the plurality of everyday life and implicitly reflect the heterogeneity of the body politic.

As I have noted, the sequences in the series that represent the contestants' lives beyond the competition are crucial to facilitating viewer knowledge, fandom and affinities with the contestants. As a 'lead in' to singing performances, and with extended profile sequences shown when individuals are eliminated, these sequences (or 'packages') depart from the studio setting and present a montage of past appearances on the programme, self narration in voice-over and narration by and images of friends and family. For example, Madam Parker features in a sequence describing her life, before moving to Australia, in a small Aotearoa/New Zealand town, Tuakau, where her family still live. As a single mother, she states how much she misses her three-year-old son and her family. The images depict her visit to the rural Maori community, on a marae (meeting house) with elders and at a *hungi* (traditional feast). It is the images, rather than the voice-over, that are suggestive of both histories of colonisation and how significant migratory flows exist between Australia and the rest of the South Pacific including Aotearoa/New Zealand.

One of the most explicit instances in the 2008 season to offer a recognition of personal pasts as collective affective legacy is the representation of Thanh Bui, a Vietnamese Australian contestant. When he is eliminated from the competition, the short montage features Bui referring to his family's past, a narrative that has been repeated across the series: 'My family came over here and they had nothing after the Vietnam War and Australia's opened their arms to us. If I've got anything to give back to Australia then I will.' This is followed by his mother's words that, in a heavy accent, profess her pride in her son. The phenomena of forced migration and the history of the Vietnamese diaspora in Australia are reflected in Bui's statement. Also present is an affirmation of national belonging and gratitude. These representations reflect the diversity that many people experience in everyday life, but is seldom narrativised on commercial television. I am suggesting an analysis of these sequences that does not involve underlining how they represent emotions (although they certainly do this) or trigger viewers' emotions. More significant is the manner in which they take forms of signification usually categorised in the affective realm and fold them into the social and the historical. These subjects and their narratives become objects of the emotions as their speech acts are aligned with the affective sphere of family pasts. These personal histories make apparent the legacies of historical events. This historical dimension is insinuated in the text and available as an additional reading, rather than explicitly stated.

While contestant's identities may be narrativised throughout the season in ways that contribute to the deliberate vernacularising of the format and facilitate viewer relationships with ordinariness and aspiration, they also, in less deliberate ways, highlight Australia's historical location. If the subjectivities represented in the programme are produced through a focus on personal histories and narratives of family pasts, they also sit within the broader address of national broadcasting and the competitive quest for an *Australian* pop star. There is an effect here at the level of the national. The representation of histories of migration recognise global and national pasts. Specifically, hinted at here are aspects of Australian nationhood that are frequently disavowed in representation. Viewers are asked to identify with multicultural Australia as it has been produced through a century of population expansion and with an imagined community that is descended from a British settler culture and yet is geographically dislocated from the centres of the West.

Australia is 'South of the East', as Audrey Yue notes, sited in and reliant on the Asia Pacific. Representations that work to highlight regional geo-historical relationships can 'disrupt the ontologies underpinning the status of Asia, Australia and Asia in Australia' (Yue 195). The narratives of migration and the transnational identities they allude to contest Eurocentric conceptions of Australian history through acknowledging the regional and the global as constituents of the national and the local. Yet because this is posed in the series through the frame of personal and familial enunciations, it calls for an affective understanding of social identities and histories. The performance of the self is rendered in the programme in a way that implicitly presents modes of everydayness that are bound up with multicultural histories and politics at the level of lived emotional experience.

The operation of emotionality, in this sense, is slightly different to that described in previous chapters; rather than configured in relation to a defined set of specific emotions, these subjects are formulated through relationships and enunciations that are aligned with affective states and cultural realms. They are delineated through their cultural associations with narratives of intimacy more broadly. Queer theory has much to offer in exploring the political ramifications of intimate family life and its bearing on social relations. In her discussion of the conceptual category of 'public feelings', Ann Cvetkovich argues: 'political identities are implicit within structures of feeling, sensibilities, everyday forms of cultural expression and affiliation that may not take the form of recognizable organizations or institutions' ('Public' 461). The notion of public feelings also attends to the legacies of racialised histories of colonisation and Cvetkovich argues that there are intersections between trauma and migration that are relevant to critiques of nationalism and globalisation. In the sequences I have discussed, histories of colonisation are present as traces within the personal narratives. More relevant here, in Cvetkovich's sense is the presence of affective collective experience, such as the experience of the Polynesian or Vietnamese diaspora, and ways of perceiving experience as a broader social phenomena rather than idiosyncratic, localised events (*An Archive* 123). Thus, the pasts represented are not simply related to and producing personal narratives but are embedded in social histories.

However, these social subjectivities are enunciated within highly structured profile sequences composed of 'sound bites', interviews and family events which have been, most likely, orchestrated for the camera. Further, these portraits are embedded in the commercial momentum of the series and the process of packaging individuals as commodities for the media and music industries. While recognition of an alternative national history may be encouraged here, this recognition occurs within the dictates of commercial television's increasingly cross-platform marketing regime. In this respect, it is perhaps inevitable that this regime will exploit cultural difference in order to produce a market of multicultural minoritarianism for the mainstream. A central problem with this marketisation is that the image and style of the ethnic other is highlighted in popular culture in ways that minimise cultural politics and any contestation to the prevailing order. Yet to understand *Australian Idol* only through this address to the mainstream is to dismiss the diversity of the audience and the different cultural spheres that align themselves with different contestants. It also underestimates the capacity of all audiences to engage in more sophisticated modes of viewing and interpretation.

Australian Idol is produced by a national, free-to-air broadcaster with a remit to reach the largest portion of the Australian audience. Although it is not a public broadcaster, the ethos of public broadcasting is relevant in some respects here. In describing the 'public service idea', Stuart Hall has argued that it need not reproduce 'the old cultural hierarchies' ('Which Public' 35). It can seek to constitute 'publics' in ways that understand broadcasting's role in re-imagining the nation as it shifts and changes, becoming 'the 'theatre' in which this cultural diversity is produced, displayed and represented, and the forum in which the terms of its associative life together are negotiated' ('Which Public' 36). This challenges a dominant public service understanding of national broadcasting, which is often described in terms of reconfiguring the past in the interests of promoting, unifying and homogenising national iconography and mythology.

The notion of a public 'associative life together' and the recognition of diverse personal histories points to what is at stake more broadly in conceptions of subjectivity in reality television. The performances in *Australian Idol* accentuate emotion and are laden with sentiment, as critiques describe, but this is accompanied by a mode of selfhood, the self as citizen, that is tuned into the relation between the self and the collective. In this case, self-mastery and self-fashioning are encouraged through discourses that locate the self within neo-liberal norms of consumption and aspiration.[5] I have argued in previous chapters that documentary subjectivities, especially the doco-auteur, demonstrate this mode of selfhood in ways that approximate Foucault's ethics or concept of care of the self.

In the *Idol* format, as with all reality examples that focus on success, stardom or the 'make-over', this takes the form of self-realisation and personal governance. Yet ways of being a subject, within this, include not only self-actualisation but also awareness of and interaction with others in ways that have consequences for modes of viewing and the representation of subjectivity. Gay Hawkins emphasises this point when she notes that 'ethics are fundamental to the multiple processes of subjectification, they allow us to judge, cultivate and order ourselves not simply in relation to wider moral interdictions but also in relation to "askesis" or sensibilities that establish the range of possibilities in perception, enactment and responsiveness to others' (414). If the contestants on *Idol* can be thought to engage in self-cultivation, crafting performances of the self that conform to the commercial demands of reality television as I have stated them, they also respond to their own, often diasporic, public spheres and backgrounds. This then feeds into the 'contact zone'[6] of the mediatised public sphere, a space where relations between centre and margin are reformulated and negotiated. This is encouraged by the fantasy of affinity (and a shared 'ordinariness') fostered between contestant and viewer, making the contact zone a more level field of encounter. In this sense, the stories told by the contestants play some small part in re-imagining the nation. In the rest of this chapter, I explore another component of the series that weaves together the terms of subjectivity, temporality and the emotions: the musical numbers in the text.

Music, nostalgia and reality television

The musical numbers are the focus of the competition's objective – the search for a pop star, decided through on-screen judging and audience votes. In this respect, the numbers offer a forum and a teleology through which self-improvement and cultivation, according to strict normalising rules of behaviour and appearance, are enacted. Yet the musical performances also play a role in structuring the *Idol* programmes and fostering viewer engagement. Integral to music is the notion of time and timing. At one level, repetition and rhythm structure linear music time. Music also structures the timing of the programme; the musical numbers/performances order each show as contestants perform and receive comments from the judges. In turn, the special themes of individual shows focus on music from a particular era or genre, such as Australian music, rock music, Motown music and the themes punctuate the time of the competition across the *Idol* season. The music organises the series in ways that make *Idol* unique in the field of reality programming.

In one respect, the temporality facilitated by the emphasis on music could be understood to re-inscribe qualities of liveness and immediacy as small increments of time, largely in the form of songs, and the localised meaning of the competition are foregrounded. However, pop music does more than simply provide order and rhythm; it engages viewers through sensual, evocative and nostalgic registers, thus furthering the complex play of emotion in the reality form. These are intensities, as Dyer describes in relation to Hollywood musicals. The *Idol* shows are not musicals but Dyer's account of the text's capacity to present feelings, which are both aesthetically and narratively authenticated is relevant here. In distinguishing between representational and non-representational signs, he discusses the use of tap dance in a range of media. Dyer emphasises the meaning of the sound of tap and 'the significance such sounds acquire from their place within the network of signs in a given culture at a given point of time' (23). As I have discussed, different signs match up with different historically and culturally determined sensibilities.

The contestants in *Idol* do not perform original music but, rather, are required to draw on a selection of well-known popular songs from the distant and recent past as a way of demonstrating their ability to diversify across genres and enhance their popular appeal. This clearly corresponds with the ethos of transfer, adaptation and recycling that is the foundation of the global television format. In this sense, songs that have succeeded in the charts are assimilated to the format and combine the pre-existing popularity of music, genres and celebrity types with the ordinariness of the contestant. This secures the *Idol* series financially and culturally, as product for consumption. Popular cultural pasts are invoked here in ways that further the interests of the commercial relationship between viewer and text. Yet this accounts for only one dimension of the dialogue the format encourages with the viewer. To work effectively in this commercial respect, the songs must also exist as intensities and relay references to the past in ways that trigger responses and desires in the audience. Simon Frith establishes the important relationship between music and perceptions of time, imagination and desire:

> Music is not, by its nature, rational or analytic; it offers us not argument but experience, and for a moment – for moments – that experience involves *ideal time*, an ideal defined by the integration of what is routinely kept separate – the individual and the social, the mind and the body, change and stillness, the different and the same, the already past and the still to come, desire and fulfilment.
>
> (emphasis in original, 157)

Frith describes a subjective temporal complexity that is pertinent to *Idol* recycling. In the remainder of this chapter, I wish to look more closely at the interweaving of time, emotion and music on television and the ways in which *Australian Idol* directs audience responses.

As Caryl Flinn observes in her study of Hollywood film music, in film theory a clear division between 'knowledge and sight' and 'intuition and sound' has cast sound in a different interpretive order, or as 'curiously "other"' (6). Flinn argues that sound, and music in particular, should be understood not as outside film's social concerns or conventions of representation, but as distinctively configured within these realms. In contrast to film scholarship, television theory has for some time been exploring the importance of sound in the role television plays in the domestic sphere and modes of distracted viewing. In ways that compare with the soap opera and other forms that emphasise listening as much as gazing, the *Idol* programmes offer pleasure in hearing the songs and the judges comments as much as pleasure in viewing the spectacle of the contestant's performances. The music functions also to recall, for some, remembered personal pasts and, more pertinently, popular pasts in ways that are collectively recognised and are supported by the constant recycling, across media platforms, of popular culture from past eras. The music structures spectatorial moments that weave together, as Frith notes, the individual and the social at the level of desire.

Aligning this example with prevalent approaches to the inter-connections between time and commodity culture would entail understanding this as an example of postmodern culture's crisis of historicity. Following this, historical time is replaced by an emphasis on spatial rather than temporal categories. The fragmented referencing of cultural styles and imagery that have come before signals the deficit of any movement forward. The scholar most associated with this critique, Fredric Jameson, describes this as 'the random canni-balization of all the styles of the past, the play of random stylistic allusion' (65) and the primacy of the 'neo'. This narrative would apprehend the *Idol* example as adhering to the blank referencing of the past as individuals and the songs they perform become muddled into a flattened experience of random and commodified popular pasts in ways that, again, resemble television's perceived eschewal of historical time. But I wish to resist the lure of viewing the *Idol* series through the lens of postmodernity, either as a cultural epoch or a conceptual field. I am interested in exploring the functions of temporality and nostalgia through more specific questions of com-munity and subjectivity and how these are formulated through the medium of television.

Nostalgia, or a longing for missing time, is the emotion connected to time that is most powerfully evoked by music. Flinn understands this capacity in reference to utopia as music has an 'ability to return [listeners] to better, allegedly more "perfect" times and memories' (9). For Flinn, both utopia and nostalgia are reliant on fantasies of a no-place but in contrast to utopia, nostalgia is a response and an emotion. The word is a combination of the Greek *nostos* (to return home) and *algos* or *algia* (sorrow, pain or a painful state). Initially a medical term, nostalgia was used first in the late seventeenth century to describe a severe form of homesickness, much like melancholia, experienced by Swiss soldiers posted in foreign lands (Radstone 119). It was only much later to emerge as a descriptor for a cultural condition pertaining to late capitalism and alienation. While many approaches, including critiques of postmodern culture, have taken nostalgia as an aspect of cultural production that denigrates representations of the past, my investigation is in agreement with Hutcheon's endeavour to account, in a more nuanced way, for the trans-ideological capacity of nostalgia (*Irony, Nostalgia* 6).

In the context of examining collective viewing experiences and the public service idea, nostalgia's connection to a sense of community is significant. Modernity sees nostalgia frequently inferring a loss of tradition, community values and simpler pre-industrial times. This is a lament for both a vanishing sense of belonging and a clear feeling of collective identification. Hutcheon frames this in terms of the desire for a return to a homeland and the homogeneity this might entail:

> In nineteenth-century Europe, homeland became articulated in terms of the nation state, and nostalgia began to take on its associations with nationalism – and chauvinism. Even its more innocent-seeming forms – such as the preparing and eating of familiar foods by immigrant groups – can be seen as a nostalgic enactment of ethnic group identity, a collective disregarding, at least temporarily, of generational and other divisions.

A symptom of nostalgia's mourning for an inaccessible past is the tendency to forgo the complexities of difference for the fantasy of belonging to a clearly identifiable, unconditionally discrete collective.

The address of *Idol* consciously works to the heart of this symptom in its endeavour to meet broadcast television's demand to maximise the audience. Songs easily become the objects of nostalgia in ways that cohere communities of viewers. In the 2008 season, *Australian Idol*'s themed nights included an Australian music night, 1980s night (with Cyndi Lauper as a special guest judge), an *Abba* night, a *Motown* night, a Michael Jackson night and a *Rolling Stones* night. The themed nights offer variety across the series while also facilitating the viewer as the subject of knowledge. In this case, it is pleasurable knowledge of popular musical pasts that is emphasised and this is intended to unify an audience in the present around collective memory. Whether the audience actually remember the popularity of *The Rolling Stones* or *Abba* in the sixties or seventies becomes relatively inconsequential – due to the prevalence of *Classic Hits* radio stations and the constant recycling and reflection on musical pasts in popular culture more broadly (especially in film and television), songs are not only hinged to a particular historical context, they also signify the recent past and present. Thus, a song can evoke a proliferation of imagined pasts and presents.

This capacity for the song to feed into nostalgia and activate multiple or mass responses in the audience becomes bound up with the success of the performance and the contestants' ability to make the right choices and, thus, properly manage the self. This is highlighted on the *Rolling Stones* night when contestant Roshani Priddis chose to sing a lesser-known hit, *Wild Horses*, from the 1973 album, *Goats Head Soup*. The judges were critical of the choice. On the following night's programme, the audience's decision about who is to be eliminated from the competition is finalised. The judges speak again and Dickson advises Priddis that she 'has to choose songs the audience can connect with'.[7]

What is at stake is the capacity of the song and the performance to evoke, for the audience, the fantasy of 'perfection and integrity in an otherwise imperfect world' (Flinn 9). Music powerfully hails a community of subjects into place and this sits well with the endeavour to achieve a broad national audience and to engender a sense that the time and place of viewing is shared with others. Yet rather than a recognition of difference, as with the personal profiles of contestants, the musical performances are more explicitly oriented towards maximising a single mass audience and, thus, foregrounding sameness and commonality. This is not necessarily the enactment of group identity in the present that Hutcheon refers to, but rather a representation of perfection and simplicity that works for an emotional attachment to a past sense of homeliness where potentially destabilising differences, such as gender or ethnicity, do not come into play. This is not explicitly a national sense of belonging, but as a nationally broadcast show, *Australian Idol* poses this as the default imagined collective. Further, nostalgia's idealisations may be projected into the past, but they arise from a sense of lack felt in the present. This results in a distinct contrast in the programme between the affective everyday lives of the contestants that fracture the notion of a singular national history and the songs that favour a simpler expression of identity and belonging. This, in turn, structures contrasting relationships between the self and the past. The viewer is hailed into place by the aesthetics of the text either as a subject of a culture of fragmentation and diversity or a subject of a culture of commonality and communal interests and desires. Both interpellations rely on affective meanings which circulate around the text's modes of enunciation.

It is important to note that this is not a straightforward collective subjectification to musical nostalgia. There is a constant challenge to the notion that songs have popular appeal in ways that transcend historical specificity and elide differences, especially generational difference. There are occasional instances when teenage contestants have been required to perform songs that may have been hits in the seventies or eighties and have professed that they have never heard the songs. In one case, 16-year-old Tom Williams (born in 1982) performed Billy Joel's *Uptown Girl*, released in 1983, for 80s night. After he attracted criticism from the judges for his performance, one of the hosts, Andrew G, asked him: 'What are you going to do to improve for next week?' Williams replied, 'I don't know; hopefully pick a song that I know. I'm from the nineties, you know, we got chucked [*sic*] with the eighties.' Hence, the notion that many viewers are familiar with the featured songs is revealed as an assumption and the generational differences across the audience, judges and contestants come into view.

Moreover, as I noted above, nostalgia need not necessarily work as a purely denigrating force, eclipsing the representation of political histories. I have described *Idol*'s musical numbers as invoking a utopian past and, thus, as homogenising, but nostalgia also has the potential to focus political desires and democratising engagements with history. Nostalgia can, conceivably, activate ordinary, everyday pasts in ways that exist in tension with official or elite historical knowledge. In his work on nostalgia and heritage culture, *Theatres of Memory*, Raphael Samuel endeavours to move beyond characterisations of nostalgia as a form of 'false consciousness' (17), endowing the emotion with the potential to re-imagine marginalised and under-class pasts. In the case of popular music, popular memory can also be employed in recalling the politicised moments that shaped or were shaped by musical histories. In the case of the *Rolling Stones*, this was the countercultural movement of the 1960s. Motown Records, the first recording company to be owned by an African American, has a particular place in the history of the commercial politics of music and race in America. There is a potential, then, for nostalgia to work though the psychical and the historical as a commemoration of the countercultural histories that are often bound up with popular music.

All the same, this potential is not realised in *Idol* and commentary around the songs frequently remains within a discourse of emotion in a way that effaces rather than activates social history. Judges do frequently discuss the origin of the song, but usually with regard to the intention of the original artist and the meaning or affect the song was designed to convey. This is posed in terms that are not explicitly linked, in the programme, to political or cultural histories. Thus, there is seldom any recourse to the actual social movements more broadly to which the songs belong. A constant refrain voiced by the contestants in response to the criticism of the judges is: 'I just really like the song.' The song as an object of feeling becomes assimilated into the activity of self-fashioning through a language of personal preference and taste, rather than an awareness of social pasts.

Yet the performances that give rise to subjectivity here do not fit into a straightforward ideological model. At different points in a single show, they tap into different audience sensibilities: from a viewer that recognises diverse cultural histories to one that escapes into the homeliness of homogeneity and commonality. Yet they do, unquestionably, pose modes of selfhood that cannot be simply reduced to the ahistorical and the singularly personal. In other words, to observe that reality television engages the feelings as a way to enhance entertainment value is only part of the story that can be told about this non-fiction mode.

Many of the documentaries explored in the previous chapters use the non-fiction form to explicitly represent the vicissitudes of the social sphere and, often, the individual's place in this sphere. *Australian Idol* would seem to be an awkward fit in this regard. The series does not reference authenticity and actuality in order to convey the realism of socio-political meaning, rather these aspects of non-fiction are used to present a true-to-life fantasy that marries the quotidian and the realm of celebrity and stardom. Nevertheless both share in the aim to create an affinity between the texts and the worlds represented; the world the contestants inhabit is the same world the audience reside in. This is the crux of the construction of subjectivity in the programme. It signals the ways in which this subjectivity enters into the realm of the social – it is entrenched in shared popular (musical) and national pasts, and thus the affect world of the public sphere.

If the performances seek out viewer sensibilities and recognition as I have discussed, the location of the viewer, their subjectivity, is also confirmed here. Berlant captures some of the tenor of this dialogue in her description of the 'intimate public sphere' as 'a space of mediation in which the personal is refracted through the general, what's salient for its consumers is that it is a place of recognition and reflection. In an intimate public sphere emotional contact, of a sort, is made' (*The Female Complaint* viii). This emotional contact is key to the spectatorial imaginary that is engendered by *Australian Idol*. In the previous chapter, I argued that *Born into Brothels* invokes the hopefulness that saturates the figuration of childhood, only to foreclose on the possibility of conceiving of material change in the film and in the children's lives. Where these child subjects are caught in survival time, without a clear pathway towards the 'good life', *Australian Idol* presents subjects that cast the viewer's imaginary backwards in order to pose a collective past (and future) that activates divergent forms of belonging.

Epilogue

Hope and documentary

> I know that you cannot live on hope alone, but
> without it life is not worth living.
>
> Harvey Milk, *The Times of Harvey Milk* (1984)

In the two concluding chapters of this book, I have explored the emotions of hope and nostalgia. The two different investigations work equally well as concluding topics. In some respects, they provide a double ending: one chapter explores what is at stake for subjectivity in the documentary expression of hope and futurity, and one looks back through the lens of nostalgia to that which is perceived to have been lost. In closing, I've chosen to return to a meditation on hope and documentary. While this offers an optimistic tone to finish on, more importantly it acknowledges an emotion that is key to the practice of non-fiction film-making – hope. This is an emotion that also shapes the representation of documentary subjects – when individuals are shown in hopeless situations, they subtly tell us that conditions could be different or, in the historical documentary, that situations cannot be repeated. These representations draw on the power of what can be accomplished if wishing, aspiring and having faith in possibility are widely maintained.

In *The Times of Harvey Milk*, despite his tragic and untimely death, the figure of Milk is made to objectify hope and futurity. Moreover, the quote above, from a well-known speech reproduced in the film, resonates with the preoccupations of the social advocacy documentary in a number of respects. Hopefulness is not the only narrative or aesthetic concern for those making and critiquing documentary, but it underpins the crucial and long-standing connection between the documentary project and narratives of liberal democracy. It is central to the fantasies that motivate a range of activities in public life. In this sense, documentary practice and reception plays one small role in the broader late modern discourses that endorse individual social agency and the affective understandings that perpetuate these discourses. Elizabeth A. Povinelli captures this when she writes: 'the ideals of liberalism are not about knowledge and its exposure to truth and revelation, but about the fantasies necessary to act in a liberal society and how these fantasies are protected and projected into social life through specific textual practices' (155). Without the fantasy that society *can* be influenced by those outside the halls of power, the task of protest or bringing to light the exclusion of others is not viable. This is a task that is crucial for much committed documentary and has been central to many of the arguments explored in this book.

Bus 174

In closing, I would like to turn to one final film. *Bus 174* (2002), directed by Felipe Lacerda and José Padilha, shows how a portrait of a single individual might play on the paradoxical relationship between hope and hopelessness, or power and powerlessness, in ways that maintain the necessary fantasies that Povinelli describes. It is a documentary that seeks to answer the question: 'How can this have happened?' The question that is intended to follow is: 'What can be done about this?' *Bus 174* begins with a single event that took place in an affluent suburb in Rio de Janeiro on 12 June 2000. The documentary works to reveal the expanding web of cause and effect that surrounds this event. On this day, a young African Brazilian man, Sandro de Nascimento, attempted to rob passengers on a bus and, for some reason, then decided to hold the passengers hostage. The stand-off paralysed police for many hours and was broadcast live on Brazilian television with the media positioned unusually close to the armed hostage-taker. The film-makers draw on this remarkable media footage to tell the story of what happened on that day and they weave it together with a broader portrait of this man's experiences.

This representation explores the environments, people and events that shaped de Nascimento's life. It encompasses the violent murder of his mother that he witnessed at age ten; his subsequent life with gangs of street kids in city slums; and his experiences of poverty, crime, drugs, police violence and Rio's harsh prison system. Despite his very transient existence, the film-makers are able to find and interview many who were close to de Nascimento, including social workers, friends and relatives. Those who were involved in the bus crisis are also interviewed, including bystanders, hostages and the ill-equipped and under-trained police involved in the stand-off. One reviewer describes the film:

> The drama has a lurid fascination, and there is a queasy, guilty thrill in watching it unfold. But the filmmakers use this slightly questionable appeal and the inherent suspense of the hostage drama to investigate the violence, the poverty and the social malaise that bedevil modern Brazil.
>
> (Scott)

There is a clear appeal to emotions in the film's address. Yet those who tried, and failed, to help de Nascimento throughout his life express a tangible sorrow. This emotion sits alongside the compelling depiction of the panicked and chaotic events on the bus.

The sadness, and even frustration, that interviewees articulate is bound up with what is inferred but not stated until the end of the documentary: de Nascimento did not survive the siege. He is an individual without future and thus without hope. Moreover, there is an ambiguity around his reasoning and his will to enter into this hopeless situation. When de Nascimento hijacked the bus he had already collected money from the passengers. During the stand-off, he expressed a desire to take revenge for the deaths of his friends in the infamous 1993 Candelária Massacre, in which police shot and murdered a group of street children sleeping outside a church. Further, while he demanded guns and a grenade, it is unclear what his aim was in sparking the event beyond an ill-considered attempt at revenge. Without a clear rationale, de Nascimento cannot be constituted as a subject of hope or futurity. The documentary paints a picture of the means by which the subject is subordinated, regulated and suppressed by social and state institutions. The investigation into de Nascimento's past clearly illustrates this. The incident on the bus appears as his single act of agency, an act that recognises and seeks to break through the social order to which he is subjectified. With too little regard for self-preservation, this presents as an unravelling of subjectivity. By building an image of this individual's life and surroundings in conjunction with the detailed event that marked its end, the film conveys the making and the unmaking of the self.[1] The hijacking can only result in de Nascimento's death.

In presenting this startling and impossibly harsh life story, the film-makers are emphasising a problem in the moral order. In *Bus 174*, the absence of the speaking subject motivates the film's agenda. It seeks to find a place in history for the subaltern and the film does this through expanding the social vista around de Nascimento. However, the film-makers choose not to organise the film in a way that directs a single reading – they leave that to the interpretive and imaginative capabilities of the audience. The many interviews create a heterogeneous set of interpretations. Those who describe the events of 12 June 2000 consistently reflect on what they believed was happening in the mind of the hijacker or how the siege would progress at a given moment. This speculation builds and multiplies, with no single perspective privileged in the documentary.

While de Nascimento's motivation cannot be known, the cameras that were near the bus and the hostages' testimonies afterwards record and retell the scene, including what seems to be de Nascimento's orchestration of the event. The hostage-taker himself understands the media appeal of emotion as he encourages the female hostages to scream, cry and appear panicked for the onlooking cameras. One reason for this may be to enhance the perception that he posed a real threat to the passengers. It also may be that he wished to heighten the media's interest and to secure a place for himself on the public stage.

The documentary infers these details but ultimately leaves them unresolved. Yet public recognition of de Nascimento's plight, and many others like him, is often referenced. One interviewee notes that there is an issue at stake that is 'bigger than Candelária and bus 174, bigger than all our everyday tragedies. Our society treats these invisible kids not as human beings but as garbage. They are cast into pigsties so that we can avoid responsibility for them.' The film attempts to recast subjectivity through de-individualising de Nascimento's predicament and locating him, and the exceptional event on the bus, within a highly stratified society rife with neglect and corruption. Even without a subjective future, due to this recasting, de Nascimento becomes a documentary object that is presented in ways that might compel hopefulness.

In many ways, what *Bus 174* represents is already widely known: there is a large African Brazilian underclass who live in great poverty; many who exist in these conditions experience and perpetuate violence, and society or the state is unable to remedy the situation. But the documentary translates this into a question of subjectivity and offers visible and auditory evidence of the relation between human actions and the social and moral order. Through constructing a collage that *shows* rather than *explains*, the film opens a space for the viewer to interpret and imagine. The aim is, in this respect, to decolonise the imagination of the audience in ways that open a path beyond the media reports and the sound bites that condense rather than expand ways of knowing. De Nascimento's actions and experiences offer an avenue through which to explore a broader set of questions about Brazilian society and its future well-being.

This points to a further problematic that I have referred to at points throughout the book. Who is the audience for the film and what are the ramifications of reading suffering across cultures? The constituency of viewers who inhabit the Brazilian public sphere are poised to read the film, and are in a position to take action in that same sphere, in a way that other audiences are not. Yet *Bus 174* also calls upon the wider international community to acknowledge the social situation it describes. The wide distribution and international success of the documentary, in one sense, testifies to this. But how is otherness structured for this audience? Does it verify what we already think we know about Brazil – it is a country that cares little about the large urban slums in which many live in abject poverty and lawlessness, outside the teleology of progress?[2] This is a perception that easily confirms the perceived relation between the civilised West and the barbaric non-West. I argue that the documentary resists this for some of the reasons that Kim Longinotto's documentaries also avoid this appeal. The film offers a multi-perspective approach to the bus 174 event, with different voices presenting this society as internally grappling with the terms of liberalism and democracy. Moreover, it is a self-ethnography in which the film-makers and the interviewees are reflecting on responsibility within their own communities.

The film plays on the problem of tolerance. Brown refers to the mechanisms by which 'intolerant' societies are opposed to 'tolerant', usually Western, nations:

This division of the world into the tolerant and the intolerant, the fundamentalist and the pluralist, the parochial and the cosmopolitan, allows the political theoretical and philosophical literature on tolerance to repeatedly pose the question 'What should be the attitude of the tolerant toward the intolerant?' as if these dire opposites truly existed, embodied in radically different entities.

(*Regulating* 189–90)

The film does not paint Brazilian society as intolerant of race and social disadvantage. It neither asks viewers to be tolerant of de Nascimento and his actions, nor does it refuse to tolerate them. Because of this, tolerance and intolerance are not assumed as default cultural positions that the viewer should assume. Rather, the documentary attempts to open up a textual schema without directing assumptions or feelings. We are not asked, specifically, to empathise with de Nascimento but rather to acknowledge, accurately, his place in the social history of the nation.

Referring to Jill Godmilow's approach to her film *Far from Poland*, Rabinowitz describes how the film-maker was 'forced to rethink the codes of documentary address – codes which naturalise the world, make sense of it, and reinforce its social relations by smoothing out contradictions' (*They Must be Represented* 31). She goes on to note that the film experience these codes provide 'can't dream. It can't provoke imagination' (*They Must be Represented* 31). Rabinowitz surmises:

This desire to dream, to provoke imagination, seems to lead the documentary away from the realm of history and truth and into the realm of art and artifice. How are we to judge historical documentaries if they call themselves dreams? In documentary, the viewer is asked to participate in a series of contracts – between film and its object, between filmmaker and audience, between reality and representation.

(*They Must be Represented* 31–2)

Throughout this book, I have sought to theorise ways of re-thinking the presentation of subjectivity in documentary. The contracts Rabinowitz describes determine how we judge documentary and these are inevitably underwritten by emotion, both as a discourse and as a feeling. This is the case whether emotions bind subjects to one another and shape the way others are perceived or offer a sensation of actuality. In both cases, imagination is paramount.

The example of *Bus 174* presents a number of the forms of selfhood I have discussed in the preceding chapters. The film-makers are citizen-subjects who enact their care for the collective through seeking to motivate a new vision of a public event. The experiences of de Nascimento are traced from childhood to adulthood, and from hopefulness to hopelessness. Perhaps most significantly, the viewer is interpellated as a subject of knowledge in a manner that requires an understanding of the relationship between the individual and the collective, artifice and truth, hope and hopelessness. *Bus 174* exemplifies the powerful ways in which documentary can capture the social self and in so doing, harness cultural sensibilities.

At a number of points throughout this book, I have argued that emotion provides an important frame through which to understand how viewers are addressed by documentary and, thus, how films might engender modes of recognition and reciprocity. I have not proposed that documentary all works with a similar intent, but rather that emotion adheres to and shapes selves differently in certain times and contexts. It can rally and sustain movements engaged in seeking social recognition for groups and individuals, but it can also obscure the interactions and contexts that position and marginalise individuals. This means, above all, that the effects of emotion can be paradoxical and uneven. They contribute to modes of documentary performance and reception in which our expectations of the world can be either reinforced or come undone.

Notes

1 Introduction: Representation and Documentary Emotion

1. Throughout this book I use the term 'narrative' to describe how a sequence of events and individuals are represented in a documentary in ways that infer a recognisable ordering of time and space. I acknowledge that many scholars limit narrative to the domain of fiction film. In employing the term I wish to emphasise the storytelling capacity of non-fiction and the diverse ways in which documentaries organise the worlds they represent to make these worlds recognisable to viewers.
2. See Perri 6 et al. for a survey of some of this scholarship.
3. A number of philosophers, most notably Hobbes and Spinoza, provide the basis for this line of thought. Political philosophy and feminist theory have, in ways that are gaining more and more theoretical momentum, sought to understand the role of the passions in political life. See Gatens, James, Honneth and Mouffe.
4. See also McGuigan, Ahmed, Brown and Spelman.
5. Stearns and Stearns term this cultural variability of emotion 'emotionology' and address the historical dimension of this at some length.
6. See Carl Plantinga and Greg M. Smith, Murray Smith, Malcolm Turvey.
7. The reason for this aversive response to pleasure may well (and understandably so) be due to the expansion of feminist film scholarship that sought to dismantle the gendered implications of scopophilia. Documentary, of course, does not exist outside gendered constructions, as will be discussed in Chapter 2.
8. Among the technologies Cowie refers to are the devices constructed by Eadward Muybridge, and, pertinently, those designed by scientists such as the stereoscope. These were integral in linking vision, pleasure and cinematic representations of actuality. While the pleasure tied to the function of display in early cinema has been well theorised, mainly in Tom Gunning's work on primitive cinema (as I will discuss at greater length in Chapter 2), the non-fiction cinema of early, scientifically inspired devices and then later 'actualities' exist as an important facet of the lineage of documentary film. Eric Barnouw is one scholar to begin his history of the non-fiction film not with the social realism of the 1920s but with the earliest cinematic technology that preceded and then included the Lumiere Brothers. Paula Rabinowitz also cites the Lumiere Brothers as the founding fathers of documentary and newsreel.

9. Although Dyer seems to open a place to discuss a history of signs, he is much more interested in the correspondence between signs and the instances of different historically and culturally determined sensibilities. My interest is in drawing out this aspect of Dyer's essay to propose an understanding of documentary that both acknowledges the stratum of pre-established relations with the form, as it is constituted through a mutating history of signs, and with intensity in ways that work at the needs and desires pertaining to a given social system.

10. With the rise in the popularity of documentary, particularly the films that follow in the wake of Michael Moore's style of film-making, the landscape of political documentary production and reception has changed markedly over the last decade. As Stella Bruzzi observes, documentary has become a global commodity (1). If the committed documentary seeks to mobilise a subject of agency, it is increasingly important in this new era of production to also account for the subject of consumption, and entertainment, that these films engage.

11. The recent book by Lisa Cartwright, *Moral Spectatorship: Technologies of Voice and Affect in Postwar Representations of the Child*, notwithstanding. In this book, Cartwright argues that 1970s and 80s feminist film theorists missed an opportunity to fully realise the importance of object relations in cinema.

12. The bad object is also the mother. For Klein all loved objects are, simultaneously, hated.

2   Pleasure and Disgust: Desire and the Female Porn Star

1. Beyond the mainstream, other examples have contributed to this revision of sexual agency, including the film-making of Jane Campion or Catherine Breillait and the figures of Susie Bright, or 'post-porn Goddess', Annie Sprinkle.

2. In this sense, my discussion is limited to the problem of how female agency and desire is produced in the text through genre conventions and popular discourse. Questions that pertain to the female viewer and her desirous relationship to pornography and the female porn star are significant, yet this particular question of difference is beyond the scope of this chapter.

3. As Gunning describes, until approximately 1906, actuality films outnumbered fictional films. It is this era of film culture that is central to his analysis.

4. Muybridge's well-known images of horses and other animals offered evidence of the nature of movement in ways that appealed to a desire for new scientific knowledge and his projections were shown in lecture halls to interested audiences of the time. This focus on zoology soon encompassed the mechanics of the human body, with naked or semi-naked pictorial accounts of men, women and children performing short tasks and activities.

5. See Kaplan (*Pornography*), Rich (*Anti-porn*) or Williams (*Hard Core*).
6. SBS Television (Special Broadcasting Service) is Australia's smaller, second public service broadcaster with a charter that stipulates that SBS must work to meet the needs of culturally diverse viewing nation.
7. See Arthurs or Boyle for more discussion of 'docuporn'.
8. See McRobbie, Walkerdine et al., Attwood, Gill and Whelelan.

3 Injury, Identity and Recognition: *Rize* and *Fix: The Story of an Addicted City*

1. For work that specifically examines documentary representations of the Holocaust and trauma, see Joshua Hirsch, Shoshana Felman or Janet Walker (who also presents insightful discussions of documentary, memory and the trauma related to incest).
2. *Not a Love Story: A Film about Pornography*, discussed in the previous chapter, is an interesting example emerging out of the women's movement.
3. Importantly, in his essay 'New Subjectivitites: Documentary and Self-Representation in the Post-verite Age', Renov describes how the social movements of the 1960s and 70s gradually became displaced by the politics of identity that were marshalled by the women's movement. The emphasis on issues of sexuality, race and ethnicity was evident in documentary by 1990, in films that expressed the 'disparate cultural identities of the makers' (*The Subject* 176). While I am not specifically discussing autobiographical films here, the body of films Renov describes contributes to the politics of the subject in documentary that I am referring to.
4. This point references Jane Gaines's argument that 'the documentary film that uses realism for political ends has a special power over the world of which it is a copy because it derives its power from that same world' ('Political' 95).
5. Although both draw on identity discourses, *Rize* and *Fix* can be placed slightly differently in relation to traditions of documentary practice. *Fix* is a product of Canada's National Film Board (NFB) and was released in the same year as *Bowling for Columbine*. The film should be contextualised less through a relation to Moore's film than a history of NFB documentary film-making and its reputation for a long-standing commitment to the production of political documentary. This commitment is evidenced by a history of production that includes Wild's own work, that of Alanis Obomsawin, George C. Stoney and Bonnie Sherr Klein among many others. Central to *Rize*, as I will discuss, is the spectacle of dance, and as such it can be positioned alongside other spectacle-oriented documentaries such as *Touching the Void*. Yet the narrative impetus of the film finds a place in the body of work that explores experiences of racialised oppression, comparable in its African American specificity to *Hoop Dreams* (1994), or the more recent *The Boys of Baraka* (2005), among others.

6. This specificity is emphasised in the film when, at one point, a piece of ethnographic footage of African tribal dance (actually sourced from one of Leni Riefenstahl's films on the Nuba, ca 1970s) is interspersed with a contemporary dance sequence. The documentary seems to be referencing, in this manner, a connection between African tribal culture and African American culture: krumping, as a response to oppression and exclusion from capitalist aspiration is a retrieval or revival of a culturally specific practice and thus is posed as a resistant activity. While this locates krumping as, perhaps, a radically specific culture, it also, through essentialising the practice, negates the agency involved in krumping as a subversive tactic, while bringing to the film, the romanticising and objectifying gaze of Riefensthal's own camera.

7. See NFB (51–2) for more details of the community outreach and marketing that accompanied the release of the film.

8. The rest of the community that is represented in *Fix* who struggle with their addiction are also represented in ways that resist articulating an explanatory trauma. However, they are given little voice in the narrative. When compared with Wilson, they become a backdrop for his charismatic character sketch. Thus they emerge as caricatures, defined solely by their drug use and by their socio-economic status.

9. This is also an unmistakably abject representation of the body of the drug user, echoing my discussion in the previous chapter. The recognition of corporeality and the boundary site of the body is emphasised as it is transgressed by the needle. This re-inscribes the eclipsing of subjectivity.

10. For example, for Scarry, physical pain provides the nation-state with control over a collective imaginary or reality. In another instance, Berlant views a politics of pain as unviable due to the way it is constantly advanced in the public arena as sentimentality, thus positing an intimate public sphere in which the personal is deployed in ways that eclipse the political. This kind of violence is one that occurs when pain, once it is recognised, is appropriated and mediated by discourses of nationhood.

4   Women, Pain and the Documentaries of Kim Longinotto

1. Film titles include *Pride of Place* (1976), *Tragic but Brave* (1994), *Rock Wives* (1996) and her recent feature documentary, *Hold Me Tight, Let Me Go* (2007).

2. Throughout this chapter, I refer largely to Longinotto as the authoring subject of the four documentaries, with the understanding that three of these works credit a co-director. In all of the documentaries that she directs, Longinotto is the principal director and nearly always the cinematographer as well. Co-directors take on different roles depending on their relationship to the production and often her collaborators do not assume responsibilities that the film industry would generally attribute to a 'director'.

3. For example, in colonial representations the figure of the veiled woman is inaccessible, mysterious and sexualised. She embodies the mystery of the Orient, inviting unveiling and possession. African women become sexualized through primitivist fantasies that encapsulate Freud's 'dark continent', also awaiting exploration and domination by a masculinist West.
4. Following the Islamic revolution of 1979, Shari'a, or Islamic law, to a great extent replaced the Westernized legal system that had, under the Shah, governed family law. Mir-Hosseini, who is an anthropologist, writes in her book, *Marriage on Trial: A Study of Islamic Family Law in Iran and Morocco*, that 'irrespective of the extent and method of reforms, the end result has been the creation of a hybrid family law, which is neither the Shari'a nor Western' (11). It was after reading this book that Longinotto began working collaboratively with Mir-Hosseini on *Divorce Iranian Style*.
5. This self is a fiction because it is a product of liberal humanism that, in turn, legitimizes other instruments of modernity such as the nation-state and egalitarian civil society. As the work of Michel Foucault has established, the self is subjected to a multitude of regulatory and disciplinary discourses. In this respect, the quest for personal fulfilment and self-maximisation involves the regulation and expression of a particular kind of subject.
6. This visibility of the relation between filmed subject and film-maker is achieved by Mir-Hosseini who not only spoke Farsi but also built close relationships with the women in the film and empathised with their plight. As Longinotto states in an interview with Sarah Teasley, 'when they're looking at us, the crew, they're actually looking at Ziba, looking at a friend [...].'
7. The question of identity in contemporary Iranian society has been most visibly represented, on an international stage, in Iranian art-house cinema. The New Iranian Cinema movement's most well-known films were made under the reformist regime of President Mohammad Khatami, from 1997 to 2005. The representation of women, and the complexity of their social position, has been central to this cinema. A significant number of important women film-makers have emerged in Iran such as Rakhshan Bani-Etemad, Tahmineh Milani and Samira Makhmalbaf, while male film-makers, such as Jafar Panahi (*The Circle* (2000), *Offside* (2006)) and Abbas Kiarostami (*Ten* (2002)) have also explored the experiences of women in contemporary Iran.
8. However, it remains unclear whether this is only a symbolic, regulatory power or a more institutionalised form of authority, as the documentary does not offer information about who is responsible for the operation of the shelter. With no reference to whether the shelter is administered by the state or by the civil society, or what other welfare services exist for these women, *Runaway* relies only upon interpersonal relationships to convey cultural meaning and complexity.
9. Since the time of writing, Longinotto has released another documentary, *Rough Aunties* (2008). This film is set in Durban, South Africa and focuses on a group of women working with an NGO and dealing with child abuse cases.

10. FGC encompasses a range of practices, not all of which can be considered mutilation, that are carried out in many different African cultures for a variety of different reasons. However, given the descriptions of FGC in the film, *The Day I will Never Forget* is concerned with the more acute practice of excision of the clitoris and the removal, to varying degrees, of the genital area that is then stitched together, often leading to infections and ensuing complications with intercourse and childbirth. In these cases, 'circumcision' is a misleading term.
11. Significantly, in the second half of the film, it is not only the legal system that enables female agency, but also Christianity, as the church makes a stand against FGC and operates shelters and schools for girls alienated from their families.
12. As Patricia White notes, there is a paradox evident in the film as the 'women's assumption of a traditionally patriarchal authority steeped in the English colonial legacy to condemn traditional (African) male power' (126) marks their appropriation of a Westernised legal system.
13. See Manga Fombad for an in depth analysis of this regime.
14. Following this event in the narrative, Amina and her estranged husband also appear before an Islamic cleric in Shari'a court. After appealing to Amina to return for a trial reunion, he certifies the couples's divorce. It is not clear in the film how much pressure, if any, Ntuba's ruling (or the camera) exerted on the cleric's decision.
15. I draw this notion of 'discovery' in observational documentary from Elizabeth Cowie.
16. Felman and Laub use this term in regard to experiences of the Holocaust, and FGC is clearly a very different experience. However, it is an example of trauma, and the documentary orients the narrative around individuals speaking of the memory and impact of the event.
17. This mutuality has been observed by a number of theorists. Chantal Mouffe, in *The Return of the Political*, believes that political theory is unable to grasp the import of the 'passions' as a force in the field of politics and thus cannot adequately account for them and the conflicts they engender. In her discussion of Spinoza, Moira Gatens writes: 'In so far as the political realm is concerned with the governance of ourselves and others, the organization of our needs and resources, our rights and obligations, it is quintessentially concerned with the passions and the imagination' (129). Gatens points out the link between human imagination, expression and a sense of political power.
18. Without knowledge of the nature of the collaboration between Longinotto and Fardhosa, those who view this scene must assume that this is the primary reason the film crew does not intervene.
19. For example, *Sisters in Law* has shown at more than 120 festivals and was the winner of the Prix Art et Essai at the Cannes Film Festival (2005) and *Divorce Iranian Style* won the Grand Prize for Best Documentary at the San Francisco International Film Festival (1999) and the Silver Hugo Award at the Chicago International Film Festival (1998).
20. See Smaill for more discussion of these circuits of distribution.

5   Loss and Care: Asian Australian Documentary

1. The events Khoo refers to occur in 2001 as the Norwegian cargo ship, the MV *Tampa*, rescued 439 Afghan asylum seekers from a distressed fishing vessel in international waters off the Australian coast. Australian authorities had been slow to respond to the vessel's distress calls. Moreover, the Australian government sought to refuse *Tampa* entry into Australian waters and, thus to refuse aid for the refugees. Insisting on their disembarkation elsewhere, military personnel were deployed to board the ship. For more discussion of the cultural and political consequences of this event, see Perera (2002).

2. This act was part of a package of legislation that was the first to be passed by the new federal parliament and while not explicitly racialised, the restrictions it put in place have become known as the beginnings of what has been termed the 'White Australia' policy that was to remain in place until 1958. For more details, see Jupp.

3. Notably, two other prominent examples of Asian Australian documentary authorship, Ayres's earlier documentary *China Dolls* (1998), and *Kidnapped!* (2005) directed by Korean Australian film-maker, Melissa Kyu-Jung Lee, also employ re-enactments to a significant degree. In the case of *Kidnapped!*, diasporic authorship is not associated with the problematic of Australian culture, but it is rather reflected in her transnational location as she explores the abduction of Japanese citizens by the North Korean regime in the 1970s and 1980s.

4. See, for example, Mulvey (2006), Davis (2004), Barthes (1981).

5. Significantly, both Cooper and Lingis draw on a notion of ethics that is indebted to the work of Emmanuel Levinas. For Levinas, human existence is relational in the sense that he focuses on the ethical responsibility of the self when facing the Other, an Other who is always 'absolutely Other' in that they can never be fully known. This is because the other cannot be defined in relation to the self, through the binary opposition between self and other, but rather is understood as having its own qualities and attributes that are not the projection of the self.

6. John Howard was the prime minister of Australia (1996–2007) and the leader of the conservative government.

7. In early 2005, Do was awarded 'Young Australian of the Year' for his community volunteer work including the work with the young actors that lead to *The Finished People*. While the publicity brought by the film arguably contributed to Do's success in gaining the award, the honour consequently further increased the notoriety of the film.

8. 'Ali' is an alias used in the documentary to protect the identity of the young asylum seeker.

9. Interviews and text on-screen are the main avenues for exploring this history. As an inter-title states, despite being a signatory to the United Nations Refugee Convention of 1951, and thus resolving to protect refugees and respect their rights, Australia is the only Western nation to detain asylum seekers indefinitely as a matter of policy.

10. This 'awkwardness' may also be, in part, a result of the small budgets the film-makers had to work with. Neither film received any funding at the production and pre-production stages from Australia's film funding infrastructure, but rather relied on local community support and goodwill from sectors of the film industry.
11. Significantly, Naficy's study is primarily concerned with first generation exilic or diasporic film-makers. Yet in these Asian Australian documentaries, it is those of the second generation, Anna Yen and Van, who voice the strongest sense of mourning specifically for the losses engendered by displacement in the movement from homeland.

6   Civic Love and Contemporary Dissent Documentary

1. I am aware that by characterising Left documentary practice in this way, I am subscribing to something of a misnomer. There is no single unified category that constitutes this phenomenon. Indeed, while many take up direct cinema methods, or an expository style, depending on the historical moment, many 'Left' documentaries also experiment with these conventions. My concern is less with particular movements and more with the *ethos* of intervention and activism.
2. Yet beyond this, Socrates also required a dedication and adherence to beliefs in such a way that "*nothing* is allowed to become so sacred or constitutive of our being that abandoning it is unthinkable" (Villa 23).
3. See Bill Nichols, or John Izod and Richard Kilborn, for further discussion of this point.
4. The social collective these documentaries endeavour to address is sometimes clearly a national collective, as in the case of *Fahrenheit 9/11*, but this collective is also almost always broader than the nation. The overriding theme of the dissent documentary is concerned with global capitalism or with the localised effects of global capital. Because of this, the sphere in which they circulate and the viewership they address is both local and global.
5. See D'Arcus for more discussion of these dimensions of protest movements.
6. YouTube especially has become a site for experimentations with semiotic play in the moving image. Another example in the South Pacific is 'engagemedia'.
7. All three documentaries achieved international theatrical distribution. *The Corporation* was produced in conjunction with a number of film funding bodies and television networks including TV Ontario. Following this, all found multiple television broadcast slots. Yet a number of anti-corporate films within this trend have also reached a popular audience through informal distribution avenues. Perhaps the most notable example is *Outfoxed: Rupert Murdoch's War On Journalism*, which was not shown widely in cinemas, but in the months leading up to the 2004 American presidential election was circulated extensively on DVD.

This distribution was successful largely due to the work of MoveOn.org, an internet-based group working in support of the American Democratic Party. While they may feed into and draw on a new media environment, these documentaries adhere to the models offered by formal distribution networks and mass consumption.

8. See Colebrook for more discussion of elitist communication and irony.

7   Children, Futurity and Hope: *Born into Brothels*

1. The foremost philosopher of hope in the twentieth century, Bloch brings Freudian approaches to an understanding of Marxist thought and argues that hope is integral not only for politics but for humankind itself. Yet Bloch's Marxist utopianism must also be understood in the context of his commitment to Stalinism and his support of the Soviet Union in the 40s and 50s. See Zipes and Miller Jones.

2. See Rose for a fuller discussion of sociological approaches to subjectivity.

3. Currie is referring to fiction narrative here, and of course in documentary the events and people are real. Yet they are not necessarily of the same order as people and events known to viewer through off-screen avenues. I argue that narrative desire and conflicts still operate in regard to documentary, albeit in slightly different ways.

4. For more discussion of this point, see Wilson.

5. The awards the documentary has received demonstrate this audience popularity. For example, the film won the Oscar for best documentary feature in 2005, the best documentary award at the Seattle International Film Festival in 2004 and the audience award at the Sundance Film Festival in 2004.

6. See Hirsch for an insightful discussion of domestic and family photography.

7. In an interview with Wendy Mitchell, the film-makers note that the foundation has raised more than US$ 100,000 by selling the children's photographs at film festivals and on its web site.

8. Frann Michael observes that the film-makers decided not to distribute the film in India, thus it has not been widely shown to local audiences. This sits in contrast to my earlier discussion of Kim Longinotto's documentaries that were distributed through formal and informal networks in the regions they depict.

9. *Let Us Now Praise Famous Men* portrays the lives of impoverished share-cropping families in the Southern states of the US in the 1930s, including Evans' black-and-white photographs of the dire living conditions they experienced. It is also a meditation on the complexities of the representation of otherness, participation and observation.

10. Some agencies were working with the film-makers but are not identified in the narrative – they appear in the background as interpreters or school administrators (Michael 58). In addition, as Michael writes: 'Of the three "boarding schools" in which some of the children have enrolled by the

end of the film – Sanlaap, Sabera, and Future Hope – Sanlaap is specifically for the children of sex workers, and the other two are for street children. This suggests, perhaps the difficulty of getting the students admitted was not, as the film implies, because children of prostitutes are so stigmatized, but because these children were fortunate enough to have homes; that is, they were relatively better off than other, homeless children in the area' (58).

11. Moreover, the film does not attempt to explore the lives of the women, systemic poverty or the microcosm that Sonagachi represents. In this respect, there is no attempt to alter perceptions around a very stigmatised portion of Indian society. The move to place the children in boarding schools extracts them from a much broader set of problems and emphasises individual ascent rather than collective enfranchisement.

12. See Dean MacCannell for a discussion of modernity and tourism. Significantly, he also notes: 'As a tourist, the individual may step out into the universal drama of modernity. As a tourist, the individual may attempt to grasp the division of labor as a phenomenon *sui generis* and become a moral witness of its masterpieces of virtue and viciousness' (7).

13. Michaels notes this framing of the adults: 'because the residents of Sonagachi are represented as unfit parents, without resources or collective organization, escape from the neighbourhood can come to seem the only possibility for saving the children [...] The film's emphasis on "good" – that is boarding school – education stresses its focus on individual rather than communal solutions' (58).

8   Nostalgia, Historical Time and Reality Television: The *Idol* Series

1. See Couldry, Morley or Feuer for examples of the way television poses links between the domestic and the public sphere.

2. This version of television temporality has also been employed to characterise the distinctions between traditional documentary and reality television. Nichols describes the 'pervasive "now" of tele-reality' in which 'social responsibility dissolves into tele-participation' (*Blurred Boundaries* 54). Here Nichols is writing in reference to an earlier phase of reality programming and his discussion draws largely on the long-running *Cops*.

3. See Moran for a greater elaboration of the global television format.

4. For more discussion of the ways this localisation occurs, see Turner, Moran or Waisbord.

5. This mode of selfhood is theorised extensively in the work of Nikolas Rose. For a discussion of how it is evident in reality television, see Tania Lewis's work on 'lifestyle experts'.

6. I draw this term from Mary Louise Pratt's work and also from José Esteban Muñoz's use of the term. Muñoz describes it as 'a space where the echoes of colonial encounters still reverberate in the contemporary

sound produced by the historically and culturally disjunctive situation of temporal and spatial copresence that is understood as the postcolonial moment' (91).
7. Dickson advises Priddis to use the internet to research her song choice to discover which songs have been significant hits in Australia at the time of release. Notably, his comment refers to past popularity and satisfies only one aspect of the song's potential to engage the audience. This is particularly important given that much of the audience for the show will have been born in the eighties and nineties.

Epilogue

1. Judith Butler theorises that subjects emerge with an attachment to forms of power and authority but, because this attachment threatens the 'I' (agency), the subject must deny or foreclose on that attachment to persist: 'To desire the conditions of one's own subordination is thus required to persist as oneself. What does it mean to embrace the very form of power – regulation, prohibition, suppression – that threatens one with dissolution in an effort, precisely, to persist in ones own existence?' (*The Psychic Life* 9). If de Nascimento is attached to the forms of institutionalised racism, material exclusion and the life of crime and provisionality that ensues, his action on the bus confronts the paradox Butler describes. He embraces forms of power but not the denial of the attachment. Without the foreclosure required, the result is the dissolution of the self.
2. This is an image of Brazil, and Rio in particular, that gained greater currency and visibility with the release of Fernando de Meirelles's *City of God* (2002). This film was, coincidentally, released the same year as *Bus 174* and to some extent, the documentary circulates in the shadow of the more well-known film.

Bibliography

Agee, James and Walker Evans, *Let Us Now Praise Famous Men: Three Tenant Families*. New York: Ballantine Books, 1966.

Ahmed, Sara. *The Cultural Politics of Emotion*. New York: Routledge, 2004.

Appadurai, Arjun. 'Hope and Democracy.' *Public Culture* 19:1 (2007): 29–34.

Armstrong, Isobel. *The Radical Aesthetic*. Malden: Blackwell Publishers, 2000.

Arthurs, Jane. *Television and Sexuality: Regulation and the Politics of Taste*. Maidenhead: Open University Press, 2004.

Ashby, Justine. 'Postfeminism in the British Frame.' *Cinema Journal* 44:2 (2005): 127–35.

Attwood, Feona. 'Sexed Up: Theorizing the Sexualization of Culture.' *Sexualities* 9:1 (2006): 77–94.

Barnouw, Erik. *Documentary: A History of the Non-Fiction Film*. Oxford: Oxford University Press, 1993.

Barthes, Roland. *Camera Lucida: Reflections on Photography*. Trans. Richard Howard. New York: Hill and Wang, 1981.

Bauman, Zygmunt. *Wasted Lives: Modernity and its Outcasts*. Oxford: Polity, 2004.

Berlant, Lauren. 'The Subject of True Feeling: Pain, Privacy, and Politics.' *Cultural Pluralism, Identity Politics, and the Law*. Eds Austin Sarat and Thomas R. Kearns. Ann Arbor: University of Michigan Press, 1999. 49–84.

____ 'Critical Inquiry, Affirmative Culture.' *Critical Inquiry* 30:2 (2004): 445–51.

____ 'Nearly Utopian, Nearly Normal: Post-Fordist Affect in La Promesse and Rosetta.' *Public Culture* 19:2 (2007): 273–301.

____ *The Female Complaint: The Unfinished Business of Sentimentality in American Culture*. Durham: Duke University Press, 2008.

Biressi, Anita and Heather Nunn. *Reality TV: Realism and Revelation*. London: Wallflower Press, 2005.

Bloch, Ernst. *The Principle of Hope*. Trans. Neville Plaice, Stephen Plaice and Paul Knight. Oxford: Blackwell, 1986.

Boyle, Karen. 'Courting Consumers And Legitimating Exploitation.' *Feminist Media Studies* 8:1 (2008): 35–50.

Brown, Wendy. *States of Injury: Power and Freedom in Late Modernity*. Princeton: Princeton University Press, 1995.

____ *Politics Out of History*. Princeton: Princeton University Press, 2001.

____ *Edgework: Critical Essays on Knowledge and Politics*. Princeton: Princeton University Press, 2005.

____ *Regulating Aversion: Tolerance in the Age of Identity and Empire*. Princeton: Princeton University Press, 2006.

Bruzzi, Stella. *New Documentary*. 2nd ed. London: Routledge, 2006.

Butler, Judith. *The Psychic Life of Power: Theories in Subjection*. Stanford: Stanford University Press, 1997.

___ 'Afterword: After Loss, What Then?' *Loss: The Politics of Mourning*. Eds David L. Eng and David Kazanjian. Berkeley: University of California Press, 2003. 467–73.

Cartwright, Lisa. *Moral Spectatorship: Technologies of Voice and Affect in Postwar Representations of the Child*. Durham: Duke University Press, 2008.

Chow, Rey. *Primitive Passions: Visuality, Sexuality, Ethnography, and Contemporary Chinese Cinema*. New York: Columbia University Press, 1995.

Colebrook, Claire. *Irony*. New York: Routledge, 2004.

Cooper, Sarah. *Selfless Cinema? Ethics and French Documentary*. London: Legenda, 2006.

Corner, John. 'Performing the Real: Documentary Diversions.' *Television and New Media* 3:3 (2002): 255–69.

Couldry, Nick. 'Liveness, "Reality", and the Mediated Habitus from Television to the Mobile Phone.' *The Communication Review* 7 (2004): 353–61.

Cowie, Elizabeth. 'The Spectacle of Actuality.' *Collecting Visible Evidence*. Eds Jane Gaines and Michael Renov. Minneapolis: University of Minnesota Press, 1999. 19–45.

Cullum, Judge Brett. 14 November 2005. 'DVD Verdict.' 12 July 2007. http://www.dvdverdict.com/reviews/rize.php.

Cunningham, Hugh. *The Children of the Poor: Representations of Childhood Since the Seventeenth Century*. Oxford: Blackwell, 1991.

Currie, Gregory. 'Narrative Desire.' *The Philosophy of Film: Introductory Text and Readings*. Eds Thomas E. Wartenberg and Angela Curran. Oxford: Blackwell Publishing, 2005. 139–47.

Cvetkovich, Ann. *An Archive of Feelings: Trauma, Sexuality, and Lesbian Public Cultures*. Durham: Duke University Press, 2003.

___ 'Public Feelings.' *South Atlantic Quarterly* 106:3 (2007): 459–68.

D'Arcus, Bruce. *Boundaries of Dissent: Protest and State Power in the Media Age*. New York: Routledge, 2006.

Davis, Therese. *The Face on the Screen: Death, Recognition and Spectatorship*. Bristol: Intellect, 2004.

De Lauretis, Teresa. *Alice Doesn't: Feminism, Semiotics, Cinema*. Bloomington: Indiana University Press, 1984.

Dodd, James. 'The Philosophical Significance of Hope.' *The Review of Metaphysics* 58 (2004): 117–46.

Dyer, Richard. *Only Entertainment*. London: Routledge, 1992.

Eng, David L. and Shinhee Han. 'A Dialogue on Racial Melancholia.' *Loss: The Politics of Mourning*. Eds David L. Eng and David Kazanjian. Berkeley: University of California Press, 2003. 343–71.

Esteban Muñoz, José. *Disidentifications: Queers of Colour and the Performance of Politics*. Minneapolis: University of Minnesota Press, 1999.

Felman, Shoshana. 'In an Era of Testimony: Claude Lanzmann's Shoah.' *Yale French Studies* 79 (1991): 39–81.

Felman, Shoshana and Dori Laub. *Testimony: Crises of Witnessing in Literature, Psychoanalysis, and History*. New York: Routledge, 1991.

Feuer, Jane. 'Concept Of Live Television: Ontology As Ideology.' *Regarding Television: Critical Approaches – An Anthology*. Ed. E. Ann Kaplan. Frederick: University Publications of America, 1983. 12–22.

Flinn, Caryl. *Strains of Utopia: Gender, Nostalgia, and Hollywood Film Music.* Princeton: Princeton University Press, 1992.

Foucault, Michel. 'What is an Author?' *Textual Strategies: Perspectives in Post-Structuralist Criticism.* Ed. Josue V. Harari. Ithaca: Cornell University Press, 1979. 141–60.

____ *Ethics: Subjectivity and Truth.* Ed. Paul Rabinow. New York: The New Press, 1994.

Fowler, Catherine. 'The Day I Will Never Forget: An Interview With Kim Longinotto.' *Women: A Cultural Review* 15:1 (2003): 101–7.

Freud, Sigmund. 'Mourning and Melancholia.' *On Metapsychology: The Theory of Psychoanalysis.* London: Penguin, 1984. 251–68.

Frith, Simon. *Performing Rites: Evaluating Popular Music.* Oxford: Oxford University Press, 1998.

Gaines, Jane. 'Political Mimesis.' *Collecting Visible Evidence.* Eds Jane M. Gaines and Michael Renov. Minneapolis: University of Minnesota Press, 1999. 84–102.

____ 'The Production of Outrage: The Iraq War and the Radical Documentary Tradition.' *Framework* 48:2 (2007): 36–55.

Gatens, Moira. *Imaginary Bodies: Ethics, Power and Corporeality.* London: Routledge, 2006.

Gill, Rosalind. 'From Sexual Objectification to Sexual Subjectification: The Resexualisation of Women's Bodies in the Media.' *Feminist Media Studies* 3:1 (2003): 100–5.

Grosz, Elizabeth. 'The Body of Signification.' *Abjection, Melancholia and Love: The Work of Julia Kristeva.* Eds John Fletcher and Andrew Benjamin. London: Routledge, 1990. 80–103.

____ *Space, Time and Perversion: The Politics of Bodies.* Sydney: Allen and Unwin, 1995.

Gunning, Tom. 'Cinema of Attraction: Early Film, Its Spectator and the Avant-garde.' *Wide Angle* 8:3–4 (1986): 63–70.

____ '"Now You See It, Now You Don't": The Temporality of the Cinema Of Attractions.' *Velvet Light Trap* Fall (1993): 3–13.

Gutierrez-Jones, Carl. *Critical Race Narratives: A Study of Race, Rhetoric, and Injury.* New York: New York University Press, 2001.

Habermas, Jurgen. 'The Public Sphere: An Encyclopedia Article.' *New German Critique* 1:3 (1974): 49–55.

Hage, Ghassan. *Against Paranoid Nationalism: Searching for Hope in a Shrinking Society.* Sydney: Pluto, 2003.

Hall, Stuart. 'Which Public, Whose Service?' *All Our Futures: The Changing Role and Purpose of the BBC.* Ed. Wilf Stevenson. London: British Film Institute, 1993. 23–38.

____ 'Introduction: Who Needs Identity?' *Questions of Cultural Identity.* Eds Stuart Hall and Paul du Gay. London: Sage Publications, 1996. 1–17.

Hansen, Christian, Catherine Needham and Bill Nichols. 'Pornography, Ethnography and the Discourses of Power.' *Representing Reality.* Bill Nichols. Bloomington: Indiana University Press, 1991.

Hansen, Miriam. 'Mass Production of the Senses: Classical Cinema as Vernacular Modernism.' *Modernism/Modernity* 6:2 (1999): 59–77.

Hart, Adam. 'DVD Re-Run Interview: Greed Is Good?; Jennifer Abbott and Mark Achbar Talk About *The Corporation*.' *Indiewire* April 2005. Accessed 2 May 2007. http://www.indiewire.com/people/people_040611corp.html.

Hawkins, Gay. 'The Ethics of Television.' *International Journal of Cultural Studies* 4:4 (2001): 412–26.

Heath, Stephen and Gillian Skirrow. 'Television: A World in Action.' *Screen* 18:2 (177): 7–59.

Hirsch, Joshua. 'Posttraumatic cinema and the Holocaust Documentary.' *Film and History* 32:1 (2002): 9–21.

____ *Afterimage: Film, Trauma, and the Holocaust.* Philadelphia: Temple University Press, 2004.

Hirsch, Marianne. *Family Frames: Photography, Narrative, and Postmemory.* Cambridge: Harvard University Press, 1997.

Holland, Patricia. *Picturing Childhood: The Myth of the Child in Popular Imagery.* London: I. B. Tauris, 2004.

Holmes, Su. 'Reality Goes Pop! Reality TV, Popular Music and Narratives of Stardom in Pop Idol.' *Television and New Media* 5:2 (2004): 147–72.

Holmlund, Chris. 'Postfeminism from A to G.' *Cinema Journal* 44:2 (2005): 116–21.

Honneth, Axel. *The Struggle for Recognition: The Moral Grammar of Social Conflicts.* Trans. Joel Anderson. Cambridge: MIT Press, 1996.

hooks, bell. *Reel to Real: Race, Sex, and Class at the Movies.* New York: Routledge, 1996.

Hutcheon, Linda. *Irony, Nostalgia, and the Postmodern.* University of Toronto, 1998. Accessed 27 October 2008. http://www.library.utoronto.ca/utel/criticism/hutchinp.html.

____ *Irony's Edge: The Theory and Politics of Irony.* London/New York: Routledge, 1995.

Izod, John and Richard Kilborn. 'The Documentary.' *The Oxford Guide to Film Studies.* Eds John Hill and Pamela Church. Oxford: Oxford University Press, 1998. 426–33.

James, Allison and Adrian L. James. *Constructing Childhood: Theory, Policy and Social Practice.* Houndmills: Palgrave Macmillan, 2004.

James, Susan. 'Passion and Politics.' *Philosophy and the Emotions.* Ed. Anthony Hatzimoysis. Cambridge: Cambridge University Press. 2003.

Jameson, Fredric. 'Postmodernism or the Cultural Logic of Late Capitalism.' *New Left Review* 146 (1984): 53–92.

Johnston, Claire. 'Women's Cinema as Counter Cinema.' *Notes on Women's Cinema.* Ed. Claire Johnston, London: Society for Education in Film and Television, 1973.

Juhasz, Alexandra. 'No Woman is an Object: Realizing the Feminist Collaborative Video.' *Camera Obscura* 18:3 (2004): 71–97.

Jupp, James. *The Australian People.* Sydney: Angus & Robertson, 1988.

Kaplan, E. Ann. 'Pornography and/as Representation.' *Enclitic* 9 (1987): 8–19.

Kaplan, E. Ann and Ban Wang. 'From Traumatic Paralysis to the Force Field of Modernity.' *Trauma and Cinema: Cross Cultural Explorations.* Eds E. Ann Kaplan and Ban Wang. Hong Kong: Hong Kong University Press, 2004. 1–22.

Kassabian, Anahid and David Kazanjian. 'Melancholic Memories and Manic Politics: Feminism, Documentary and the Armenian Diaspora.' *Feminism and Documentary*. Eds Janet Walker and Diane Waldman. Minneapolis: University of Minnesota Press, 1999. 202–23.

Kavka, M. and Amy West. 'Temporalities of the Real.' *Understanding Reality Television*. Eds Su Holmes and Deborah Jermyn. London: Routledge, 2004. 136–53.

Khoo, Tseen. 'Introduction: Locating Asian Australian Cultures.' *Journal of Intercultural Studies* 27:1–2 (2006): 1–9.

Kian-Thiebaut, Azadeh. 'From Islamization to the Individualisation of Women in Post-revolutionary Iran.' *Women, Religion and Culture in Iran*. Eds Sarah Ansari and Vanessa Martin. London: Curzon, 2002. 127–42.

Kipnis, Laura. '(Male) Desire and (Female) Disgust: Reading *Hustler*.' *Cultural Studies*. Eds Lawrence Grossberg, Cary Nelson and Paula Treichler. New York: Routledge, 1992. 373–91.

Klein, Melanie. *The Selected Melanie Klein*. Ed. Juliet Mitchell. London: Penguin, 1991.

Kristeva, Julia. *Powers of Horror. An Essay on Abjection*. Trans. Leon S. Roudiez. New York: Columbia University Press, 1982.

Laub, Dori. 'Bearing Witness or the Vicissitudes of Listening,' in *Testimony: Crises of Witnessing in Literature, Psychoanalysis, and History*, Shoshana Felman and Dori Laub, M.D. New York: Routledge, 1991. 57–74.

Lesage, Julia. 'The Political Aesthetics of the Feminist Documentary Film.' *Issues in Feminist Film Criticism*. Ed. Patricia Erens. Bloomington: Indiana University Press, 1990. 222–37.

Lewis, Tania. *Smart Living: Lifestyle Media and Popular Expertise*. New York: Peter Lang, 2008.

Lingis, Alphonso. *The Community of Those Who Have Nothing in Common*. Bloomington: Indiana University Press, 1994.

Lury, Karen. 'The Child in Film and Television: Introduction.' *Screen* 46:3 (2005): 307–14.

MacCannell, Dean. *The Tourist: A New Theory of the Leisure Class*. 2nd ed. California: University of California Press, 1989.

Manga Fombad, Charles. 'The Scope for Uniform National Laws in Cameroon.' *The Journal of Modern African Studies* 29:3 (1991): 443–56.

Marks, Laura U. 'Fetishes and Fossils: Notes on Documentary and Materiality.' *Feminism and Documentary*. Eds Diane Waldman and Janet Walker. Minneapolis: University of Minnesota Press, 1999. 224–44.

Margulies, Ivone. 'Exemplary Bodies: Reenactment in *Love in the City, Sons*, and *Close Up*.' *Rights of Realism: Essays on Corporeal Cinema*. Ed. Ivone Margulies. Durham: Duke University Press, 2002.

McGuigan, Jim. 'The Cultural Public Sphere.' *European Journal of Cultural Studies* 8:4 (2005): 427–43.

McNair, Brian. *Mediated Sex: Pornography and Postmodern Culture*. London: Arnold, 1996.

_____ *Striptease Culture: Sex, Media and the Democratisation of Desire*. London: Routledge, 2002.

McRobbie, Angela. 'Post-Feminism and Popular Culture.' *Feminist Media Studies* 4:3 (2004): 255–64.

Metz, Christian. 'The Imaginary Signifier.' *Screen* 16:2 (1975): 14–76.

Michel, Frann. 'From "Their Eves" to "New Eves": Suffering Victims and Cultivated Aesthetics in *Born into Brothels*.' *Post Script: Essays in Film and Humanities* 26.3 (2007): 53–62.

Miller Jones, John. *Assembling (Post)modernism: The Utopian Philosophy of Ernst Bloch*. New York: Peter Lang, 1995.

Miller, Susan B. *Disgust: The Gatekeeper Emotion*. Hillsdale, NJ: Analytic Press, 2004.

Miller, William I. *The Anatomy of Disgust*. Cambridge: Harvard University Press, 1997.

Mir-Hosseini, Ziba. *Marriage on Trial: A Study of Islamic Family Law in Iran and Morocco*. London: I. B. Tauris, 2000.

____ 'Negotiating the Politics of Gender in Iran: An Ethnography of a Documentary.' *New Iranian Cinema: Politics, Representation and Identity*. Ed. Richard Tapper. London: I. B. Tauris, 2002.

Mitchell, Wendy. 'Cameras on Unseen Calcutta; Zana Briski and Ross Kauffman's *Born into Brothels*.' *People*. Accessed 2 October 2008. http://www.indiewire.com/people/people_041209born.html.

Moore, Lindsey. 'Women in a Widening Frame: (Cross) Cultural Projection, Spectatorship, and Iranian Cinema.' *Camera Obscura* 59 (2005): 1–33.

Moran, Albert. *Understanding the Global TV Format*. With Justin Malbon. Bristol: Intellect Books, 2006.

Morgan, David. 'Pain: The Unrelieved Condition of Modernity.' *European Journal of Social Theory* 5:3 (2002): 307–22.

Morley, David. *Home Territories: Media, Mobility and Identity*. London: Routledge, 2000.

Mouffe, Chantal. *The Return of the Political*. London: Verso, 2005.

Mulvey, Laura. 'Visual Pleasure and Narrative Cinema.' *Screen* 16:3 (1975): 6–18.

____ *Death 24 x a Second: Stillness and the Moving Image*. London: Reaktion Books, 2006.

Munsterberg, Hugo. *The Film: A Psychological Study; The Silent Photoplay in 1916*. Foreword by Richard Griffith. New York: Dover Publications, 1970.

Naficy, Hamid. *An Accented Cinema: Exilic and Diasporic Filmmaking*. Princeton: Princeton University Press, 2001.

NFB (National Film Board). *Breaking New Ground: A Framework for Measuring the Social Impact of Documentaries*. Toronto: National Film Board of Canada, 2005.

Nichols, Bill. *Representing Reality*. Bloomington: Indiana University Press, 1991.

____ *Blurred Boundaries: Questions of Meaning in Contemporary Culture*. Bloomington: Indiana University Press, 1994. 55–68.

____ 'Historical Consciousness and the Viewer: *Who Killed Vincent Chin?*' *The Persistence of History: Cinema, Television and the Modern Event*. Ed. Vivian Sobchack. New York: Routledge, 1996. 55–68.

_____ *Introduction to Documentary*. Bloomington: Indiana University Press, 2001.

Nowell-Smith, Geoffrey. 'On History and the Cinema.' *Screen* 31:2 (1990): 160–71.

O'Hehir, Andrew. 'Beyond the Multiplex.' *Salon: Arts and Entertainment*, 2 March 2005. Accessed 6 January 2009. http://dir.salon.com/story/ent/movies/review/2005/02/03/btm/index.html.

Paasonen, Susanna. 'Strange Bedfellows: Pornography, Affect and Feminist Reading.' *Feminist Theory* 8:1 (2007): 43–57.

Perera, Suvendrini. 'What is a Camp ...?' *Borderlands*, 1 (2002a). http://www.borderlandsejournal.adelaide.edu.au/vol1no1_2002/perera_camp.html.

_____ 'A Line in the Sea: The *Tampa*, Boat Stories and the Border.' *Cultural Studies Review* 8:1 (2002): 11–27.

Perri 6, Susannah Radstone, Corinne Squire and Amal Treacher. 'Introduction.' *Public Emotions*. Eds Perri 6, Susannah Radstone, Corinne Squire and Amal Treacher. Basingstoke: Palgrave Macmillan, 2007. 1–33.

Pevere, Geoff. '*Fix: Story of an Addicted City.*' 17 October 2003.*Toronto Star*. Accessed 25 April 2006. http://www.thestar.com/NASApp/cs/Content Server?&pagename=thestar/Layout/Article_Type1&c=Article&cid=10 66384937191&call_pageid=1022183557980&col=1022183560753.

Plantinga, Carl. 'Notes on Spectator Emotion and Ideological Film Criticism.' *Film Theory and Philosophy*. Eds Robert Allen and Murray Smith. Oxford: Oxford University Press, 1997. 372–93.

Plantinga, Carl and Greg M. Smith, eds. *Passionate Views: Film, Cognition and Emotion*. Baltimore: Johns Hopkins University Press, 1999.

Povinelli, Elizabeth A. *The Cunning of Recognition: Indigenous Alterities and the Making of Australian Multiculturalism*. Durham: Duke University Press, 2002.

Pratt, Mary Louise. *Imperial Eyes: Travel Writing and Transculturation*. London: Routledge, 1992.

Rabinowitz, Paula. *They Must Be Represented: The Politics of Documentary*. London: Verso, 1994.

_____ 'Sentimental Contracts: Dreams and Documents of American Labour.' *Feminism and Documentary*. Eds Janet Walker and Diane Waldman. Minneapolis: University of Minnesota Press, 1999. 43–63.

Radstone, Susannah. *The Sexual Politics of Time: Confession, Nostalgia, Memory*. London: Routledge, 2007.

Renov, Michael. 'Toward a Poetics of Documentary.' *Theorising Documentary*. Ed. Michael Renov. New York: Routledge, 1993. 12–36.

_____ *The Subject of Documentary*. Minneapolis: University of Minnesota Press, 2004.

Rich, B. Ruby. 'Anti-porn: Soft Issue, Hard World.' *Feminist Review* 13 (1983): 56–67.

_____ 'Documentary Disciplines: An Introduction.' *Cinema Journal* 46:1 (2006): 108–15.

Roscoe, Jane. 'Television: Friend or Foe of Australian Documentary?' *Media, Culture & Society* 26:2 (2004): 288–95.

Rose, Nikolas, *Inventing Our Selves: Psychology, Power and Personhood.* New York: Cambridge University Press, 1996.

_____ *Governing the Soul: The Shaping of the Self.* 2nd ed. London: Free Association Press, 1999.

Russell, Catherine. *Experimental Ethnography: The Work of Film in the Age of Video.* Durham: Duke University Press, 1999.

Samuel, Raphael. *Theatres of Memory: Past and Present in Contemporary Culture* Vol. 1. London: Verso, 1994.

Scarry, Elaine. *The Body in Pain.* New York: Oxford University Press, 1985.

Schwartz, Bill. 'Media Times/Historical Times.' *Screen* 45:2 (2004): 93–105.

Scott, A. O. 'Film Festival Review: Dissection of a Crime Leaves Brazil Exposed.' *The New York Times.* 27 March 2003. Accessed 12 March 2009. http://www.nytimes.com/2003/03/27/movies/film-festival-review-dissection-of-a-crime-leaves-brazil-exposed.html.

Shapiro, Michael J. *Cinematic Political Thought: Narrating Race, Nation and Gender.* New York: New York University Press, 1999.

Sleightholme, Carolyn and Indrani Sinha. *Guilty Without Trial: Women in the Sex Trade in Calcutta.* New Brunswick: Rutgers University Press, 1997.

Smaill, Belinda. 'Interview with Kim Longinotto.' *Studies in Documentary Film* 1:2 (2007): 177–87.

Smith, Greg M. 'Local Emotions, Global Moods, and Film Structure.' *Passionate Views: Film, Cognition, and Emotion.* Eds Carl Plantinga and Greg M. Smith. Baltimore: Johns Hopkins University Press, 1999. 103–26.

Smith, Murray. *Engaging Characters: Fiction, Emotion, and the Cinema.* Oxford: Clarendon Press, 1995.

Smith, Roberta. 'From Children Raised in Brothels, Glimpses of Life's Possibilities.' *The New York Times* 12 August 2005: E2: 31.

Snyder, C. R., ed. *Handbook of Hope: Theory, Measures & Applications.* San Diego: Academic Press, 2000.

Spelman, Elizabeth. *Fruits of Sorrow: Framing Our Attention to Suffering.* Boston: Beacon Press, 1997.

Spivak, Gayatri Chakravorty. 'Translation as Culture.' *Parallax* 6:1 (2000): 13–24.

Staiger, Janet. 'Authorship Approaches.' *Authorship and Film.* Eds David A. Gerstner and Janet Staiger. New York: Routledge, 2003. 27–57.

Stearns, Peter N. and Carol Z. Stearns. 'Emotionology: Clarifying the History of Emotions and Emotional Standards.' *The American Historical Review* 90:4 (1985): 813–36.

Tasker, Yvonne and Diane Negra. 'Postfeminism and the Archive for the Future.' *Camera Obscura* 21:2 (2006): 171–6.

Teasley, Sarah. 'Interview with Kim Longinotto.' *Documentary Box* 16 (2000) Yamagata International Documentary Film Festival. Accessed 15 January 2009. http://www.yidff.jp/docbox/16/box16-2-1-e.html.

Tobing Rony, Fatimah. *The Third Eye: Race, Cinema, and Ethnographic Spectacle.* Durham, NC: Duke University Press, 1996.

Trinh, T. Minh-ha. *When the Moon Waxes Red: Representation, Gender and Cultural Politics.* New York: Routledge, 1991.

Turner, Graeme. 'Cultural identity, Soap Narrative, and Reality TV.' *Television and New Media* 6:4 (2005): 215–422.

Turvey, Malcolm. 'Seeing Theory: On Perception and Emotional Response in Current Film Theory.' *Film Theory and Philosophy*. Robert Allen and Murray Smith. Ed. Oxford: Oxford University Press, 1997. 431–56.

Villa, Dana. *Socratic Citizenship*. Princeton: Princeton University Press, 2001.

Wahlberg, Malin. *Documentary Time: Film and Phenomenology*. Minneapolis: University of Minnesota Press, 2008.

Waisbord, Silvio. 'McTV: Understanding the Global Popularity of Television Formats.' *Television and New Media* 5:4 (2004): 359–83.

Walkerdine, Valerie, Helen Lucey and June Melody. *Growing Up Girl: Psychosocial Explorations of Gender and Class*. New York: New York University Press, 2001.

Walker, Janet. *Trauma Cinema: Documenting Incest and the Holocaust*. Berkley: University of California Press, 2005.

Waugh, Thomas, ed. *Show Us Life: Toward a History and Aesthetics of the Committed Documentary*. Metuchen: Scarecrow Press, 1984.

Whelehan, Imelda. *Overloaded: Popular Culture and the Future of Feminism*. London: Women's Press Ltd., 2000.

White, Patricia. 'Cinema Solidarity: The Documentary Practice of Kim Longinotto.' *Cinema Journal* 46:1 (2006): 120–8.

Williams, Linda. *Hard Core: Power, Pleasure, and the 'Frenzy of the Visible'*. Berkeley: University of California Press, 1989.

____ 'Film Bodies: Gender, Genre and Excess.' *Film Quarterly* 44:4 (1991): 2–13.

____ 'Mirrors without Memories: Truth, History and the New Documentary.' *Film Quarterly* 46:3 (1993) 9–21.

____ 'Porn Studies: Proliferating Pornographies On/Scene.' *Porn Studies*. Ed. Linda Williams. Durham: Duke University Press, 2004. 1–25.

Williams, Patricia. 'Metro Broadcasting, Inc. v. FCC: Regrouping in Singular Times.' *Critical Race Theory: The Key Writings That Formed the Movement*. Eds Kimberle Crenshaw, Neil Gotanda, Garry Peller and Kendall Thomas. New York: The New Press, 1995. 191–204.

Williams, Raymond. *The Long Revolution*. New York: Columbia University Press, 1961.

Wilson, Emma. 'Children, Emotion and Viewing in Contemporary European Film.' *Screen* 46:3 (2005): 329–52.

Winston, Brian. 'The Tradition of the Victim in Griersonian Documentary.' *Image Ethics: The Moral Rights of Subjects in Photographs, Film, and Television*. Eds Larry Gross, John Stuart Katz and Jay Ruby. New York: Oxford University Press, 1988. 34–58.

____ *Claiming the Real: The Documentary Film Revisited*. London: BFI Publishing, 1995.

Whiteman, David. 'Out of the Theatres and into the Streets: A Coalition Model of the Political Impact of Documentary Film and Video.' *Political Communication* 21 (2004): 51–69.

Wood, Helen and Lisa Taylor. 'Feeling Sentimental about Television and Audiences.' *Cinema Journal* 47:3 (2008): 144–51.

Yue, Audrey. 'Asian Australian Cinema, Asian-Australian Modernity.' *Diaspora: Negotiating Asian-Australia*. Eds Helen Gilbert, Tseen Khoo and Jacqueline Lo. St Lucia: University of Queensland Press, 2001. 190–9.

Zipes, Jack. 'Ernst Bloch and the Obscenity of Hope.' *New German Critique* 45 (1988): 3–8.

Index